FORCES OF POWER

FORCES OF POWER

by

WILLIAM L. TAUB

GROSSET & DUNLAP
A FILMWAYS COMPANY
Publishers • New York

This book is dedicated to the memories of the beloved deceased members of my family:

Mary and Samuel Taub, my mother and father;
Beatrice Taub, my sister;
Henry J. Taub, my brother, who died February 8, 1979;
and Max M. Kurman, my brother-in-law;
and my good friend Flor Trujillo.

CONTENTS

1

THE PHOENIX BIRD RISES

It was April 18, 1952, and my rented limousine was racing through the Mojave twilight. Between the mountain ranges that rimmed the horizon a strange mirage was beginning to emerge from the desert floor. It began as a dim artificial glow low in the sky, and as the car approached, it started to blaze, brighter than the Northern Lights, a pulsating hot neon oasis in the lonely desert: Las Vegas.

In the back seat of the car I struggled into my formal jacket and stuffed pearl studs into my ruffled shirt, wondering where on the list of strange things I'd done for clients I would rate dressing in the back of a limousine. Not very high, I guessed.

Soon we were humming down the Strip on Highway 91, past the rows of billboards whose constantly changing names were one of the few ways of marking the passage of time in Vegas. The names on those billboards were beginning to rival Broadway's: Jimmy Durante, Bert Lahr, Milton Berle, Georgia Gibbs, Lena Horne. Once no top name would consider playing in a raw honky-tonk town in the middle of a desert, but time, and an enormous influx of money, was changing all that.

Meyer Lansky, Bugsy Siegel, Johnny Roselli, and the Teamsters Union pension fund trustees: none of these names

1

appeared on the billboards, and very few people knew back then that Las Vegas's other name was Syndicate City.

The billboards began to rush by, intermingled with the nightclub signs: El Rancho Vegas, the Flamingo, Eartha Kitt, Lili St. Cyr, Wilbur Clark's Desert Inn, Joe E. Lewis. Then the car had to slow down for a heavy traffic jam approaching the nightclub up ahead. I was due there at 8:30 and the traffic jam was partially my responsibility. Now I was afraid I'd be late.

"Don't worry about a thing, Mr. Taub. We'll get you there on time," my driver said.

He did, but just barely. The limousine pulled up in front of the Last Frontier, an outlandish replica of the Old West, right down to the solid mahogany bar with real bullet holes and a bordello with wax madam and beckoning girls. I stepped out into the bands of multicolored floodlights and moved through the huge crowd of club-goers all trying to get into the Ramona Room before 8:30.

By some miracle I ran into Marian Saunders, my guest for the evening, and we stopped for a moment in front of the marquee outside the Ramona Room. The bold block letters said a lot, but they couldn't begin to tell the whole story.

Inside the Ramona Room was a scene of glittering pandemonium as waiters rushed around serving everyone before the show. I congratulated myself on the turnout. The right names were there, names personifying privilege, glamour, power, wealth, together with the lesser-known names who decided who got the privilege and who didn't. They were all eager to see the Las Vegas opening of the Eighth Wonder of the World, the daughter of a laundress from East St. Louis, Illinois, who had been causing so much trouble wherever she went, and bewitching audiences onstage. They had come to watch her show Las Vegas how it was done.

"And now the Last Frontier, in association with William L. Taub, is proud to present—THE FABULOUS JOSEPHINE BAKER!" Applause drowned out the opening measures of the overture as the curtains parted to reveal an immense white staircase at the top of which stood an all-white Josephine. She wore a long Elizabeth Arden gown of silk and sequins that shimmered under the spotlights, and her lips were sparkling as well as the hand microphone she held close to them. White plumes towered above her.

Even her skin was white, a makeup feat that took several hours to perfect before each performance. Slowly, sinuously, she moved down the stairs.

"Je reviens," she sang. "I've come back."

That she had. Josephine Baker, the darling of Paris and the Continent for twenty-five years, had in 1951 begun a sensational comeback in her native country, only to see her tour disintegrate before the year was out. She had been the target of a lot of hatred, but instead of returning to France in humiliation, she had stayed to fight, and that night she faced an adoring audience in her own country. I considered it something of a miracle, and one I had been instrumental in making happen.

I was introduced to Josephine in the late forties by Flor Trujillo, daughter of the dictator. Flor was then working at the Dominican Embassy in Paris. Both Josephine and Flor possessed a wonderful vitality, beauty, and lust for life, and it was natural that they become friends.

Those were exciting years in Paris. Everyone who had survived the war was making up for the bad times, and the night life was lavish and unrestrained. Josephine remained queen of the nightclub scene and enjoyed near sainthood because of her activities in the French Resistance. Her favorite pieces of jewelry were the three medals presented to her by her fellow member of the Resistance, General de Gaulle, and she incorporated her wartime experiences into her nightclub act, telling her audiences how she had crossed the borders of occupied countries with secret messages for the Allies written in invisible ink on her music. I sat in the audience and thought how effective a courier she must have been. She was known all over Europe, and it was more likely she would have been asked for her autograph than searched.

One night I brought up a subject that had been on my mind since I first met her. "Josephine, you've always been so successful in Europe," I said. "Why don't you consider an American tour?"

She wouldn't hear of it. Why should she risk touring a country where she'd never had anything but trouble when she was having such a lovely time in Europe? Josephine had come to Paris with the *Revue Negre* when she was nineteen and had gone back to the United States only two times in all the intervening years. Neither time had been a happy one.

As soon as I brought up the subject, I realized it was a touchy one. It had been many years since Josephine had been exposed to the kind of prejudice she had known in her native country. She had no desire to relive bad memories. One of her earliest was of a race riot in her home town of East St. Louis. When the trouble escalated into a mass rout of the town's black community, Josephine and her family were among the terrified people who had to run a gauntlet of armed whites to reach a bridge that led to St. Louis and safety.

The Baker family made it to the bridge, but in a way Josephine never stopped running. The nightmares of her childhood were later replaced by insomnia. Anyone close to Jo had to be willing to put up with her after-midnight telephone calls that could last until dawn's early light.

In spite of Josephine's resistance to the idea of an American comeback, I couldn't let it go. She was a consummate performer and had changed her style over the years to keep up with the times. In the twenties, billed as "The Black Venus who drives men mad," she danced on a huge mirror wearing only a short dress and sang "Ave Maria" clad in a girdle of bananas. How she managed to be both scandalous and in good taste at the same time was one of those mysteries of show business. Only Josephine could have gotten away with the outrageous things she did.

Gradually she added more elegance to her style, although the flamboyance remained. She could be still seen on an afternoon walking down the Champs Élysées with a pet leopard on a jeweled leash.

This was the Josephine I met in the forties—elegant, flamboyant, larger than life. One night she was brimming over with enthusiasm about a chateau she had bought called Les Milandes. She was going to change its name to La Place Josephine. (Several years later I would have cause to regret her penchant for renaming things Josephine.) Along with her passion for renovation was despair over how much it was going to cost her to outfit her quaint medieval village with all the modern conveniences. "I've got to get my hands on a lot of money," she said.

Again I broached the subject of an American tour. If the

renovation of Les Milandes was going to cost her a fortune, the United States was the best place to make it, I said. She was apprehensive but more willing this time to listen to my ideas. I wanted to present her as an international institution rather than a black woman entertainer. The incredible effect she had on audiences would offset any bad press she might receive, I told her, for aside from the race issue, there was potential trouble with the Hearst syndicate. For some reason they regarded her wartime activities with suspicion.

"Think about it, Josephine," I said. "Things are different now back home." I later hoped she never held those words against me.

Other business interests demanded my attention, however, and we went our separate ways. In 1951 Josephine did stage a comeback, a one-woman concert and nightclub tour. For months she rocked the country—but not in the way she had intended.

Things began well. She played as many as four performances a day, always to packed houses, and boasted of receiving over a hundred marriage proposals from important men. Her act was even more lavish than it had been in Paris, although the near nudity was gone. Her famous bananas had been replaced by gowns designed by Dior, Rochas, and Balenciaga. Wherever she played, she was a sensation.

Then I started reading about her on the front page rather than in the entertainment section. It started in Miami, which was rigidly segregated. Josephine had managed to receive a non-discrimination clause in her contract, and on opening night at Copa City she played to a cheering integrated audience. "This is a very significant occasion for us," she announced, "and by 'us' I mean the human race." Then the NAACP sponsored a Josephine Baker Day in Harlem. Thousands attended. It must have seemed to Josephine, who was such an optimist anyway, that times really had changed.

But the backlash had already begun. The wild exuberance of Baker Day annoyed certain people in the press, and Josephine's own political naïveté didn't help matters. Always ready with the grand gesture, she had sent truckloads of food and gifts into slum neighborhoods, an act of generosity that came out tinged with red in the tabloids.

Then came the famous snub at the Stork Club in October 1951. When I heard about that and thought about the volatile personalities involved, I knew all hell was going to break loose, and it did. Josephine had been refused service in the Cub Room of the Stork Club, that sanctum sanctorum of stars, celebrities, and syndicated columnists. Walter Winchell, who had been seen at his table during the incident, swore up and down he hadn't been there.

The Stork Club was the last place in town to create a scene, nor had anyone ever dared challenge owner Sherman Billingsley's tacit discrimination against Jews and blacks. Apparently Josephine had thought her international show business credentials would make her an exception.

The uproar began. The NAACP picketed the club, sworn statements and counterstatements appeared in the newspapers, and then Walter Winchell took off his gloves and went after Josephine, accusing her of being anti-Jewish, a fascist, and a communist. Josephine sued Winchell, the King Syndicate, and the Hearst chain, and then appealed to President Truman for help.

I had been Truman's emissary to Iran much of that year, helping resolve a conflict between England and Iran over petroleum rights. One day I received a call from the United States. It was someone close to Jo who was also a friend of mine. Had I heard about Josephine's troubles? Yes, I said. Hadn't everybody? Then he asked me whether I would consider going to California and using my show business acumen to negotiate some new appearances for her. I said I'd have to think about it seriously.

I made some inquiries and found out how bad things had become since the Stork Club incident. Jo was spending more time appearing at civil rights gatherings than she was performing. She was no longer regarded as an entertainer but as a troublemaker, and club owners were afraid to have anything to do with her. One by one her concert and nightclub contracts were being annulled. A quarter-of-a-million-dollar film contract had gone up in smoke. By the end of 1951 not one commitment remained intact. In the face of an unleashed Hearst press everyone was running scared.

Given the obstacles, I didn't feel I could do anything to help.

Then I recalled my first meeting with Jo in Paris and my feeling that with the right approach Jo could overcome her bad press. The situation was considerably worse now than when we had first discussed a comeback, but perhaps not impossible. I decided to see what I could do. I flew to the West Coast and immediately began negotiating with club owners.

In February 1952 I booked Josephine into the El Patio in Mexico City and took out a full-page ad in *Variety* announcing her sold-out success there. I put her on a salary of $7,500 a week plus expenses and contacted Jake Kozloff of the Last Frontier and Abe Schiller of the Flamingo Hotel, two of Las Vegas's hottest night spots. Schiller responded first, offering to book her for three weeks, but later Kozloff made an even more attractive offer, $12,500 a week for four weeks, and many other extras, also, which I pursued. These negotiations were delicate and complicated. I found myself flying between Mexico City, where Josephine was working, and Las Vegas via Los Angeles, where I was making some inroads in reviving her film career.

Las Vegas in the early morning is like a Christmas tree with its lights turned off, a dull place for an early riser and non-gambler like me. I quickly learned to adjust my arrival time in order to conduct business the Vegas way, which is after the lights go back on. The contract with Kozloff was signed at last, complete with Jo's now-mandatory nondiscrimination clause. It was time to arrange for Josephine and her entourage to arrive from Mexico, complete with secretary, French maid, two musicians, and twenty-four wardrobe cases.

Meanwhile I pursued other outlets for her in television, product endorsements, and of course films. Convincing Hollywood to get involved with Josephine Baker would require my most persuasive powers. With considerable trepidation I approached Darryl Zanuck at 20th Century–Fox, whom I had known a long time. I also talked to Howard Hughes at RKO. I knew what they were up against, for bucking the Hearst enterprise was no laughing matter. The careers of entertainers far less controversial than Baker had been snuffed out by the reigning pooh-bahs in the King Syndicate.

Consequently I was not surprised when Hughes turned me down and Zanuck backed off. I was able to change Zanuck's mind only after hours of persuasion. Whether it was eloquence on my part or sheer exhaustion on his, I'll never know, but he came around. Any remaining doubts he had would all be erased when Jo performed for a month at Ciro's to sold-out acclaim.

By early April, with the Vegas debut only weeks away, I started to have second thoughts about Jo's wardrobe. The world's leading dress designers had always vied for the privilege of providing her costumes, as they were then assured maximum exposure to a wide audience of buyers. Josephine had always preferred the French designers such as Balmain, Schiaparelli, and Dior, but I thought it would be a diplomatic gesture to choose an American-based designer for a change. I decided to buy her a whole new wardrobe from Elizabeth Arden, who had Count Fernando Sarmi in her employ, and instructed Jo to wire her measurements to Arden's salon in New York City. Sarmi, along with Miss Arden and Monsieur Jacques, her chief hair-dresser, would all be in Las Vegas on opening night to make sure Josephine looked her best.

My correspondence piled up as I shuttled between New York and Los Angeles, with frequent stops in Las Vegas, checking with dress designers, hairdressers, coordinating a thousand and one details including the shipment of two white Birds of Paradise for her act. Josephine was famous for her menagerie and was currently traveling with a pet monkey. I took the zoo-keeping in stride along with all the rest. Baker was meticulous about every detail. So was I. If her Las Vegas act was to be the success of the age, everything had to be perfect. Our diligence paid off.

"J'ai deux amours, mon pays et Paris," Josephine sang her finale in that husky, intimate voice of hers, and for the first time in many weeks I found myself relaxing. Basking might be a bet-ter word as I looked around the room that night and took in the tumult. I had done the impossible—I had gotten Josephine a distinguished audience in an elegant club. The rest was all Josephine, and she never failed to turn an audience into a mass of devout Baker worshipers. Her act became the hottest ticket in the country, and getting into the Ramona Room had become as

difficult for the nightclub-goer as it had been for Jo in the first place.

On May 1, 1952, Josephine was to open at Ciro's on Sunset Strip in Hollywood. I wanted her opening to rival any event in Hollywood history. Her wardrobe alone would put even the most glamorous star's to shame. If the producers and major directors could see Josephine at her finest, I felt, her act would be an entrée into a career as an international film star.

There were black entertainers working in Hollywood in the early fifties, but their roles reflected the prevailing racial attitudes in the country. There was only one way to initiate change in Hollywood, and that was at the box office. Therefore, it was box-office glamour I intended to showcase.

To opening night at Ciro's I invited every important producer, director, and film executive in town as well as the brightest stars of the time. My telephone in the Beverly Hills Hotel rang incessantly with pleas for tickets. It was a very heady experience producing the hottest act in Hollywood.

On May 2 the limousines in front of Ciro's were causing traffic jams up and down Sunset Strip. Josephine's fellow performers had turned out in force. At my table that night were Darryl Zanuck and his entourage, among them a shy, soft-spoken unknown named Marilyn Monroe. Zanuck was interested in having her work for Fox. Although her credentials at the time were limited to a few lackluster movies and the title "Miss Cheesecake of 1951," Zanuck saw her potential, and he brought her to the opening to show her off. I could see she was entranced by Josephine's act.

Afterward Marilyn approached me.

"Mr. Taub, I really enjoyed the show. Josephine is so beautiful. Do you think I could meet her?"

The crush of well-wishers backstage was unbelievable, but we managed to wedge our way into Jo's dressing room, where I made the introductions. The result was instant friendship.

In a few years Josephine Baker would become one of the world's most enthusiastic mothers, adopting homeless waifs from all over the world. Marilyn, on the other hand, spent her whole life searching for substitute mothers and fathers. I think what happened that night was an exchange of two people's very strong needs.

Later that night Marilyn asked me whether she could come back the following night.

"Come as often as you like. You're my guest," I told her.

While Josephine was at Ciro's, I pursued my discussions with Zanuck, attempting to convince him to give Jo a role in *Gentlemen Prefer Blondes,* a film version of the long-running Anita Loos Broadway show in which Betty Grable was to star. Our discussions were arduous, sometimes lasting until three in the morning as I presented my arguments to what seemed like relays of Fox executives as well as Zanuck himself. I emerged from one of these marathons with a victory. Jo had been given a co-starring role. Not only that, but she had insisted Marilyn be given a part too, and Zanuck had agreed. It was Marilyn's sizzling performance in *Gentlemen Prefer Blondes* that sent her on the way to the top, and I know she never forgot Josephine's support. It was an unusual act of generosity in an industry not known for such behavior, but that was how the lady was.

I was soon to see another side of Josephine Baker that would send me reeling. By the end of the Ciro's engagement, a tentative film offer had been worked out. Jo would play herself and be billed as co-star with Betty Grable. Her salary would be $6,500 a week with a four-week minimum. Any recording she would do would be billed at $1,000 a day. I was sure I could do even better as the movie approached production. Meanwhile Josephine had swung through the East, playing Chicago and New York clubs like the Rainbow Room and the Latin Quarter. Our contract was to terminate in mid-June, when Jo would start her South American tour.

Jo was in high spirits because the money was rolling in. Les Milandes was getting a new roof, a new plumbing and heating system, and a J-shaped pool. She was excited about everything —her chateau, her film debut, her plans to adopt children . . . everything was going her way.

One evening as we were discussing some minor personnel problems in the touring group and reminiscing about her successes in Las Vegas and at Ciro's, she brought up the Fox contract.

"You know, Bill, I've been thinking about the Fox deal, and I think they made a mistake with the title," she said.

"How so?"

She gave me one of the looks she used on people who were too dim-witted to see the obvious.

"The title's all wrong," she said.

"But, Jo, that's the name of the show. Anita Loos wrote it that way. It ran on Broadway for years. Everybody knows it as *Gentlemen Prefer Blondes.*"

"Bill," she said, beginning to lose her patience, "I'm not blond."

"But, Jo, you're supposed to appear as yourself. You're not acting as anyone else. Doesn't that make sense?"

There was an ominous pause. I was afraid I was beginning to see the light.

"The name of the movie should be *Gentlemen Prefer Josephine Baker.*"

"What??"

"Why not? I think that's a perfect title."

"That's the craziest damn thing I ever heard. You can't go and change an established title just like that."

"Now just one minute, Bill," she said, heating up, "I don't understand why it's so difficult for you to see this my way. Titles are changed all the time. The contract will just have to be changed. I won't sign unless it's *Gentlemen Prefer Josephine Baker.* It's perfect. I can work it into my act."

I had a sinking feeling the argument was already over.

"Look, Jo, this is absurd. When I went to Fox to negotiate this contract I talked myself hoarse convincing them you were the soul of reason. They took me at my word. If I went to Zanuck now and asked him to change the title to *Gentlemen Prefer Josephine Baker,* he'd laugh me right out of his office, and by God I wouldn't blame him!"

She wouldn't budge. *Gentlemen Prefer Blondes* was made with its original title but without Josephine.

I was destined to go another round with Josephine in 1960, when I produced her engagement at the Huntington Hartford Theatre in Los Angeles. There she was embraced by Charles de Gaulle and admired by President John Kennedy, who confessed he had been in love with her since he first saw her in Paris in 1940.

But that June in 1952, nothing would have convinced me I would ever again have a relationship with Josephine other than as admirer, preferably from afar. With many regrets but as amicably as possible, I kissed the fabulous Josephine Baker good-bye.

Many of the people who were to weave themselves in and out of my life over the years were present during the Josephine Baker episode: Flor Trujillo, Howard Hughes, Charles de Gaulle, John Kennedy, Marilyn Monroe. In turn, these people were to link me with others who played prominent roles in my adventures: Richard Nixon, Madame Mao Tse-tung, James Hoffa, the Kennedys, Aristotle Onassis.

It was my friendship with Flor Trujillo that would cause me to become involved with Richard Nixon in a pursuit across Europe of the Trujillo family fortune. This early episode in a series of confrontations with Nixon over many years taught me lessons I would find most helpful in later involvements with him.

In 1971 I went another round with Richard Nixon, this time privately at the White House. We discussed the conditions under which Jimmy Hoffa would be pardoned. Less than two years later, when I, along with the rest of the country, heard the news that our President had taped every conversation that took place in the Oval Office, I knew it wouldn't be long before I was called to testify before the Watergate prosecution team. I also knew when I did that the axe would fall and Richard Nixon would be impeached. I went before the prosecution team during the preliminary hearings and came away with the feeling they were doing everything possible to prevent the impeachment of the President. Later I was told this was indeed the case, as their primary concern was the stability of the country.

The tape of my conversation with Nixon was one of several that were suppressed because their contents contained undeniable grounds for impeachment. In late November 1971 the President of the United States called me to his private office to conduct his own private business. The transaction under discussion involved billions of dollars.

I introduced Marilyn Monroe to Yves Montand and regretted the tragic results. Montand, in turn, played an important role in the film Z, which cost me a murky entanglement with the Greek junta, the Central Intelligence Agency, and the

U.S. State Department. I became the proverbial Man Who Knew Too Much, and my knowledge nearly cost me my life in an assassination attempt on a deserted road in the French Alps.

From the *Z* story and its sequel came an introduction to Madame Mao Tse-tung and a secret trip to Peking two months before Nixon's official visit in 1972. Madame Mao made reference to a fortune in gold bars worth around one hundred million dollars, which I already knew lay in a vault on Wall Street. After my conversation with Madame Mao that day concerning a treasure that, in her words, was "soon to come home to its rightful owner" via those special diplomatic channels that are immune to all inspection, there was no doubt in my mind about who the courier was going to be.

Howard Hughes, who thought Josephine Baker was too hot to handle, tried a few years later to involve me in a scheme so outrageous it nearly succeeded. He planned to dupe the Vatican into unwittingly participating in clandestine global surveillance for the benefit of himself and the CIA: a new satellite, sanctified by the Pope, and free from all regulation. For once he failed.

James Hoffa assumed people would work miracles for him if he yelled loud enough. I worked one for him in 1963, pitting myself against the power of the Department of Justice and the personal wrath of Attorney General Robert Kennedy. I had seventy-two hours to raise $45 million in surety bonds for him through a man in Switzerland. I was still on the ground at the TWA terminal in New York when it started to snow. I beat the deadline by ten minutes, and in his gratitude Jimmy Hoffa withheld my fee, using it as leverage for future miracles he might want me to perform.

I almost succeeded in 1972, this time involving Jimmy in a visit to Hanoi to arrange for the release of twelve prisoners of war with behind-the-scenes assistance from North Vietnamese peace negotiator Le Duc Tho and Madame Mao herself, as well as a very ambivalent, then suddenly very helpful Richard Nixon. It was Hoffa himself who caused the failure. He wouldn't get on the plane that would take him to Hanoi because he said he "smelled a trap." At the time I thought he was a very paranoid man, but after he vanished I changed my mind about Hoffa and his instincts.

My knowledge of the events leading up to the disappearance of James Hoffa is being revealed here for the first time. I know who killed Hoffa and I know why. My knowledge is based on my close relationship with the man over many years. I knew him—how he thought, how he reacted. I knew his habits, his plans, and who his enemies were.

Ten days before Hoffa's disappearance he insisted I call him from a New York telephone booth. I did, and on that stifling July night his news turned my blood to ice. James Hoffa had plans to have someone "disappear." Those plans backfired and were the cause of his death.

The events of my life feature not me so much as a cast of characters who play their roles in repertory fashion. Status and fortunes change. Bit players become leads. Adversaries become allies. And loyal friends become the loyal opposition.

In my dealings with people in high places, I have watched the secret exchange of vast amounts of money for favors among those whose fortunes are large enough and whose power is far-reaching enough to make them impervious to control by law. I have watched government manipulated from within and without for the purpose of personal aggrandizement and ideological zeal, and have seen the all-pervasive system of hidden connections that makes the world go round. I know the system will never change unless we know the names of the people who adhere to the maxim that he who governs the most makes the least noise.

Many of the characters in my story are now dead. Others have fallen from power. They have all had their say, and now it is time to have mine.

2

EARLY NIXON

Throughout my life I have had many encounters with Richard Nixon in his roles as Vice President, private citizen, attorney, President, and fallen leader. Sometimes the encounters were direct confrontations; other times I would be made aware of Nixon's participation only by chance. As far as I'm concerned, Richard Nixon has always been the same, predictably so. As I look back to my first encounter with him, I feel not unlike an art patron viewing one of the master's early works.

My first experience with him came through my friendship with Dwight Eisenhower, which had begun in Paris, long before Eisenhower became President. At that time I was living in Paris, representing Josephine Baker, Charles Trenet, and a number of other French entertainers.

A mutual friend brought Maurice Chevalier to see me about representing him in his battle to enter the United States. He had been accused of being a collaborator and had been denied a visa. It was an unfair charge, but it made good headlines and a lot of people used it for political mileage.

I agreed to represent Chevalier, although I knew my efforts would pit me against some old friends in Washington. I spent much time at his penthouse at 14 Avenue Foch in Paris and his country home in Marne-le-Coquette, familiarizing myself with Chevalier's activities during the war. During one of those visits I met Dwight Eisenhower.

The two men had become friends and card-playing buddies during the war while Eisenhower headed NATO and lived in Paris. Eisenhower, more than anyone else, knew Maurice Chevalier was no collaborator. He made no secret of his opinion of those who accused his friend of cooperating with the Nazis.

Besides their love of cards, the two men shared such pleasures as painting and cooking. Both Ike and Chevalier considered themselves superior cooks, and they often traded dinners. I shared many of these evenings of good food, wine, and conversation, and a friendship developed among us that transcended professional concerns.

In my efforts to win Chevalier permission to re-enter the United States, I found myself in a battle against some very powerful political figures as well as the U.S. Department of Justice. On August 22, 1953, after many long months of negotiation, Chevalier received a letter from Ed Sullivan, written from Sullivan's Paris hotel. It read:

Dear Maurice,

Before flying to New York this afternoon, I talked to Bill Taub about a date or two on my TV show. I'd love to use you and of course you'd be a sensational success.

Delighted to learn that Taub has cleared up your visa problem with Senator Pat McCarran and France because we have missed you in America.

Taub's reputation in New York is that he is a conscientious, loyal, energetic representative and his work with McCarran on your behalf indicates this to be completely true.

Awaiting your arrival in New York eagerly, Madame joins with me in every warm expression.

Always,
Ed Sullivan

Eisenhower exulted as much as Chevalier and I when that letter arrived, for it seemed more official than the one sent by the U.S. government.

My friendship with Eisenhower continued after his election to the White House. It was the very nature of our relationship that prompted a call, some years later, from Clifford Folger, chairman of the Republican National Finance Committee. The Republican Convention had just renominated Eisenhower and Nixon, and Folger told me an emergency had developed. Ike had just come out of his ileitis operation and was physically and emotionally depressed. He wanted to withdraw from the race. The mere thought sent spasms of fear through the ranks of the Republican faithful. None of the Washington crowd had been able to bring him out of his mood.

Folger knew I was a kind of bridge between the two worlds Ike enjoyed. He hoped I might be able to find a way to penetrate Eisenhower's dark mood, and I agreed to visit the White House for breakfast. When I met the President, it was quickly apparent he was more than depressed. He was smoldering with resentment. Never a political man, he had always been unhappy with the shoddy expediency of politics. As we talked, his anger burst forth. He felt he had been pressured into seeking reelection and pressured into keeping Nixon on the ticket.

"I don't want to run on the same ticket with that man," he told me. "I should never have let them talk me into it. He's totally self-serving and he's always into something. To him, honesty is just one more mask to wear at the right time."

I listened and let him sputter out his anger, then told him his old card-playing buddy, Chevalier, would soon be in the United States to co-star in the film *Gigi* with my good friend Hermione Gingold at Metro-Goldwyn-Mayer. His mood brightened at once, and we were soon into happy recollections of other times and places. But his words about Richard Nixon, uttered in a moment of angry confidence, stayed with me.

Eisenhower did not withdraw and the ticket was reelected. At the inaugural ball I would have my first confrontation with Richard M. Nixon. Mamie Eisenhower had graciously agreed to invite a friend of mine, the well-known New York fashion designer Frank Perullo, to create her gowns for the inaugural balls. Because of personal problems, Perullo was unable to complete the assignment, but I wanted to express my appreciation to Mamie. While in Paris I bought her a beaded evening bag and sent it to her upon returning home.

Eisenhower had offered me the ambassadorship to Luxembourg. Business commitments made it impossible for me to accept, so I suggested the name of an old friend, Carrie Munn. Perle Mesta was just concluding her ambassadorship to Luxembourg, and I felt the post ought to be held by another woman. Eisenhower agreed, and it was arranged that Carrie Munn would attend the inaugural ball as my guest at my table. Carrie was a Palm Beach socialite fashion designer.

While I was at the Shoreham Hotel the Sunday before the inauguration, Bernard Shanley, Eisenhower's appointments secretary, called. President and Mrs. Eisenhower were inviting me to tea that afternoon. It was emphasized that the invitation was private, and I was to come alone.

After I arrived, Mamie stayed only a few minutes and then left me alone with the President. The conversation that followed both moved and disturbed me. Eisenhower, in his time of triumph, seemed to be experiencing another mood of depression. He told me how much he appreciated my friendship and in particular my visit to him when he was feeling so poorly after his ileitis operation. Then he told me what was really troubling him.

"I don't expect to live out the full term of my presidency," he told me. "I'm really concerned about my health."

"Mr. President, I'm sure you'll live many long years," I said.

His face remained somber. "I hope so," he said. "I wouldn't want to leave the presidency in that man's hands." He stared into space for a moment, then reached into his pocket and pulled out a sheet of paper. "I'm going to give you a list of names I'd like you to have," he said. "These are people who have been very close to me. If any of them can ever be of assistance to you, I want you to feel free to call upon them."

He handed me the sheet of paper and I glanced at it. There were some thirty names and addresses on it. The list was a virtual guidebook to the most prominent people in the world, nationally and internationally, in banking, industry, commerce, and government. As I folded the list into my pocket, I knew I would treasure it whether or not I ever had reason to call a single one of those names.

"I've got something else for you," he said, and from a

nearby table he handed me a carved ivory elephant. "This has been part of my collection for years. I want you to have it."

There were tears in Eisenhower's eyes when I left that afternoon. They were not caused by an attack of sentiment. Rather, he was beset with highly mixed feelings about his coming term, upset by the prospect of prolonged associations he deplored. Dwight Eisenhower preferred to look backward rather than forward.

I went to the inaugural ball a few nights later feeling concern for the man about to spend four more years as President. He and Mamie were already in the presidential box when I arrived, and it was Mamie who first spied me at my table with Carrie Munn and my other guests. She held up the beaded bag I had brought her from Paris, gave a little wave with it, and I was relieved to see Eisenhower seemed his old cheerful self. A little while later Clifford Folger came to my table.

The President wanted me to join him in the presidential box. I expected to stop only for a moment and took Carrie Munn with me, but Eisenhower rose and greeted us warmly and insisted we sit down next to him. Unfortunately, Richard and Pat Nixon were sitting there. Some hurried conversation followed. Then the Nixons got up and moved two rows back to sit beside the Folger party. President Eisenhower motioned to the empty seats, and Carrie Munn and I sat down where the Nixons had been. I glanced back and caught a glimpse of Richard Nixon's face. It was tight with anger. The little mechanical smile in no way matched his eyes.

The incident had been a manifestation of Dwight Eisenhower's words to me in private. Aside from the necessities of office, he wanted as little to do with Nixon as possible. At the inaugural celebration he had leaped at the chance to reminisce with those he felt most comfortable with about times when he felt more in his element. Later Mamie took me aside and with typical sensitivity suggested I dance with Pat Nixon. I agreed at once. I had felt somewhat embarrassed by the incident and disturbed at Nixon's inability to take it in stride. I approached Pat and asked her to dance. I was coldly turned aside by her and determinedly ignored by Nixon.

To me, the incident was but a passing unpleasantry. I was to learn that no unpleasantry ever passed with Nixon. My next contact with him came a few years later. He had run for the presidency and lost to John Kennedy and, with much public fanfare, had joined the law firm of Mudge, Rose, Guthrie, and Alexander. I was surprised to receive an invitation to a cocktail party given by Mudge, Rose in honor of their new partner.

I had not had a chance to reply to the invitation when I received a telephone call from Rose Mary Woods in behalf of Mudge, Rose. "Mr. Taub, we haven't heard from you about the cocktail party for the Vice President," she said. When I didn't give her a direct reply, she suggested that, in lieu of a gift, a check be sent.

"A check?" I said. "For what?"

She hesitated a moment before answering. "The firm is buying Mr. Nixon an apartment at 812 Fifth Avenue." There was another delicate pause. "It's suggested checks should be for a minimum of a hundred dollars."

"I understand," I murmured and managed to put the phone down without further comment. The building at 812 Fifth Avenue was the one in which Nelson Rockefeller then lived. I certainly did understand. The purpose of the cocktail party was not to honor the new partner so much as to raise the purchase price for his apartment. I returned the RSVP card with the "shall not" box checked. I was sure it would be as carefully noted as those that contained acceptances.

I never learned just whose idea that venture was, but with the benefit of hindsight, I'm sure it was a warming-up exercise in the art of personal aggrandizement that would culminate in the purchase of Nixon's palatial residences in Florida and California.

An association with Richard Nixon in Spain, which took place not long after the cocktail party incident, would be an alliance of sorts. Like the alliances to come, it would be fashioned more of necessity than desire. Yet I hoped for the best. I was an optimist then.

The joint venture with Nixon concerned the pursuit of a huge fortune purloined by the brothers of our respective clients, Flor and Angelita Trujillo. Angelita had hired the firm of Mudge, Rose, and I was representing my good friend Flor. Their father, the Generalissimo of the Dominican Republic, had been assassinated.

On a spring night in 1961 two men who had been working out of the Miami area made a trip to the Dominican Republic in a disguised plane. They brought with them guns, ammunition, and a plan for the assassination of Rafael Trujillo. Their plan succeeded, and after the assassination his two sons, Ramfis and Rhadames, fled the country with the remainder of the Trujillo fortune, a good part of which had already been removed to other countries, among them France, Spain, Liechtenstein, and Switzerland. The fortune had been amassed by the Generalissimo. While he reigned as head of the Dominican Republic, he controlled forty-eight companies, including an auto distributorship, a paint factory, a match factory, and a sugar mill.

Trujillo also owned 60 percent of the land, much of it sugar-producing. It was said that in the Dominican Republic not one dollar ever changed hands, whether in a bank or a bordello, without a portion finding its way into the private coffers of Trujillo.

The exact amount of the Trujillo fortune was not (and still is not) known, but the best estimates ranged from $150 million to $1 billion. It was a very broad range, but even at the conservative end a very considerable amount of money was involved. When their brothers absconded with the fortune, Flor Trujillo and her half-sister, Angelita, immediately took separate actions to obtain their shares.

It was clear I would have to work closely with Nixon in pursuit of that fortune when I arrived in Spain. Recalling my previous brushes with him, I viewed this prospect with something less than pleasure.

When I arrived in Spain, I had already addressed myself to the practicalities of the task. As Ramfis was believed to control the largest part of the fortune, it was decided to go after him first.* Ramfis had taken up residence in Spain, where the political climate was favorable. His father and General Franco had been very close friends, and Ramfis apparently felt he could pursue his usual lavish pleasures there to a fare-thee-well.

He had been born into privilege, and his taste for glamorous film stars had become legendary. Among those most

---

*Generalissimo Trujillo always said, "Power is golden." His son Ramfis said, "Power is gold."

often linked with Ramfis Trujillo were Kim Novak, Joan Collins, and Zsa Zsa Gabor.

Outside Madrid Ramfis Trujillo owned a castlelike home where he kept a garageful of fast and expensive cars and a stable of fine polo ponies. He also had a large yacht, an office, and an apartment in Madrid. I knew Ramfis would be disinclined to give up anything that might diminish his lifestyle, but there are ways to approach any problem. I had formulated a plan that took in the political facts of life and the climate of Spain as I knew it.

I was not a newcomer to Spain and its ways. Over the years I had made many friends on different levels of Spanish society. I also represented the family of Queen Fabiola of Belgium, who was of Spanish birth and of royal blood. In Spain, I knew, one did not run roughshod over social and political sensitivities.

My plans centered around obtaining the assistance of two men. One was Dr. Christobal Martinez-Bordiu, a world-renowned open-heart surgeon, Marquis of Villa Verde and husband of General Franco's only daughter, Carmencita. Under the auspices of IBM, I had produced a film for Spanish television of Dr. Bordieu performing open-heart surgery. It was one of the first, if not the first, of its kind ever produced, and General Franco was very proud of it.

The other man was former Spanish Ambassador to the United States Antonio Garrigues, who had been Spain's envoy to the Vatican as well as General Franco's attorney. Both these men were eminently positioned, socially and politically, to cooperate with me in my approach to the problem. Both agreed to help. Dr. Bordieu even arranged for me to stay at the Phoenicia Hotel on the Grand Villa, an establishment open only to members of the Spanish nobility and their guests.

Nixon, I learned, was staying at the Ritz and working out of the U.S. Embassy in Madrid. The day after I landed in Madrid, I arranged a meeting with Nixon. I saw no value in working at cross-purposes to achieve the same end, and I believed a strategy session was the first order of business. We met at the Ritz, where Nixon arrived in an embassy car, and even before we began to talk I could feel a brusque antagonism emanating from him. I outlined what I felt was the best way to proceed, assuming he would be happy to take advantage of my knowledge of the country and my connections. It became clear he had no such intention.

"I'd like to try to arrange a personal meeting with Ramfis," I began.

"Why?" Nixon said.

"I think he might listen to reason if an appeal is made to his better nature, his sense of family pride," I explained. "There are people here who could contact him and make the initial overtures. I've always believed you can catch more flies with honey than with vinegar."

"That's nonsense," Nixon said. "He and his brother stole the money for themselves. The man's no more than a common thief. It's as simple as that."

"Not over here, it's not," I argued.

Nixon looked at me severely, leaned forward, and gave me a short lecture on Spain that was remarkable for its ignorance, to say nothing of its insensitivity.

"This has got to be handled forcefully. These people understand authority," he said. "Ramfis Trujillo must be arrested, imprisoned, and extradited. I'll insist the Spanish authorities do just that."

"I doubt they'll do anything of the kind," I said.

"Of course they'll do exactly that. I'll lean hard. I'll go through every channel there is. I'll have our ambassador use every bit of his influence."

"In this matter, I doubt he'll have much influence," I remarked.

"Then I'll use my own. I'm hardly an ordinary little attorney pleading his case, remember."

I continued to express disagreement with his approach, but he wouldn't budge. It was plain by his tolerant smile that he thought I had a problem. Not only was I timid but I had very little understanding of power. It was obvious Richard Nixon was about to gather his vice presidential robes about him to face down the Spanish government.

We agreed to keep in contact, but I had already given up thoughts of a truly cooperative effort. In fact, after what I had just seen, I wanted to stay as far away from Nixon as possible. This turned out to be easier said than done.

I began to follow my plan. I lunched with Antonio Garrigues in his law offices, and with Dr. Bordieu over a glass of Manzanilla, and presented my thoughts to both men. They promised to do all they could, which I knew would be considerable. The wheels had been set in motion. Now all I had to do was to listen, and remain available while they initiated their own moves. In Spain delicacy is a highly esteemed quality, even in the bullring. It is only the bull that charges.

From time to time I saw Nixon at the Ritz. I also received word he had put through a formal request for the arrest of Ramfis Trujillo and that he was pushing the demand through official channels. My own moves bore fruit first. I was informed Ramfis had agreed to see me. After all, I was no stranger to him. I couldn't count the number of times I'd seen him during the years I had met with his father. I was driven to his estate outside Madrid where two armed guards met me at the gate. In addition to the guards, some forty bloodhounds patrolled the property to ensure Ramfis's privacy.

He met me in a living room filled with dark heavy-footed Spanish furniture, and at once I was introduced to the problem of guilt by association.

"How dare you come here and try to have me thrown in jail?" Ramfis shouted.

"I had nothing to do with that," I answered quickly. He was tall, suave, a Latin Errol Flynn type; a sneer came easily to the lips of Ramfis Trujillo.

"You are his countryman. You are both here for the same purpose. You meet and talk about it," he said.

"I told you, I've had nothing to do with his actions. And I didn't come here to talk about Mr. Nixon. I came to talk about you and Flor."

My attempt at brushing aside Nixon failed. "Do you know what that man has been doing?" Ramfis raged. "He's been trying to have an order signed to put me in jail. He's been going around to everybody—pushing, pestering, threatening. Who the hell does he think he is?"

I said nothing as he went on for a full fifteen minutes. Finally I found a chance to break in. "I want to talk about the money, Ramfis," I said. "You and Rhadames have no right to all of it. Flor is entitled to her share."

"I want nothing to do with her. I'll give her nothing,

absolutely nothing," he shot back. "She's the one who's behind all this, stirring everyone up." Once he and Flor had been very attached to each other, but Ramfis had chosen to become enraged at the one he had been closest to in the family. I argued the case for a while longer, but it was apparent Ramfis was in no mood to be reached by pleas to his better nature. I decided it was best to leave. Knowing the mercurial Trujillo temperament as well as I did, I thought tomorrow the wind might blow from another direction, and I wanted to leave the door open for another meeting.

"Think about this," I suggested. "And we'll sit down again soon."

"We'll sit down again never," he roared. "I will give nothing. No settlements, nothing. You can tell that to your Mr. Nixon."

I didn't bother to protest he was not "my" Mr. Nixon, but as I was driven back to Madrid I had a few choice silent words for the man. I called him as soon as I reached the hotel. When I finally got through to him he agreed to meet me at the Ritz. I saw no purpose in trying to arrange a clandestine meeting. It had become obvious I was being watched as well as he, and any clumsy attempt at secrecy would only make matters more suspicious. I wasted no time with Nixon once we met.

"You're lousing up the works," I began, and that was a gentler version of what I really wanted to say. I recounted my meeting with Ramfis and his fury at the Nixon moves.

"He's worried," Nixon said.

I stared at him. "He's not worried. He's just mad as hell," I said. "This isn't America. It's not even France or Germany. Things are done differently here. There are all sorts of deep ties, friendships—"

Nixon ignored my words and cut in, "I've finally gotten directly to Franco. My demands are on his desk now, and I expect action any minute."

I could only stare at him in amazement. "Aren't you aware of the fact that Franco and Generalissimo Trujillo were the very closest of friends?"

"That's all past history," he answered.

It was hopeless, I realized. He knew nothing about the Spanish character, and perhaps even less about friendship. I told him the meeting was over and left, hoping his demands had not actually reached Franco. For the next few days that hope grew as I learned Nixon was still pounding tables and making demands. When later in the week I received a call from Antonio Garrigues to attend a meeting in his office concerning the Trujillo matter, I responded at once. Perhaps the approaching debacle could still be avoided.

When I arrived at the meeting, I was surprised to find my friend Dr. Bordiu was also there. As I sat down with General Franco's attorney and his son-in-law, they informed me of certain developments that they considered both ominous and urgent. With almost apologetic regrets for the unpleasant realities of their message, they gave me the bad news, in true keeping with the cultured Spanish gentleman's belief that if poor wine must be served, it can at least be presented in the best manner.

"General Franco has just signed a decree forbidding the arrest or extradition of Ramfis Trujillo," Señor Garrigues said. "There has been no crime committed in this country by Ramfis Trujillo. He is, in fact, an honored guest here under the protection of General Franco. The General is most disturbed at the attempts and the methods used to try to have him placed under arrest."

"Mr. Nixon is not the Vice President now, and in Spain he never was," Dr. Bordieu interjected with a little half-smile. "General Franco resents his attitude. But regardless of the personalities involved, the General has not been pro-American since the days of our civil war when so much support for the Loyalists came from your country. The involvement of American agents in the slaying of Generalissimo Trujillo has not made him any more sympathetic to your country or your cause here."

Then Antonio Garrigues leaned forward and touched my hand. "I am sorry to have to put it so unpleasantly, my friend, but I have been told it would be best for Mr. Nixon to leave Spain. If he continues in his ways, he may violate certain civil laws he may not be aware of and find himself arrested rather than Ramfis. I hope you will kindly impress this upon him."

Although both these old friends were too civilized to phrase it in Ramfis Trujillo's terms, I was made aware without a word exchanged between us that they also felt, by the very nature of our mutual pursuit, that Richard Nixon was my problem. They also said something else. There would be no money coming from Ramfis Trujillo.

I thanked them for their help and their advice and returned at once to my apartment at the Phoenicia. It took me a while to get hold of Nixon, but the tone of my voice convinced him to come to a meeting immediately. I told him exactly what had been said. The warning had been clear enough, but just in case, I made it clearer.

"You've cooked your goose but good," I told him. "I've been trying to tell you it's a different ball game here. It's Franco's ball park. He owns the ball and both teams, and he makes up the rules and he always wins. You'd better leave Spain right away."

Nixon muttered something, but the color had drained from his face. Suddenly he was a very frightened man.

"Go to Paris," I said. "I'll be there in a few days. The rules will be different there, and we can move against Rhadames."

Nixon rose and walked from the table without a backward glance, without a word of thanks for my warning. I excused the lapse as the oversight of a badly shaken man.

In a few days I left Spain for France. Upon my arrival at the Ritz in Paris, I contacted Jean François, the international banker at the Banque Romande in Geneva, Switzerland, where he was chairman of the board. Because of his position in banking circles, Jean François probably knew more about the flow of the Trujillo monies than anyone, including the Trujillos. He had been appointed to assist in the pursuit of the monies held by Rhadames.

France was a different country with a different set of personal and political allegiances. The situation was more hopeful than in Spain, and strategic plans were made for the arrest of Rhadames. Jean François was held in high esteem by President de Gaulle, and I was a personal friend of the General as well. Nonetheless, facilitating moves through the French courts for the arrest encompassed bitter legal problems because our counsel was taking every precaution to prevent obstacles put in our way by lesser authorities with ties to the battery of lawyers Rhadames had employed.

With the tacit assistance of the Ministry of Justice, Rhadames Trujillo was finally arrested and extradited to Switzerland. In Geneva he tried several legal maneuvers to obtain his freedom. These were merely a smokescreen, for the promise of financial reward and the power of the Trujillo money were his real weapons. However, Jean François was an eminently qualified Swiss banker who also functioned in the Geneva courts, and he was determined to triumph over Rhadames.

Rhadames was unsuccessful in his attempts to free himself and finally agreed to a settlement of several million dollars in exchange for his release. The pursuit was finally over. While the technical, legal, and financial details were being thrashed out in Paris and Geneva, I had a final meeting with Richard Nixon over the settlement. In Spain he had been an obstruction. In France his efforts had been virtually nonexistent. But by then I realized I should be grateful for his low profile.

As far as I knew, Nixon hadn't spent his own money for a dinner, a taxi, or a chocolate bar. He hadn't made a telephone call that wasn't charged to someone else. He had made no real contribution to the victory. In fact, he had almost undermined it in Spain. Nevertheless, he received for his efforts a check for $1,625,000. When he began to complain about his expenses, I told him I thought he should take the money and run. He took it and went his way and I went mine.

He never did find time to express any appreciation for what I or anyone else had done to bring about the settlement. He returned to Mudge, Rose a hero. They were well satisfied with the accomplishment of their new partner. As for me, I had learned a lesson about Richard Nixon.

There would be other lessons learned, other questions answered. They would concern the killers of Rafael Trujillo. Years later I was to have separate encounters with two of the men from Miami who had carried out the assassination of Trujillo, and they both claimed to have done the job for the Central Intelligence Agency.

The first encounter was very disturbing. As my visitor calmly described how he had been paid by the CIA to murder her father, Flor Trujillo sat on a couch across from him, her face rigid with horror and contempt. The second encounter, which was by long-distance telephone, was more of the hair-raising variety. The man who threatened me at the other end of the wire was discovered a few months later curled inside an oil drum floating off the coast of Florida. His name was Johnny Roselli.

In 1962, however, the killers of Rafael Trujillo had no identity. I certainly would not have connected the assassination with an agency of my government. In fact, I would have dismissed such a theory as a spy-thriller invention. That was many years ago. Today I am a much more cynical man.

3

THE DEATH OF MARILYN MONROE

In the summer of 1962, as I was preparing to go to the Riviera, I spent my Saturdays at the New York Athletic Club. One afternoon I was in the steam room when an emergency call came from my housekeeper. I was to telephone Spyros Skouras, president of 20th Century-Fox, at his home in Westchester.

Skouras had just been released from the hospital, and he sounded very weak and troubled. "Bill, can you get away? I've got to see you at once. I'll send a car to bring you up to Westchester."

I said I would come. Skouras was one friend I would try to move mountains for. Besides, I knew he was in big trouble. The filming of *Cleopatra* had cost his studio an astronomical sum that had not been recouped at the box office. Then, to make matters worse, Marilyn Monroe had just walked off the set of *Something's Got to Give* and refused to return.

Fox was preparing a $34-million breach-of-contract suit against her. In two weeks there would be a board of directors meeting at Fox, and there was a good chance that because of these financial disasters Skouras would be ousted. It was no wonder he was so distraught.

He was resting in his living room when I arrived. We talked

at length about the possibility of convincing Marilyn to return to the filming of *Something's Got to Give*. I hadn't been in touch with her very much that year, so I had no idea what kind of shape she was in. However, since breaking her contract, she had more or less dropped out of sight, and I knew Marilyn well enough to be worried about her reclusive behavior. It wasn't like her to shut herself off from her friends.

I told Skouras everything I knew about Marilyn that made it unlikely she would ever complete the film in Hollywood. It took a long time.

My role as Marilyn's confidant and dispenser of brotherly advice went back a long time. In the early fifties, when her marriage to Joe DiMaggio was about to break up, we made a flight from New York to California. She sat next to me for most of the trip, confessing that her marriage to DiMaggio was a wretched failure, while Joe rode alone a few seats ahead of us.

After the divorce she decided she wanted to live in New York, far from what she called the Hollywood leeches who were bleeding her financially and making an emotional wreck of her. She would often sit on the floor of my apartment, hair disheveled, wearing a dirty black sweater and jeans, tears running off her mascaraed lashes, and talk and talk. As she talked, her plans for a new life began to formulate. She was going to create a new style of living for herself in New York—new friends not involved in movie making, new interests of a more intellectual nature. I watched her slowly evolve from a distraught and indecisive woman into a self-confident one, brimming over with plans for a fresh start.

The first order of business was to help her find an apartment. I made inquiries among my fellow tenants in the building where I was living on Park Avenue, and found an acquaintance who was looking to sublet for a year or two. Marilyn and I went down to the second floor and went through the apartment. It was perfect, right down to the walls that were painted in the shades of jade and mauve so flattering to Marilyn. She was ecstatic. My acquaintance agreed to sublet for one year, and I told Marilyn she could stay with me for the week or so it would take her to get settled. We shook hands all around and had drinks.

That same afternoon Milton Greene called Marilyn at my apartment. Greene and his wife had formed a film production

company with Marilyn. She told him the great news about finding an apartment. He was shocked to hear she was staying with
me and insisted on seeing the apartment at once. Almost immediately he and Mrs. Greene appeared at my door, and we all
marched back down to the second floor to show the apartment
to the Greenes. When Milton discovered it had only one
bedroom, he told Marilyn it wouldn't do. She needed an apartment with two bedrooms, one for her and one for them.

Marilyn meekly complied. It wasn't long after that she
moved into the Greenes' house in Westport, Connecticut, to
prepare for the shooting of *The Prince and the Showgirl,* in
which she co-starred with Laurence Olivier. Terence Rattigan
had written the screenplay. It didn't do well, and Marilyn soon
escaped from the protective Greenes to Arthur Miller, whom
she had met through her new mentors. She and Arthur married,
and for a long time I saw little of her. Who knows? Had I urged
her to stay, Marilyn might have become Mrs. William L. Taub
instead of Mrs. Arthur Miller.

She came back into my life in 1960 when I was involved
with Yves Montand and Simone Signoret. They needed help
with a visa problem similar to the help I had given Maurice
Chevalier. The Montands had been denied entry visas because
in the eyes of U.S. Immigration and the Department of Justice,
their political activity in Europe stamped them as anti-American. Some people even considered them active Communists. I
was retained by 20th Century–Fox to petition Immigration and
Justice to give them permission to enter the country. I was successful, and Montand appeared on Broadway soon after as a
singer with a five-piece band. Then came the introduction I
would live to regret. On Montand's opening night I escorted
Marilyn Monroe backstage to meet Yves. He was tall, sexy, ur-
bane, and very French. Marilyn flipped.

Shortly after they met, Marilyn went to California to make
Let's Make Love. The production was delayed because of a
problem casting the leading man. Then I had one of my
brainstorms. I called Spyros Skouras and said, "Why don't you
co-star Yves Montand opposite Marilyn? I think the
chemistry's right." He thought I was stark, raving mad. I had
barely been able to get Montand into the country, and now I
wanted him to star in a Hollywood film? However, Skouras had

often questioned my sanity before and then come around, and he eventually changed his mind about this. Yves became Marilyn's co-star.

It was a cozy group that wound up in neighboring suites at the Beverly Hills Hotel. I was in one because I had Josephine Baker under a recording contract for 20th Century–Fox. Marilyn was next door with Arthur Miller, and the Montands were across the hall. We had many hilarious dinners and late-night visits back and forth. But little by little the atmosphere became volatile. What with the smoldering glances, the murmured innuendos, and the not-so-subtle simultaneous disappearances of Marilyn and Yves, I expected an explosion momentarily.

Then Arthur Miller left to work on the screenplay of *The Misfits,* Simone Signoret returned to France to do a film, and stars exploded over the Beverly Hills Hotel. It was obvious to me that Marilyn had fallen hard, this time with a passionate equal rather than a Pygmalion or a father substitute. This was pure eros, and if there are any doubts, I suggest staying up to catch the movie they made together the next time it appears on "The Late Show."

Marilyn once dreamed of going to Paris with Josephine Baker. The girl who knew nothing about Continental living would become a woman of culture and sophistication under Josephine's tutelage. The dream never materialized after Josephine backed out of *Gentlemen Prefer Blondes,* but now it was revived, with a twist: this time she would discover Europe as Mrs. Yves Montand.

One night I answered the telephone and heard the voice of Simone Signoret blistering its way from Paris through the Atlantic cable, across the North American continent, and into my unsuspecting ear. If anything happened between her husband and Marilyn, it would be my fault, she yelled, because I had brought them together.

I left for New York and Europe, but was back in Hollywood for Josephine Baker's opening at the Huntington Hartford Theatre. A picture that hangs on my wall, taken at the celebration following her opening night, will always haunt me. Yves and Marilyn are seated together at Josephine's premiere, Marilyn glowing like a bride-to-be and Yves gazing inscrutably into the camera. It was the last I saw of her for some time.

When the film was finished, Yves left for Paris. Marilyn threw him a champagne party at the airport in New York and called me afterward, hardly able to control her excitement. Yves, she told me, was going to Paris to divorce Simone and she was going to divorce Arthur Miller. When they had shed their respective mates, they would marry.

In the meantime she had a contractual obligation to work with Miller on the filming of *The Misfits,* which would take place in Nevada. Arthur had written the screenplay. They came and went in separate cars, I heard.

Then in August Marilyn suddenly walked off the set and checked into a Los Angeles hospital, claiming she was suffering from exhaustion. The truth was she had just received the shattering news that Yves Montand had changed his mind. He was in Hollywood with his wife. He wouldn't return her calls. Worst of all, Simone Signoret had told the press she was sorry for Marilyn.

The Montands returned to Paris, and the unraveling of Marilyn's life began. Five days after the filming of *The Misfits* was completed, the Millers announced their separation. By January 1961 Marilyn was divorced again. The year that had begun so unhappily would continue to be a bad one. Her mother died, Marilyn suffered a gallbladder attack, Arthur Miller remarried. She became involved in a very heady entanglement with President John F. Kennedy that she was emotionally ill-equipped to handle. The little girl who sang "Happy Birthday" to the President at Madison Square Garden that year was eating herself alive with anxiety. She was thirty-five years old and felt she had been deserted by everyone.

When I had finished relating my story, Skouras agreed the likelihood of my convincing Marilyn to return to the set of *Something's Got to Give* was very slim indeed. He saw there was little chance she could handle working on that movie if the location remained in Hollywood. There were too many painful memories, too many reminders of *Let's Make Love.* Even the director, George Cukor, was the same.

"Isn't there any way you could move the location to some other place?"

"Like Paris?" Skouras sighed. "No. No chance in the world. This film has already exceeded its budget so much we'll never recoup our losses. And the worst of it is Dean Martin won't finish the film with anyone but Marilyn. If you don't talk her into going back to work, we'll have no choice but to scrap it."

Still, he wanted me to try. I said I would.

"Let's forget our troubles and go upstairs and watch *West Side Story*," he said, suddenly his old ebullient self. I'd seen *West Side Story* a thousand times, but to oblige him I followed him to his screening room.

Fifteen minutes into the film he was sound asleep. I tiptoed out, said my good night to Mrs. Skouras, and went back to New York, trying hard to figure out how I could convince Marilyn to do something I was positive she didn't want to do.

I called her from New York on a Saturday night in July. She wasn't home, and I left a message with her answering service and went out to dinner with Marian Saunders. Marian Saunders, married to the cousin of Madame Chiang Kai-shek, was considered New York's most stunning El Morocco patron and my constant date. I returned around midnight and Marilyn called me shortly after. She sounded awful. Her voice was a barely audible monotone that kept fading away. She was obviously in no condition to discuss going back to work on that film or any other.

I called Skouras the following day and told him of our conversation. I was sad for him and sad for her. Two weeks later I flew to Geneva and then to France. One night Hymie Zoll, head of the William Morris office in London, knocked on my door. "I have some very distressing news," he said. "I just heard Marilyn Monroe committed suicide."

Along with the other friends Marilyn had turned to for emotional support, I had the feeling there was something I should have said but didn't during my final conversation with her, something that might have prevented her death. It didn't make me feel any better to be told mine was a typical response to the suicide of a friend.

In retrospect, it seems to me it was the series of bitter disappointments during the final two years of her life, particularly the rejection by Montand and the public humiliation that followed, that caused Marilyn's death. It is my belief that the many unhappy experiences she suffered would have done in a far more emotionally stable person than Marilyn Monroe ever was.

4

SEVENTY-TWO HOURS

The restaurant was Delmonico's on Beaver and South William streets in lower Manhattan. It was a gray February afternoon in 1963. I knew where I was and what date it was, but I wasn't so sure about the man across the table from me.

"Now, say that to me again," I said. "Seventy-two hours to raise forty-five million dollars in surety bonds?"

My host nodded, the very picture of sanity. He was a member of a distinguished Wall Street law firm, and I had come to meet him for lunch at his request. He had chosen a corner table set apart from the rest of the diners. "That's it," he said. "It's come to that. Time is about to run out on Jimmy and the Teamsters.".

He was referring to the crisis facing James Hoffa and the Teamsters Union. I was not unfamiliar with it. The papers had been full of it. Hoffa and other officials of the Teamsters Union had been unable to obtain the bonding required under the Landrum-Griffin Act of 1959. The act had grown out of the investigations of the Senate McClellan Committee on abuses of power by top labor officials, a committee on which Robert Kennedy had served.

Under the provisions of the Landrum-Griffin Act, all union officials were required to post bonds with the federal government and became personally open to prosecution for a wide variety of offenses. Hoffa had been bonded under the act after it had become law, but Bob Kennedy was only a Senator's brother then. Now he was a President's brother and Attorney General of the United States, and he saw the Landrum-Griffin Act as the perfect vehicle to engineer the downfall of Jimmy Hoffa and the Teamsters Union.

"Is this why you called me down here?" I said.

My host nodded. "We think you could help us, yes."

"What makes you think that?"

"A lot of things. For one, you have an agreement with Havas Conseil International to represent them."

"Havas is a commercial agency," I countered.

"But it's owned by the French government. Let me go to the next point, which is you also represent the Steel Corporation of Europe, which has direct ties to the Rothschilds and the de Gaulles. It all interlocks very nicely. But more important to us is your personal relationship with President de Gaulle himself," he said.

I didn't say anything. I was waiting for him to get to the specifics. The man across the table from me continued his rundown of my résumé. "I understand you are also a personal friend of Professor Paul Keller, the head of the Swiss Reinsurance Company in Zurich."

"Things do get around," I said.

"Come on, Bill. We've done our homework on this."

He was right. I was the man for the job because of a peculiar combination of experience, friendships, and business connections that were crucial to the situation. I did have an excellent personal relationship with Charles de Gaulle. Together with Émile Hebey, I was co-chairman of the preparations under way to honor the Legion of Honor Society in Paris, one of de Gaulle's favorite projects, and it was through de Gaulle that I had become a friend of Professor Keller.

"All right," I said. "You've done your homework. Now what are you really trying to tell me?"

"That we have exhausted all our sources within the United States. We think you can open doors for us in other countries. We think you're the only one who can do it within the time limitation. You have the particular credentials we need right now."

"Possibly," I said cautiously. "But seventy-two hours in which to raise forty-five million dollars in bonding is pretty ridiculous."

"I agree, but that's what it's down to now. You can make shortcuts. You've done it before. The plain fact is unless James Hoffa comes up with the bonding, he and all the others are out and the Teamsters Union is finished."

I could only shrug in mild sympathy. I had never met Jimmy Hoffa and the affairs of the Teamsters Union were not among my concerns.

"I'm afraid it's just not in the cards," I told him. "Certainly not with that deadline. Besides, there are other reasons why I don't think I can take it on."

"Look," he urged, "I've only outlined the core of the problem for you. Do me a favor and at least think about it."

I agreed I would, mostly out of courtesy, and the lunch came to an end. I bundled up against the raw, damp February cold and walked from the restaurant to the subway to return uptown to my office. After finding a seat, I mulled over our conversation, which had been more an interrogation than a dialogue. There were aspects to the problem he had outlined that I found far more disturbing than the Teamsters' dilemma. What bothered me most was the manipulation. There is always the temptation by people in high office to use their powers autocratically, and then rationalize their actions because they were motivated by concern for the good of all.

In this case the Attorney General of the United States was doing precisely that. He was using his office in a naked display of extra-legal power hardly less ruthless than Jimmy Hoffa's own use of power within his union. Perhaps Bobby Kennedy's years on the McClellan Committee had given him with the permanent character of a prosecutor. Or perhaps his personal philosophy of government was essentially autocratic. In any case, he was using the law in an unlawful way, making the Landrum-Griffin Act his own special weapon to destroy Jimmy Hoffa.

Robert Kennedy wrote a very thorough manual on how to misuse government agencies before the Nixon administration perfected the technique. Although the Attorney General vigorously denied exerting any improper or illegal pressures on the Teamsters Union, the facts presented a different picture.

Under the Landrum-Griffin Act, every union official had to be bonded. No bond, no office. The amount of the bond varied according to the importance of the official's position in the union. Bonding also had to be provided for each position held, and many union officials held a variety of posts. Companies that furnish bonds to the federal government must hold a "Certificate of Authority as Acceptable Reinsuring Companies." These certificates are insured by the Treasury Department under an Act of Congress.

When Bob Kennedy began to use the Landrum-Griffin Act for his personal crusade against Hoffa, there were 210 certified companies in the United States. Some were subsidiaries of larger parent companies, but all functioned independently and held independent certification. The group included all the major insurance and bonding companies in the country.

Suddenly not a single one of those 210 companies would supply the necessary bonds for Hoffa and the Teamsters. This mass refusal was all the more strange since the Surety Association of America had recently recommended the Teamsters Union be given the lowest rates allowed under the law because of its no-loss bonding record.

The truth was Bobby Kennedy had reached every single company. He had told them all not to supply bonds to Hoffa and the Teamsters. He had invoked the office of the Attorney General, with the full weight of its potential powers of retribution—which were enormous—to use the Landrum-Griffin Act in a thoroughly illegal way. Not one company dared risk defying the clear intent of the highest law officer in the land.

This abuse of power, as I saw it, struck at the foundations of the national integrity. It replaced a government of law with a government of power and personal retribution. It was bad, no matter who was on the receiving end, and I returned to my office still thinking about the implications of the entire unsavory business. I had been back less than a half-hour when the telephone rang. The call was from my luncheon host. Would I meet another gentleman at a midtown office close to my own?

"There are some interesting proposals coming to you direct

from Jimmy Hoffa," he said. "I wish you would go and at least listen, Bill. You said you'd think about it and you ought to hear them out first."

Feeling ambivalent, I agreed to meet them, went downstairs, and hailed a taxi. At the midtown office I met, among others, Angelo DeSpirito, who introduced himself as the personal representative of Jimmy Hoffa. Not more than five feet five inches tall and weighing about two hundred pounds, he had an appropriately round face. He wasted no time in coming to the point.

"You know the problem, I've been told," he began.

"I know the outlines, not the details."

"Jimmy's back is to the wall and everybody else is there with him," DeSpirito said. "Jimmy told me to talk business with you. He's proposing an arrangement whereby you'll handle this for a percentage of the total bonding monies involved."

He then sketched out the details of the proposal. There were huge sums involved, and even a very small percentage came to $263,000, based on DeSpirito's preliminary figures. It was not an amount to shrug off, and I decided I had to give the proposal greater consideration. But something was bothering me and DeSpirito picked up on it at once.

"What's the matter?" he asked. "The percentage not enough?"

"No, it's not that," I said. The entire matter had raised some very important personal conflicts for me. I knew before anything could be decided, they would have to be resolved.

"I can't answer you now," I told DeSpirito. "I'll have to get back to you later this evening or tomorrow."

"Every minute counts. Every goddamn second is made out of sweat."

"I can't promise you anything. I might not be able to help you at all. There are things I've got to see about first, and even if I can take it on, seventy-two hours and forty-five million dollars may be out of reach. All I can say is I'll let you know as quickly as I can."

DeSpirito looked unhappy. His shoulders lifted in a resigned half-shrug. "Okay. There's no place else to go anyway," he murmured. I was waiting for him to put on his coat when he looked at me, his pudgy face suddenly full of alarm. "No—you go on ahead," he said. "Christ, I don't want to be seen with you now."

I stared at him. "That little bastard has a tail on everybody all the time," he explained.

"Bobby Kennedy?"

"Yes, he's got every Justice Department agent there is on the case," he said. "Jimmy's being watched twenty-four hours a day, at home, at his office, everywhere. They put a tail on anybody he sees or even stops to talk to on the street. One of the bonding companies Jimmy used to do business with has an agent camping outside its door."

DeSpirito's revelation did nothing to make me feel better. I left, alone, and returned to my office, looking back over my shoulder a number of times on the way. Bob Kennedy's behavior was suddenly not a matter of abstract principle but a personal affront.

When I finally sat down at my desk, I started to reach for the telephone to make a call to the offices of Joseph Kennedy at 230 Park Avenue, but I couldn't make myself dial.

I had had the good fortune to meet Joseph P. Kennedy early in my career. He became one of the three men I considered my mentors, the other two being Walter O'Hara of Rhode Island, and J. Howard McGrath, onetime governor of Rhode Island, U.S. senator, and Attorney General under President Truman.

Joseph Kennedy was a man of many activities that spanned the business and entertainment worlds as well as the world of international politics. When he died, his estate was somewhere in the neighborhood of $300 million.

He was already well on his way to amassing that fortune when I first met him. A close personal bond developed between Kennedy and me despite the differences in age, temperament, and background. I was able to fulfill the tasks he gave me and solve problems he tossed out, sometimes almost mischievously, to see what solutions I could come up with.

More important to Joseph Kennedy was my ability to measure up to the trust and confidence he extended. In turn, he gave freely of his experience, wisdom, and the almost magical power of the Kennedy name.

What I remembered more than anything else, however, as

I sat with one hand on the phone, was Joseph Kennedy's hatred and fear of the growing power of the Teamsters. "Too damned much money in one place," he often said. Some said his hatred was unreasonable, a personal obsession, but reasonable or not, it was very real and he had inculcated Bobby with it long before Jimmy Hoffa became a force on the labor scene.

My friendship with Joseph Kennedy was not past history. I was still in frequent touch with him on a great number of matters, and he was of great value to me. Therefore, it was with a sense of loyalty, friendship, and a very large measure of respect that I picked up the phone and placed the call to his offices.

I was very disappointed to learn he was out of the country and couldn't be reached. Wrestling with what to do next, I finally decided to try John Kennedy at the White House. Perhaps he knew where his father could be reached. If not, I wanted his reaction to my proposals.

My next call was to an old friend, Senator George Smathers. If anyone could get to John Kennedy quickly, it was he. John Kennedy breakfasted with the leadership of the Democratic party every Tuesday morning. When breakfast ended, George Smathers always stayed on for a drink or two, even though it was morning, and matters of greater confidentiality were taken up then.

When that call also failed to get through, I began to feel more negative about the entire matter. By the time I did reach Smathers, Angelo DeSpirito's paranoia had infected me and I found myself afraid to discuss the matter over the phone. Instead I told Smathers I had something very urgent to talk to him about. He asked if I could fly down to Washington to meet with him. I agreed, mindful of the time, which suddenly seemed to be racing by.

A few hours later I was sitting across from Smathers telling him the details of the proposal that had been made to me. "Of course, I don't even know if I can pull it off," I confessed. "But I do know this. I'm not going to do a damn thing unless I get some feedback from Jack Kennedy or his father."

"I understand," George Smathers said. "I'll get back to you on this."

"When?" I pressed.

"Tonight, late, or tomorrow morning," he answered.

I sighed. The clock kept ticking and I kept experiencing delay after delay. The entire matter was looking less possible than ever. Deciding there was no point in staying in Washington, I caught the last flight back to New York. I slept very poorly that night. I kept wondering what answer I'd get from Jack Kennedy, and if it would reflect his father's thoughts or his brother's crusade. I finally managed to fall asleep after deciding the time factor might well make the answer academic.

George Smathers kept his word and phoned me early the following morning. "I spoke to the President," he said. "I'm to tell you if you can make a buck out of it, go ahead."

Smathers picked up on my long silence. "You're surprised?"

"I guess so. He could just possibly be scuttling the best laid plans of Bobby," I said.

"Bobby has his vendettas. The President has his priorities," George said carefully. "Think about that little talk we had a few weeks ago."

Smathers rang off. Then his suggestion exploded in my head and I had a new interpretation of Jack Kennedy's go-ahead. I remembered very clearly the recent talk I'd had with Smathers. It had been in Miami, where I was taking a few days' rest after the Trujillo chase.

"I was just talking to Jack Kennedy a little while ago," he said to me. "He sends you his congratulations. He said his father told him about your new agreement to represent Libya."

"That's very nice of him. Thank him for me when you talk to him again," I had answered. George sat back in his chair. When George Smathers became terribly relaxed, I knew he had something important to say.

"De Gaulle is very interested in Libya since he lost Algeria," he began.

"And John Kennedy is very interested in both de Gaulle and Libya," I returned.

"You can damn well say that again. You know our relations with de Gaulle aren't good. In fact, they're lousy. De Gaulle is being uncooperative about a lot of things and secretive about a lot more."

"What about Charles Bohlen?"

Smathers frowned. "Ambassador Bohlen can't get his foot in the door over in Paris. He's not getting the kind of information Washington wants. It's not good, not good at all. And now the Libyans are acting up."

"You mean about our airbase there?" I said, and he nodded angrily.

"It's a political thing, of course. They're getting some internal pressure, but they're also using it as a lever. Frankly, Kennedy wants to improve our relations with both de Gaulle and Libya, but he needs to know more inside thinking to do that. Hell, we're out in left field now in both places."

Then Smathers leaned forward. "You'll be acting for the Libyan government on a number of levels. We both know that a lot of what's going on will include the French and may well be a bellwether to what they're planning. A lot of things will come to your attention. It would be good if you could keep me informed in a very private way of anything you feel is important that comes your way. I'm now a member of the Senate Banking Committee and I hope to become a member of the Foreign Relations Committee too. The President believes your assistance would be most helpful all around."

"How do I keep you privately informed?" I asked.

"When you write to me from Paris, Libya, Geneva, or wherever you might be, write directly to my Senate office. On the back of each envelope just put the initial *T*. My administrative assistant, Scott Peake, will see to it those envelopes come to me unopened. We need help in smoothing the waters all over and you'll be in a position to give us that help."

That was the conversation that now illuminated Jack Kennedy's message to me. He wanted me to continue as his European–Libyan–de Gaulle pipeline, and he would green-light anything for that purpose. I later learned he was certain there wasn't sufficient time to meet the bonding deadline anyway, but the fact that I'd tried to clear such a financial opportunity through Kennedy family channels had only improved my position as confidant.

In any case, I had received the Kennedy imprimatur as well as a blessing from the President of the United States. I immediately placed a call to Zurich, to Professor Paul Keller of the Swiss Reinsurance Company. I had solved my first problem, and now I needed some answers on the second. There was no point to further talks with DeSpirito or anyone else if the time factor and the money required made the quest impossible.

The call went through more quickly than usual, and in minutes I heard Paul Keller's familiar voice.

"I have a very important matter to discuss with you," I began. "It requires the strictest confidence and a very large amount of money is involved. The problem relates to the Landrum-Griffin Act here in the United States."

As I had anticipated from a man in his position, Keller was thoroughly familiar with the Landrum-Griffin Act. It was clear he knew at once the substance of my call.

"Time is everything," I told him. I chose my words carefully, aware he would place the proper meaning on each one. "I'm prepared to make an emergency trip to Zurich if you feel such a trip could be of assistance in the matter."

He was silent for about five seconds. Then he said, "I can see you up until twelve noon tomorrow. After that I will be gone on my annual skiing trip in Austria." He paused again. "I will need to know now whether you will be coming, however."

"I'll see you in Zurich by noon tomorrow," I said and ended the call, assured I had understood his cryptic reply. He had meant something could be done, but he would need the time while I was en route to Zurich to make the necessary moves with the necessary people. The next step was to get in touch with Angelo DeSpirito. I did this through the Madison Avenue offices where we had held our first meeting, and another meeting was arranged at once. A member of the Wall Street law firm through which I had originally been approached also attended this time.

"I'm prepared to try my best," I told DeSpirito, but I didn't tell him the President had given me the go-ahead.

DeSpirito became excited at once. "Great, great," he kept repeating. "But what about time? Jesus, there's not much left."

"I'm aware of that," I said. "There won't be any time to spare. Everything will have to go like clockwork. There are a lot of things I'll need for my negotiations over there."

"Just tell me what you want," he said, and I gave him a list of particulars: financial statements, affidavits, the names of the officials to be bonded, the totals for each one, and the cumulative totals, plus authorizations and all the other pertinent information. He took the items down and we proceeded to work out the details of the original proposal.

"We've got to call Jimmy," he said excitedly when we had concluded the agreement. "I've got to tell him this."

"Don't tell him he's home safe," I said. "Because he isn't. Any number of things could go wrong."

"Okay, but we've got to call him. He's the only one who can give you the things you'll need," he said.

"All right, call him," I replied, gesturing to the phone on the desk.

I watched DeSpirito's round face take on an expression of horror. "Are you crazy? Not from here," he said. "I might just as well call Bobby Kennedy direct."

I frowned. DeSpirito obviously did not feel he was indulging in paranoia. "Do you really think these phones are tapped?"

"From the minute they saw me come up here," he said. "We'll go outside and call."

"Then Justice Department agents could be outside watching for you," I protested.

"We'll have to risk it. They can't tap anything outside," he said, and moving like a squat tank, he led the way down the corridor to the elevator. Once outside, we went to a drugstore on the corner of Madison Avenue and Forty-first Street where there were two phone booths. I found myself glancing furtively at passersby as we entered the store.

DeSpirito made his call, talked for a few moments, and then handed the phone to me. "This is Jimmy Hoffa," he said.

"I took the phone and stepped into the booth. "Hello—" I began.

"You think you can get it for us?" Hoffa said. It was my first experience with Jimmy Hoffa's abruptness on the phone. "Do you realize our asses are all in a sling if you don't come through for us?" He talked as though I were to blame for the mess he was in. "It will be the end of the Teamsters."

"I'm not sure I understand that," I said. "Why will it be the end of the Teamsters?"

"Have you ever heard of George Meany?" Hoffa shot back. "That old bastard is just waiting to pick up the pieces."

"I'll do all I can," I said. "Mr. DeSpirito has given you the list of documents I'll need, I take it."

"I've got a private plane waiting to fly you to Washington. You can pick up all the financial statements and other things here," he said.

"That's impossible. I can't fly down to Washington, not even by private plane," I protested. "I have things to do here in New York and people to contact before I leave. Everything has to be ready to go like precision clockwork if this is to have any chance of succeeding."

"I want to sit down with you and go over this thing first," Hoffa insisted.

My patience was wearing very thin. "Look, either you want me to go to Zurich or come to see you in Washington. I can't do both," I told him. Then Hoffa asked to talk to DeSpirito and I handed the phone back to him.

They finally agreed on a course of action. DeSpirito would go to Zurich with me. He would take care of the travel arrangements. I held back my objections to his coming along. I wanted to go alone. There were delicate understandings to be orchestrated, and he would be in the way. On the other hand, he might be of help in answering unexpected questions. It was a mixed blessing, but I decided to let matters stand. Jimmy Hoffa asked DeSpirito to return the phone to me.

"Where do you live, Bill?" Hoffa asked, managing to sound almost gracious.

"At 605 Park Avenue," I said.

"Angelo will pick you up there in a limousine and go to Idlewild with you," he said, referring to the New York airport now named Kennedy International. "At Idlewild, at seven o'clock sharp tonight, someone will meet you. When you show your passport, that man will give you everything, all the documents you'll need in Zurich."

"Very good," I said, but Jimmy Hoffa had already hung up.

DeSpirito and I agreed on final plans and left the drugstore together. I headed for my office and he went his way. As he walked down the avenue, I glanced back in time to see a man in a black overcoat step from a doorway and walk after him. Just a coincidence? I wondered.

I went back to my office feeling very insecure. How quickly

one can grow paranoid, I muttered to myself. Yet the feeling was not unjustified. I knew Washington. Secrets were seldom really secret. The Attorney General's office had many ears. Had Bobby Kennedy gotten wind of this last-ditch attempt to circumvent his blitz of the Teamsters? He had shown no reluctance to misuse his power before and I was sure he wouldn't stop now.

Back at my office, I put thoughts of Bob Kennedy out of my mind. There was a more sobering truth on the face of the clock on my desk. The seventy-two hours had now shrunk to forty. I made some rapid calculations of the time needed to do all that had to be done. It would be close, too close. I began to gather the things I would need and was just about to leave for my apartment when DeSpirito called. He had secured passage on Alitalia to Zurich but meeting plans had been changed. The limousine would pick me up as arranged, but he would meet me at the airport. I hung up and hurried home to pack.

When I went downstairs to wait for the limousine, my wavering optimism took a plunge. It had started to snow. The limousine arrived and I watched the snow thicken as we drove to Idlewild. I was feeling gloomy by the time I arrived at the Alitalia terminal and saw DeSpirito waiting there. The limousine that brought me drove off, but DeSpirito had his wait.

"I think we're in trouble," he said. "Alitalia says they don't know when our flight will be able to leave."

Before I could answer, a man approached. He was tall, unsmiling, wearing an overcoat. "Are you William Taub?" he asked. I was amazed at the stab of apprehension that went through me. Overnight I had become suspicious of everyone.

"Yes," I said.

"Do you have a passport to show me?" he asked, and I felt relieved at once. He was Hoffa's courier. I took out my passport and handed it to him. He scanned it carefully, then drew a large manila envelope from beneath his coat and gave it to me. I opened it and gave the contents a quick glance, enough to confirm they were the financial statements and other documents I had asked for. He gave me a receipt to sign and was just walking away when the Alitalia desk made an announcement over the public address system.

"Alitalia is canceling all evening flights due to weather conditions," the voice intoned. "The airport is being closed."

After all the maneuvering and secrecy, after all the wheels had been set in motion on both sides of the Atlantic Ocean, it appeared we were about to be done in by an act of God. Suddenly I felt mobilized. The situation had become so hopeless it was time for a desperate act.

"Put the bags in your limousine, Angelo," I said. "We're going to TWA."

"You're crazy," he said. "If the airport is being closed and Alitalia isn't flying, nobody's flying."

"Maybe, but let's see. What have we got to lose?"

We hurried through the thickening snow to the waiting limousine that sped us the quarter-mile to the TWA terminal. We flung open the car doors and headed for the entrance. Then I heard a familiar voice call my name. I turned to see a very large man with a florid face, one of the TWA superintendents I'd come to know during the countless trips I made in and out of that airport. He came over at once.

"What are you doing here in this snowstorm, Mr. Taub?"

"Pat, are you flying?" I said.

"Where are you going?"

"We're trying to get to Zurich."

His brows drew together. "We've got a couple of flights trying to clear. They've been on and off a half-dozen times. We could try to get you near Zurich at least."

"How near?"

"We've got a flight to London and one to Paris waiting to get a clearance," he answered.

"If we can get to Paris, we can get to Zurich," I said.

He picked up our bags. "I'll put you on the flight to Paris and take care of your bags," he said. "Why don't you go into the lounge and have a drink. When we get clearance to take off, we'll page you."

DeSpirito looked like a man who had just won a reprieve from the gallows. I felt encouraged too, but we were still on the ground, it was still snowing, and we had no assurance the plane would leave. More important, precious minutes were being sliced from the calculations I had already revised so many times.

I sat in a lounge chair to examine more closely the contents of the envelope Hoffa's courier had given me. DeSpirito went to the bar. I had only glanced at the material when I realized with a sinking feeling that the most important item of all was missing —formal authorization for me to act for the Teamsters in the bonding. DeSpirito returned at that moment with two bottles of champagne.

"What are you going to do with those?" I asked.

"You and I are going to drink them," he said. I held up the envelope.

"You'd better find out where the authorization is before you drink anything," I said. "It's not here, and without it we'd just be going over for the ride."

DeSpirito nearly threw down the two bottles of champagne and headed for the phone at the far end of the lounge. He made his call and I watched his arms gesticulate wildly. Someone was getting holy hell at the other end of the line. Then he hung up and came back to me. "Somebody goofed," he said. "The authorization will be cabled to you in Zurich, at the hotel you mentioned to me this afternoon."

"The Baur au Lac," I said. "It had better be there. I won't move without it, and the Swiss won't talk pennies without it."

"It'll be there," DeSpirito assured me. He started to open the champagne as I went back to examining the material in the manila envelope, casting nervous glances at the lounge clock. I couldn't believe we were still sitting there.

The list of Teamster officials to be bonded consisted of 114 individuals wearing anywhere from one to six hats, and each hat required separate bonding. My preliminary estimates showed General President Jimmy Hoffa would require at least $2.5 million in bonds. I saw the name of one Frank Fitzsimmons on the list. He was then thirteenth vice president, but held other posts such as clerical officer and trustee as well. He required at least $1.5 million. I saw other names that in years to come would appear, disappear, and reappear in accounts of Teamster affairs: John T. O'Brien, Einar Mohn, John English, Harold Gibbons, Thomas Flynn—all in varying ranks of vice president.

I also noted the name of Anthony Provenzano, a twelfth vice president. He needed $500,000 in bonding. However, I noted his salary was far higher than that of the other vice presidents of similar rank. In total, the amount came perilously close to the original figure given me of $45 million. I put the material back into the envelope, looked at the clock, and groaned. It was

10:30. We had lost three more hours.

While I was going through the papers DeSpirito had gone through both bottles of champagne. "When in hell are we going to leave?" I muttered. Are we going to leave at all, I thought. I went outside to hunt down my TWA friend. He nearly exploded when he saw me.

"Oh my God, Mr. Taub. Where have you been? We've been paging you all over the place. The plane left."

I stared at him. I could almost hear Bobby Kennedy laughing. "We've been in the goddamn lounge," I said. "We didn't hear anybody page us."

Later I learned the weather had played tricks with the terminal's electric system. The address system in the lounge had not worked. I turned to see DeSpirito panting over to us. He looked sick. "Where are our bags?" I asked my TWA friend.

"On the way to Paris," he said. I nodded calmly. That figured. Our bags were on the plane and we were still on the ground. I was left with my briefcase, the manila envelope, and the clothes I wore. I hadn't a comb, a toothbrush, or an extra shirt, and the airport shops had all long since closed.

"There's one last plane trying to get off," he said. "It's a flight to London. If the weather breaks even for fifteen minutes, the pilot intends to try to fly. We'll put you on that plane. In London there's a direct flight to Zurich that connects with this plane."

"If it gets there in time," I said.

"We'll radio London and have them hold the Zurich flight as long as possible. We'll take you off one plane and put you right on the other. And we'll get your bags in Paris and reroute them to Zurich."

This was our last chance. There'd be no more waiting in the lounge. I had my TWA friend take us directly to the plane, where we settled into our seats to wait for takeoff. The snow continued to fall and time continued to slip away.

But the storm did break long enough for the plane to take off. It was the first positive thing that had happened since we had arrived at the airport many hours before. I caught some sleep in short catnaps as the plane rose above the storm and headed over the Atlantic. Each time I woke to glance at my watch, I saw it was becoming less and less likely that I could reach Professor Keller by noon. DeSpirito, watching my anxiety grow, tried to say something comforting.

"He'll wait. They'll make a bundle on the premiums for this," he said.

"You're wrong," I said. "You don't know the Swiss. If you were coming from the moon with a hundred-million-dollar deal and had an appointment at noon and arrived at 12:05 just as they were leaving for lunch, by God, they'd go to lunch. They're the most methodical people in the world."

The plane flew into dawn and then into morning. It was a few minutes before eight as we landed at Heathrow Airport in London. TWA had kept its promise. The Swissair flight to Zurich had been held and DeSpirito and I raced to get our tickets. He wanted first-class seats because his bulk made him uncomfortable in cramped quarters. They didn't have anything in first class and he began to argue. I cut him off. "We'll take any seats on that plane," I said, and then we ran to the boarding area, where the Swissair flight was ready to taxi onto the runway, and made our way to the economy section. DeSpirito sat down in a window seat and I took the seat beside him.

We had less than two hours left. I could no longer fight my feelings of dejection. I had been making mental calculations of the time left, and there simply wasn't enough of it. The flight was scheduled to take one and a half hours. It would probably take at least ten to fifteen minutes to get off the plane and wait in line for a taxi. Another ten minutes at least to the Baur au Lac Hotel to get the authorization cable, and then perhaps another twenty to the offices of Professor Keller. My calculations were adjusted still further downward when the pilot announced strong headwinds would add another ten minutes to our flying time. I saw everything going down the drain.

Shifting in my seat, I glanced at the woman sitting across from me. She wore a leopardskin coat and her sleek black hair was pulled back from her face. Her profile looked familiar. Feeling my eyes on her, she turned to look at me and we recognized each other at once. She was the Princess Ashraf Pahlevi, twin sister of the Shah of Iran. I had met her often when I was in her country mediating a dispute between Britain and Iran over petroleum. It turned out she also had been forced to fly economy. I introduced her to DeSpirito.

"I'm on my way to Zurich to pick up my children. They've been on a skiing trip," she said. "Where are you going?"

"To the Baur au Lac Hotel in Zurich," I said. "As quickly as I can."

"My chauffeur and the ambassador are meeting me at the airport. May I give you a ride to the hotel?" she asked.

"We'd appreciate that," I said, trying not to leap for joy. I saw a gain of at least ten minutes. Maybe, I murmured silently, maybe we could still make it. When we landed, we followed her to a long gray Cadillac limousine that sped us to the hotel. I checked my watch and found we had cut twelve minutes.

At the Baur au Lac, I raced to the desk. The cablegram from Jimmy Hoffa was there. By God, we might make it yet, I said to myself as I ran from the lobby. I had no time to shave or freshen up, not even to get a drink of water or a shine.

"Bill Taub—wake up," I heard.

Turning around, I realized I had forgotten all about Angelo. "Stay here," I said. "Get registered and wait for me."

I ran for the entrance and a waiting taxi. My luck was changing, that was for certain. Clutching the wire of authorization in one hand and my briefcase in the other, I catapulted myself into the back seat and shouted my destination to the driver. Then I uttered a small prayer that my watch was right. It read ten minutes to twelve.

The ten minutes were down to three when I burst into the reception room of the Swiss Reinsurance Company. Professor Keller received me at once and I hastened to explain my wrinkled and hollow-eyed appearance. I put the cable of authorization in front of him, took out the manila envelope with all the other documents, and told him how much was needed and for whom. He spread all the papers out on his desk and studied them in silence for a few minutes.

Professor Keller was impeccably starched and pressed and groomed, a typecast Prussian banker if there ever was one. I felt as if I had just been riding the rails across country, and tried to look dignified as he perused the papers before him. His face showed nothing, but two things were immediately obvious. He had a mind trained to grasp financial intricacies in one quick sweep of the eye, and he had already familiarized himself with the probabilities of my visit. He was unruffled, perhaps even unimpressed, by the scope of the transaction.

Finally he looked up and spoke to me in German. "It can be done," he announced. He glanced at his watch and stood up. "I'm sorry I must leave so quickly, but I did tell you I could not stay beyond noon," he said apologetically. "My secretary will take you to an associate who will work with you on the exact procedures necessary to complete the transaction."

We shook hands, I expressed my appreciation, and he was on his way to Austria for his skiing trip. I looked at the clock. It read exactly 12:05. His secretary showed me into an adjoining office where another man sat down with all the papers I had brought. He told me how the matter had to be handled and what still had to be done.

"Our understanding is this matter must be held in strictest confidence until it is completed," he said. "Therefore, the necessary communications will not be transmitted from Switzerland." He acknowledged the surprise on my face. "Please understand the matter will be handled from Paris. This will all be explained in detail when you arrive there."

He then had copies made of everything I had brought, and we discussed details for another hour and a half. It was obvious he was going to say no more about the necessity for flying to their Paris office in order to complete the bonding.

When I returned to the Baur au Lac I was feeling uneasy. DeSpirito answered the door in his undershorts, half asleep. He snapped awake when he saw who it was.

"Did you get it?" he asked.

"It's not finished. Get dressed. We're leaving for Paris," I told him.

His face fell. "What happened?"

I could only shrug. "They're afraid of something," I said. "I can smell it. I don't know what or why, but we're going to do whatever they say to do."

I waited while he dressed. As our bags still hadn't arrived, I arranged for them to be rerouted back to Paris as soon as they arrived in Zurich, and then made reservations on the next flight to Paris. DeSpirito continued to press for answers.

"Keller said it could be done," I told him, "but it's only been set in motion. It'll go right down to the wire."

"Christ, it sure will. There's only a few hours left," he groaned.

He followed me out of the room and we went to the airport to make the flight. I longed for a hot shower and a shave, but had to settle for washing my face in the airport men's room, then grabbing some coffee and croissants.

The necessity for the trip to Paris still disturbed me. There had been something in the tone of voice of Keller's aide that bothered me, and the ominous feeling stayed with me all the way to Paris.

I kept an apartment at the Raphael Hotel. Realizing the rest of the negotiations might well be highly delicate, I thought it best to settle DeSpirito elsewhere in case I had to make some very confidential telephone calls. I secured a room for him at the Hotel George Cinq and told him I would reach him later.

Then I went directly to the offices of the French subsidiary of the Swiss company. They were expecting me, of course, and my first question was why the transaction had been switched to Paris.

"Communications from Zurich are subject to interception," I was told. "We have been informed your Attorney General's office has put an intercept order on all communications from major Swiss financial sources. Of course, we must avoid that."

That explained everything. Somehow word had reached Bobby Kennedy that something was afoot. But he was casting about. Obviously he had no specific information.

"Here in Paris we have a special code to our New York company that cannot be intercepted," my informant continued. "The bonds will be technically posted from the New York company. Your documents, which reached us from Zurich, have already been transmitted in code to New York, along with the financial authorizations. New York has by now begun to file the bonds with the proper agencies in Washington. Unfortunately, the procedures take a lot of time."

"Will the deadline be met?" I asked.

He gave the Gallic shrug, palms up. "I don't know," he said. "I hope so. Furnishing this huge sum in so short a time has required very top-level attention and clearance."

"I see," was my answer, for now I knew precisely what his words meant, as well as why the transaction was being sent through the French office. I saw the clear likelihood that the transaction had received the blessing of Charles de Gaulle himself.

"We will not have long to wait for the answer," he continued. "Your deadline is only an hour away. We will inform you the minute we hear anything."

"I'm at the Raphael," I said, thanked him, and left.

Although I was totally exhausted, I couldn't sleep in the apartment. I couldn't even nap. DeSpirito called and insisted on coming over to wait with me. When the telephone rang again, I leaped for it.

"It is done. The bonds are posted," I was told. I looked at my watch, then at DeSpirito, who was practically pulling on my sleeve.

"Angelo," I said, "we did it, with ten minutes to spare."

Several months later, while dining with friends at La Caravelle in New York, I caught a glimpse of Joseph P. Kennedy sitting at a table with a group of people. I had been seated only a few minutes when a bottle of wine arrived. "From Ambassador Kennedy," the waiter said. There was a note attached. It read: "I did not like what you did."

5

REPRISALS

When I secured the bonds for Jimmy Hoffa and the Teamsters I had no idea Bobby Kennedy would view it as a personal defeat. That was, however, exactly how he felt, and he reacted with characteristic vengeance. Bob Kennedy was an Old Testament man.

I stayed on in Paris to help with preparations for the Legion of Honor concert, and then traveled to Libya. There I entered into negotiations on the contract whereby I would represent Libya in all commercial activities, especially petroleum interests, which had become my expertise.

Libya had become very important to France at that time, and was becoming an increasingly difficult problem for the Kennedy administration. Having lost Algeria, the French wanted to replace that loss with a close Libyan alliance. As de Gaulle's relations with the United States were at a low ebb, he pushed the Libya ties at the expense of America.

The Libyan authorities were coming under severe internal pressure to expel the American airbase in their country, a demand intensified by substantial behind-the-scenes French influence. These issues were in the forefront of international politics when my representation of Libya was confirmed by letter from the Crown Prince of Libya.

The letter of agreement in hand, I returned at once to New York to prepare the documents and gather the information needed for the Justice Department. When an American citizen agrees to represent a foreign government, a notification of intent must be filed with the United States government under the terms of the Foreign Agent Registration Act. Such a filing requires the submission of a detailed personal and business statement and a financial accounting. It involves answering questions on dozens upon dozens of government forms. It is an arduous business and I attended to it personally.

The purpose of the Foreign Agent Registration Act is to prevent foreign governments from lobbying through secret ties with American citizens. It was a forerunner of the present and more general Public Disclosures Act. When I completed the filing in Washington, I returned to Libya for discussions on problems the Libyans considered paramount. One concern was their desire to gain an audience with President Kennedy. The Libyans wanted to improve relations with both America and France, but they felt the Kennedy administration underrated Libya's power on the world scene. At the same time, they were under severe pressure from de Gaulle to forge closer ties with France. The Libyans felt an invitation from President Kennedy would help them resist French pressure while affording them a chance to change the President's views regarding their country. At that time the airbase problem was still open to resolution.

On one of many trips between Washington and Paris, Geneva and Tripoli, I met in Washington with Senator George Smathers and told him what the Libyans wanted. Smathers took the message to Kennedy, who responded negatively. His decision seemed to push the Libyans in the direction the French wanted. In time Libya expelled the American airbase and cemented ties with France.

I was at a lunch meeting in Tripoli when I received an urgent call from an associate in Washington. "Get back here," he told me. "You've got troubles."

"What kind of troubles?" I asked.

"They say you did not register properly as an agent for Libya."

"That's nonsense. I filed everything."

"They say the file's not complete enough."

"Who says so?"

"What's the matter with you, Bill? Who's the Attorney General?" Suddenly everything made an unsavory kind of sense: this was the opening gun in Robert Kennedy's pursuit of vengeance. Still, at that time, I did not realize the extent of his personal anger.

"The whole thing's ridiculous," I told my associate. "I'm too busy to come back on this kind of foolishness. Everything's been properly filed and that's all there is to it."

Unfortunately, I was dead wrong. Only a few days had gone by when I got another telephone call. "The witch-hunt is on, Bill," I heard. "You'd better get back here."

"But there's nothing wrong with the filing."

"Maybe not, but you'd better tend to this."

"I can't. Things are too involved here."

"Look, I was told orders have come directly from the top to revoke your passport if you don't come back," he warned. That brought me up short. Orders directly from the top—the dimensions of the retaliation were becoming clear, and I had to do something about it.

I compromised with a fast trip to Rome and the American Embassy there. At the consular section I had a cable sent to the Justice Department in Washington informing them they had full and complete filing under the Registration Act. Word came back quickly. I was to return and appear at a hearing on the matter.

The not-so-fine handwriting of Bobby Kennedy was discernible in these actions. I made a disclaimer of any wrongdoing in an official communication from the American Embassy and, feeling I had done enough, returned to Libya. A day or two later word reached me that my associates and friends in Washington were being subjected to extensive questioning and bothersome requests about their knowledge of my activities. Unwilling to place anyone in that position, and having received still another phone call, this time reporting I was being threatened with an indictment, I cut short my affairs in Libya and returned to Washington.

There I met with the Assistant Attorney General who had been handling the case. It was quickly apparent he had been programmed. No matter what I did, no matter how fully and rapidly I met the department's requests and answered their questions, nothing satisfied him. Every day another request arrived, another form had to be filled out, additional personal information had to be documented. They had more material on me than ten people ordinarily provided under the terms of the Registration Act, yet the demands and questionnaires continued to descend. I was spending most of my time ferreting through my past and dredging up answers for their forms. Nothing was sufficient. There was always another point to be clarified, additional information to find, more time to be spent. I felt as if I were walking through one of Kafka's nightmares.

Bobby Kennedy was clearly in search of a technicality on which he could turn down my registration and perhaps mount a prosecution. I had only to miss one of his deadlines to provide an excuse. As he well knew, his campaign was creating an intolerable climate. One cannot work while being constantly bedeviled and investigated. Every time I left the country, I was afraid the time would be seized to make some move I would not be on hand to counter. The pressure was making it impossible for me to work freely and properly in Libya's behalf. Perhaps most important, the constant investigation was affecting my reputation.

In his pursuit of vengeance, Bobby Kennedy was to receive an indirect dividend, one he had no way of expecting. The $263,000 bonding fee had not yet been paid by the Teamsters. On March 21 I met with Frank Muehlenholtz, a Teamster official, at the Teamster offices in Washington. He apologized for the delay in payment, a matter of organizational red tape, he implied. He also said Jimmy Hoffa had wanted to be at our meeting but had had to go to Miami. While the full payment was being prepared, Muehlenholtz said, I would be given a check for $25,000 for "out-of-pocket expenses." He called a secretary in and instructed her to prepare the check.

While waiting for her to return with the check, we talked about generalities until he rose, excused himself, and left the room. He came back ten minutes later and said the gentleman who had to sign the check was still not back but was expected soon. Coffee was ordered and I grew apprehensive. It was important that I get back to New York, and the weather forecast had predicted very heavy snow approaching blizzard proportions for the Washington area. I'd had enough of playing games of chance with snowstorms for that season, and I wanted to get out of the airport before the storm struck. We had finished our coffee and run out of talk, and still no check arrived. Muehlenholtz left the office again and returned a little later shaking his head.

"Look, I've got to get out of here. Put the check in the mail, will you?" I suggested.

"Absolutely," I was told and left the Teamster offices to find it had already begun to snow. I reached the airport and boarded a plane just in time.

When the check still hadn't arrived in New York by March 26, I decided on direct action. On telephoning Miami, I learned the Teamsters were at a convention and Hoffa was unavailable. John English, secretary-treasurer of the union, informed me, however, that the check had been "ordered out."

By April 12, still no check had arrived. I tried to reach Hoffa again and was told he was in Philadelphia on business. I also learned he had hired a law firm to look into the matter of the bonding fee. I was told he'd been informed the figures had been compounded incorrectly. The story was patent nonsense. Hoffa was holding up payment of the fee, but I couldn't understand why. I decided to wait and watch, confident the reasons would become manifest.

Meanwhile, Bob Kennedy's demands for more and more personal information continued. There seemed no end to the harassment and protest was pointless. I had no desire to single-handedly take on the Justice Department. In addition, President Kennedy's refusal to invite the Libyans to a meeting had caused American-Libyan relations to deteriorate to the point where representation of Libya was simply not worth the attacks and persecution I was suffering. Regretfully I informed the Libyan government I was resigning as a representative of their country. Bobby Kennedy had received his first pound of flesh.

Still the Hoffa fee remained unpaid. Other affairs kept me very busy and I went to southern France on an extended business trip. In late fall I returned to New York to find the newspapers full of the impending trial of Jimmy Hoffa and a host of co-defendants in Chattanooga on the charge of jury tampering.

Robert Kennedy had put the full power of the Justice Department into preparation for the trial, determined to do what he'd failed to do through the bonding. This time he would get Hoffa.

Early in November 1963 Professor Vittorio Valletta, chairman of the board of Fiat of Turin, Italy, visited America. He was asked to lunch at the White House with President Kennedy. Since it was to be a social occasion, and since I was an old friend of Professor Valletta as well as of others who were to attend, I was also invited. During that lunch I had the opportunity to ask President Kennedy why his brother had subjected me to such personal harassment.

"Bobby hates to lose," Jack Kennedy said. "I was told all about the problems you had and I'm sorry about that, but I never interfere with Bobby's concerns." Jack Kennedy brushed that topic aside because he wanted to talk about Marilyn Monroe. He asked me why I thought she had killed herself. I told him about the conversation we had had shortly before she died and how she had never recovered from the rejection by Montand.

Marilyn Monroe had been dead for more than fifteen months. Yet he seemed to be still disturbed by the death of this woman who had been only one of his many amusements. John Kennedy liked to play. I think he may have felt some remorse about having been intimately involved with Marilyn while remaining totally oblivious of her suffering.

Then Kennedy informed me he was about to go off on a barnstorming tour in Texas. "You're lucky," he said. "You don't make your living in politics." He leaned back and surveyed me. "Where did you get that great color?" he said.

"My tan? Southern France. But I thought that had worn off weeks ago."

"No, it's still there," he said and we went in to lunch. Four days later I was taken ill in New York while attending a meeting. As I was being driven home, I felt so bad I was taken to a hospital where I learned the reason for my "great tan." I had yellow jaundice and infectious hepatitis. Soon after my hospitalization I heard the news that John Kennedy had been assassinated. That night my own illness affected me less than the shocking event that had taken place in Texas. Later, as from my hospital bed I watched the funeral of the thirty-fifth President of the United States on television, I recalled our conversation of a few days before. Every word took on new importance now that he was gone. One comment in particular kept going through my mind like an elegy: *You're lucky. You don't make your living in politics.*

Infectious hepatitis compounded by jaundice requires a quiet recuperation. Instead, my hospital room became like a Wall Street office because of the number of calls that came in. Many of those calls came from Jimmy Hoffa's people in Washington. They wanted me to go down to Chattanooga. Hoffa, they said, wanted very much to talk to me about the bonding fee and "related matters." My inquiries about these related matters always drew vague replies. I declined. I was too ill.

Harry Berke was head of the Hoffa legal team at his trial for jury tampering. He and Jacques Schiffer, another lawyer for the Teamster defendants, took up the refrain and began calling. Quiet recuperation had become a near impossibility. Del Webb, owner of the New York Yankees and an old friend, visited me at the hospital and suggested I go to his Mountain Shadows Hotel in Scottsdale, Arizona, where I could get away from the telephone and rest. I accepted at once and flew with him in his private plane to Scottsdale.

Unfortunately, Harry Berke tracked me down and continued to press me to come to Chattanooga. It seemed two of Hoffa's co-defendants, Allen Dorfman and Nicholas Tweel, had been suggesting various moves on which Hoffa wanted my opinion.

All the reasons I'd been given seemed a little foggy and I refused again. Meanwhile, I continued to be dogged by bad luck. I broke my foot and decided to leave Mountain Shadows and return to New York for medical treatment. While changing planes in Chicago, I was paged. It was Harry Berke on the line and he wanted me to fly immediately to Tennessee. Hoffa was growing more nervous. The government was putting on a strong case.

"What does he really want?" I asked.

Berke's answer slipped and slid around the truth and then it came out. I had outmaneuvered Bob Kennedy once for Hoffa. He wanted me to do it again. He believed I could use my friendship with Joseph Kennedy to prevail upon him to call off Bobby. This tortured reasoning was so unrealistic as to become almost laughable. But it made one thing clear. It explained why Jimmy Hoffa had held back my bonding fee. He had feared this trial from the beginning, and he had looked upon me as his secret weapon. To ensure my cooperation, he had held back my fee and now dangled it before me. I told Berke the idea was ludicrous. Joseph Kennedy would not call off Bobby for anyone.

I didn't tell Berke I had already discussed going to Chattanooga with J. Howard McGrath. As a former Attorney General himself, McGrath was very much in touch with the events developing in Chattanooga and he said flatly, "Stay away from there. I'd rather see you forfeit the whole damned fee than go anywhere near there."

I finally got the message through to Harry Berke that I wasn't going to Tennessee. Obtaining the bonds had been a legitimate undertaking. Moreover, it was a task that touched on issues that transcended the bonds themselves. Becoming involved in Jimmy Hoffa's criminal trial was another matter entirely, and I wanted no part of it.

Hoffa was furious at my refusal. The trial was a labyrinthian affair full of charges based on evidence from wiretapping, bugging, surveillance, countersurveillance, and every kind of electronic listening device then available. Nevertheless, it ended in Jimmy Hoffa's conviction, and his rage was herculean. He saw the conviction as Bob Kennedy's personal victory over him and felt I could have helped him against his enemy. In retaliation he ordered an indefinite suspension of any payment on the bonding fee.

I have never been sorry I obtained the bonding for Jimmy Hoffa. There were issues important to justice that were served, albeit indirectly. But that day when Hoffa's enraged reactions reached me, I thought of the words of the King of Epirus after he'd lost most of his army in defeating the Romans. "One more such victory and I am lost," he said. I understood exactly how he felt.

Years later I found out about another reprisal that had been planned in this tale of vengeance and countervengeance. I was informed by several high Teamster officials that Hoffa had twice tried to have Robert Kennedy murdered.

Kennedy drove a convertible. Hoffa arranged to have a bomb thrown into it. The man he hired botched the job and threw the bomb into the wrong car.

Then Hoffa came up with the idea of having a bomb thrown into Bobby's swimming pool. The Robert Kennedys had announced a poolside party at Hickory Hill for some members of the bar association. I was told Hoffa had sent someone to throw the bomb into the pool during the party, but the Kennedys had called it off for some reason. "You have no idea how pissed off at Bob Kennedy Jimmy was," my informant said.

6

A STAR IN THE SKY FOR HOWARD HUGHES

Monumental wealth can sometimes spawn monumental delusions. In 1966 Howard Hughes reached out for power with a grandiose plan few people would have imagined let alone tried to bring about.

But Howard Hughes was not an ordinary man with ordinary dreams. Nor did he do anything by whim. He enjoyed success too much to let it rest on chance. He applied the same meticulous attention to detail in all his acquisitions, whether they were airlines, actresses, or the gambling casino empires he later used as havens for his reclusive lifestyle. His inaccessibility was not a matter of whim either. It was a means of operating secretly, beyond the reach of government, as well as a shelter from the contamination he feared all around him.

In all things Hughes watched, calculated, planned his moves. Consequently, it was not by chance that he involved me in perhaps the strangest, grandest, and least known of all his schemes.

I first met Howard Hughes during World War II. At that time I served under Harry Hopkins, Franklin Roosevelt's White House consultant, on the conversion of civilian plants into war production. The Hughes plants were building aircraft and parts, and as we searched for more factories suitable for wartime conversion, my work put me into almost daily contact with Hughes. At one point I was spending so much time away from New York that I gave Hughes a key to my apartment for his use during his frequent trips to the city. Arriving late and unexpectedly one night, I entered the apartment to find Hughes and a young actress in bed and belatedly realized the problems that accompany giving out extra keys.

After the war I saw Howard Hughes only infrequently. It had been many years since I had seen him at all when I got the call and was driven to his Bel Air home in California. The results of that meeting would reveal that the same forces and the same names continued to intertwine in a shadowy circle dance.

Richard Nixon was one such name. Although I was not aware of it then, he and Hughes went back a long way. Nixon's 1972 reelection campaign was not the first time he'd received $100,000 in secret from Howard Hughes. As early as 1956 Hughes had secretly furnished Nixon with $100,000 to fight Harold Stassen's dump-Nixon campaign. That same year Hughes lent Nixon's brother, Donald, $205,000 for a hamburger restaurant chain. Also, many Watergate investigators believed, but were unable to prove, that banker Charles (Bebe) Rebozo, Nixon's closest confidant, was using his Florida bank to launder cash receipts from Hughes-owned gambling casinos.

The CIA was another of the names that surfaced. The Central Intelligence Agency had close ties to the Hughes empire, as events have shown it to have with other powerful corporations. One-time Hughes aide Robert Maheu, testifying in 1974, reported Hughes had come to the conclusion long ago that any problems he might have with governmental agencies would be minimized if he were to become a "front" for the CIA. That belief proved correct for more than a quarter of a century. Hughes and the CIA established a cozy working arrangement in the late 1940s, when his companies produced specialized material for the CIA. The alliance continued up to the very recent Glomar Explorer operation the CIA conducted under the umbrella of a Hughes sea-mining project.

Other corporations and individuals have leaped into self-serving alliances with the CIA, with favors paid all around. Watergate will not be remembered as a chronicle of specific misdeeds but as the modern Pandora's box that, once opened, revealed a stunning network of connections, interconnections, ties, obligations, favors, liaisons, and unholy alliances.

A confluence of events set the stage for my meeting with Hughes at his Bel Air home. The first of these events proved to be a prelude to the illegal use of corporate power that would one day be revealed in all its sordidness. It began with a phone call from Joseph Kennedy while I was in California. The bonding incident had not affected our business or personal relationship. At the time I represented several foreign film stars and was associated in many endeavors with J. Howard McGrath, who was now counsel to Loew's, Inc., and Metro-Goldwyn-Mayer. Joseph Kennedy asked me to return to New York to meet with Antonio Sala, the attorney for Minerva Films of Rome. Although the largest film producer in Italy, Minerva was badly in need of new capital. Aware of Joseph Kennedy's long interest in the motion picture industry, Minerva Films had come to him for help.

Kennedy wanted a detailed analysis of Minerva's creative assets and financial scope, and he felt I was best suited to look into the matter. I returned to New York where it was arranged that I would go to Rome with Antonio Sala to explore the possibility of an alliance between Minerva and an American film company. At that time American motion picture executives had little knowledge of foreign films, one of the negative factors that needed evaluation.

The visit to Rome was to last only a week; it lengthened into months. While there I renewed my acquaintance with a number of friends at the Vatican. One was Cardinal Ottaviani, whom I'd first met some ten years earlier through Professor Valletta of Fiat. On that occasion Cardinal Ottaviani had talked to me about an orphanage for boys sponsored by him and Pope Pius XII, and I had contributed a year's supply of free motion pictures to the orphanage.

It was not generally known, even in the film industry, that the Vatican operated some three thousand commercial movie theaters in many parts of the world through ACEC-SAS, the Catholic League of Exhibitors of the Roman Catholic Church. For ten years I had been representing the Vatican in negotiations for films suitable for exhibition in these theaters.

When the work on the Minerva project came to an end, I returned to America with a full report for Joseph Kennedy. No new capital from American film sources was ever committed, and in time Minerva Films went bankrupt. Soon after my return to this country, I got a phone call from the State Department. Three representatives of the Soviet Motion Picture organization, SOVEX, had arrived in America to open United States–Soviet motion picture trade. Because of my extensive work with European film production, I was asked to meet with the Soviet representatives.

In Washington I met with three Russian motion picture producers and an official from the Soviet Embassy. After preliminary discussions, the Russians came to New York for further meetings on one particular film SOVEX was offering, *Sleeping Beauty,* the first complete color film of a ballet. It starred the great Russian dancer Maya Plisetskaya. I knew the film was ideal for two areas of exhibition: American television, where it would be a real first, and the Vatican chain of theaters. It would be a precedent-breaking step forward in Soviet–Vatican cultural exchange.

Although the SOVEX representatives were talking to others during their visit, they quickly recognized the benefits of my proposals in behalf of the Vatican. Culture is never without political overtones in the Soviet Union. We had a preliminary meeting of minds, and there followed a series of phone calls between my New York apartment and Rome. Since there were many who frowned upon any cooperation with the Soviets, it was important that plans for the film be kept extremely confidential. All projected dates, financial arrangements, exhibition terms, and other practical considerations were discussed with only one individual in the Vatican circle. Finally, when all the important details had been thrashed out via transatlantic phone, a formal agreement was reached between SOVEX and me, in my capacity as acting representative of the Vatican chain of exhibitors.

On January 26, 1966, I arrived—secretly, I thought—in Rome to begin technical discussions for furnishing the film through the Vatican theater chain. The first thing I learned was that it was no secret I was in Rome. Then I found out the terms that had been discussed by telephone with only one man, a gentleman of absolute integrity, were known to others. It turned out that other confidential information was far from confidential. I was bewildered. How had personal telephone discussions come to be almost public knowledge? How had my plans become known in advance? I discussed this strange turn of events with the man who had been a party to all the preliminary discussions for the Vatican, and he could offer no explanation.

There was an answer I had initially refused to consider: My telephone in New York had been tapped. It was a stunning realization but no other conclusion was possible. I thought perhaps the reason had to do with my working closely with the SOVEX representatives. As the agreement had been signed by me and the Vatican but not yet by the SOVEX people, I decided to go to Moscow to complete the signing. On January 30 I flew from Rome to Moscow. There, at the SOVEX offices, I received my next big surprise: The contract for *Sleeping Beauty* had been withdrawn.

In reply to my protests, I was simply told that "other interested parties" had been chosen. I waved the agreement we had reached and received only shrugs. Higher authorities had canceled the deal. There was no recourse. SOVEX was an official agency of the Soviet government, and suing the Russian government would be a meaningless legal exercise. It became clear I had received all the answers I would get, and I returned to Rome, and a few days later, to New York.

Still mystified and angry, I was determined to get to the bottom of the affair. Suddenly things fell into place. I discussed the matter with J. Howard McGrath. As a former Attorney General, he was in an excellent position to know what might be done. He agreed wholeheartedly that a rawly illegal deed of such magnitude should not be permitted to go unchallenged. The implications of this invasion of my constitutional right to privacy posed a threat to every telephone user in America.

It was decided I should file a formal complaint of illegal wiretapping with the Public Service Commission of the State of New York. Since the phone calls had been transatlantic, a complaint was also filed with the Federal Communications Commission in Washington.

Partly because of my wiretapping complaint, the merger between ITT and ABC, which had already been approved, was reopened at the petition of the Justice Department's antitrust division. On September 19, 1966, the Federal Communications Commission held a hearing on my specific complaint as it pertained to the commission's overall review of the ITT-ABC merger approval.

The hearing proved to be more illuminating than anyone could have suspected. It detailed the interlocking maneuvers of ABC, Bell Telephone, and ITT in violation of individual and constitutional rights. The hearing was the first public indication of another symbiotic relationship, that between the CIA and ITT. That strange partnership, revealed more fully in the disclosures of the ITT-CIA role in the downfall of the Allende government in Chile, was not an isolated, overnight working arrangement.

That ABC was nervous about the hearing was obvious from the presence of Leonard Goldenson, chairman of the network, and some fifteen other officers and counsel. The importance ITT attached to the proceedings was made clear by the representation of ITT officials. Leading the group was the president of ITT, Harold Geneen, a gentleman who prefers to stay out of the public eye.

The hearings resulted in a withdrawal of the ABC-ITT merger approval. It was an indirect victory perhaps, but a victory nonetheless.

After the Soviet cancellation of the *Sleeping Beauty* agreement, the Vatican decided to publicize its chain of commercial theaters and my work in acquiring films for it. The official announcement received wide publicity in motion picture industry trade journals, as did reports of my trips to California to acquire films. On one such trip I planned to go to the opening of the new and opulent Las Vegas casino, Caesar's Palace. The Teamsters' pension fund had provided funds for the construction of the gambling showplace and the Teamsters held a $40 million mortgage on the casino. The opening was to be a big affair, and J. Howard McGrath, who was unable to attend, asked me to go in his place.

Unfortunately, I never got to Las Vegas on that trip. Late on the night of my arrival in California, I became ill. The physician at the Century-Plaza Hotel informed me that I had had a heart attack.

After an extended stay in a hospital, I returned to the Century-Plaza for convalescence. While I was there, Irving Kahn came to see me. Kahn informed me that he was associated with a company called TelePrompter, and that TelePrompter and Howard Hughes shared certain business interests. Tele-Prompter, he said, had a large contract with the Archdiocese of Brooklyn for closed-circuit educational materials and other instructional programs. Once in my hotel room, he seemed to lose the urgency he had conveyed on the phone while setting up the appointment. I could not, in fact, discover the exact reason for his visit. He explored in rather general terms my feelings about Vatican interest in closed-circuit educational materials, and he asked questions about my relationships within Vatican circles. The meeting seemed rather pointless.

Soon after, however, I received a visit from two more gentlemen who said they were personal representatives of Howard Hughes. Their discussion was somewhat less general. Howard Hughes was interested in a plan to pioneer a communications system based on microwave linkage that would avoid normal communication methods and thus the supervision of the Federal Communications Commission. This microwave system was to be beamed through a satellite put in orbit expressly for this purpose. They asked if I thought the Vatican would be interested in becoming part of this breakthrough in communications.

My response was vague. I had no idea how the Vatican would view such a proposal, and moreover, I was not ready, physically or mentally, to tackle the idea. They left with the usual comments about contacting me again and I tabled the matter in my mind. Not long after, I received medical clearance to return to New York and my own physician.

After a period of convalescence in New York, I returned to California. I was staying at the Bel Air Hotel when Robert Maheu, still Howard Hughes's right-hand man and privy to everything Hughes thought and did, came to see me and invite me to a private meeting with Hughes. As much out of curiosity as anything else, I agreed.

The Hughes passion for secrecy had already reached semi-recluse proportions. I was driven in a limousine with window curtains tightly drawn to a location in Bel Air not very far from the hotel. Then I was taken inside a large house so sparsely furnished it seemed as if the occupant were in the process of moving out. Two or three men were discreetly placed in the hallways and I glimpsed a woman who may have been Jean Peters. I was shown into a vast and minimally furnished living room where Hughes greeted me with a quick smile. He was considerably thinner than when I'd last seen him years before. He wore a loose sport shirt and had a thin, somewhat scraggly goatee. His voice had developed a raspy quality.

"It's been a long time, Bill," he said. "But I've been reading about you. How are you feeling?"

"Better," I answered.

"Good," he said. "Seeing as how we're practically neighbors here, I thought it best to get together personally with you." No more intermediaries, I thought silently. "Besides, what I want to talk about with you has to be in strict confidence. It's about the satellite proposal."

He leaned forward urgently. "This is something for the Vatican, Bill. You know what this could do for them."

"No, I don't, really," I replied.

"It'd be a real coup," Hughes said. "The Church using the newest means of communication to bring its message to the world. Why, the possibilities are endless. A satellite launched from Vatican soil, a new star in the sky."

"What's the position of the FCC on this kind of thing?" I asked.

Hughes flashed an expression of horror. "The FCC won't have a damn thing to do with it. I haven't spoken to anyone in Washington about it. This is strictly confidential."

"Just who will own the satellite? How will this all work?"

"It'll be launched from Vatican soil. My technical experts will operate it, of course. The Vatican can use it for anything they like. Any kind of message linkup anywhere in the world will be possible. They could avoid all censorship problems everywhere."

"But technical control would be in your hands," I pressed.

"It'd have to be. They don't have the experts for that. We'd work out some kind of joint ownership. I haven't gotten into the practical details yet. What I need now is their agreement to proceed. That's why I wanted to see you. You're obviously in a position of trust. They have you acquiring films for their chain of theaters. That means they have confidence in your judgment and evaluation of communications media. I want you to carry the ball on this personally, directly to the Pope. It's too big for lower-level discussion."

Hughes had been both enthusiastic about the idea and vague on details. I decided I wanted more time to consider the matter. On the face of it, the idea held a certain excitement. It could open up vast new possibilities for good.

"Let me think a little about this," I said.

Hughes nodded. "The more you think about it, the more excited you'll get over it," he promised. "Just tell the Vatican that I'm prepared to do whatever has to be done."

I was familiar enough with the Howard Hughes way of saying things to know he was telling me that money was no object. He was convinced that given enough money, he could buy and sell anything and anyone. Yet the idea was intriguing and I turned it over in my mind as I was driven back to the hotel in the curtained limousine. Paul VI now sat in St. Peter's chair, and he had begun his reign as an innovative and aggressive Pope. His visit to India, and contemplated visit to America, were only two indications that he looked toward a more modern role for the Church in the world. The satellite idea, I thought, might appeal to such a man, and I decided to consider the proposal very carefully.

When Robert Maheu called me a few days later for my decision, I was still wrestling with the idea. I told him I needed more details on the concrete matters of control, ownership, and responsibility. Maheu got back to me the next day with vague, unsatisfactory answers. He refused to be pinned down on anything beyond the generalities Hughes had given me. I decided the project needed further thinking. While working on other matters, I had an opportunity to make some very discreet inquiries and was bothered to learn that the Hughes satellite was not as confidential as I'd been led to believe. There were intimations that Hughes had discussed his satellite project with others.

Wary, yet intrigued by the idea, I decided to go to Rome on my own and discuss the proposal with a highly respected authority in the Vatican. It was decided that the general idea would be submitted for a preliminary reaction. All the details I could muster, which were not many, were included in the presentation. The answer came back quickly. The Vatican was not interested. The project, it was felt, had political overtones.

Later I was filled in on the reasons for the rejection. The Vatican, it seemed, wanted nothing to do with a project in which Howard Hughes would be involved. Furthermore, the Vatican was very aware that the Hughes enterprise had many CIA associations. That was an element I had not given enough attention to, probably because I had not thoroughly recovered from my illness and was not functioning at top efficiency.

But I returned from my trip to Rome determined to investigate the satellite project further before getting back to Hughes. Less discreet this time, I found out that the secret project Hughes had held back for the right co-sponsor had not been held back at all. He had, through his emissaries, approached a number of governments with the project and had been turned down by all. However, the true dimensions of what he had wanted me to accomplish for him only struck me when I tried to see him.

Howard Hughes was no longer in the almost unfurnished house in Bel Air. He had been taken, in the middle of the night, to a railroad car waiting just outside Los Angeles, and from there by train to the Massachusetts General Hospital in Boston. CIA agents had spirited him from the house and into absolute seclusion in Boston. One more name popped up in this incident: Johnny Roselli had been one of those who had transported Hughes from the house to the railroad car. The CIA, Howard Hughes, Johnny Roselli—an official agency of the United States, private corporate interests, and the underworld. The same people surfaced again and again, like the tentacles of an octopus.

I kept hearing Howard Hughes's words about his satellite. *The Vatican can use it for anything they like. Any kind of message linkup anywhere in the world . . . avoid all censorship problems.* It was clear in hindsight that those possibilities would have been equally available to his CIA associates. The satellite orbited under the flag of the Vatican would have been an ideal front for the CIA's communication experts. It was a grim thought. Had I been more thoroughly taken in, or had the Vatican been less wise, it could have happened. Howard Hughes and the CIA would have had the most respectable disguise for their activities that could be devised.

But it hadn't happened and I was grateful for that. A short while after my attempt to see Hughes, I returned to New York. I had been back only a few days when a call came from Rose Mary Woods. Richard Nixon had been trying to reach me on the West Coast and wanted me to come to his New York offices for a visit. She intimated it was on a matter of considerable importance. Though as far as I knew, nothing I was doing was of interest to Richard Nixon, I went to see him as a matter of courtesy. Another surprise awaited me there.

"I called you down to hear what reaction you got during your trip to Rome," Nixon began in his usual peremptory way.

"Reaction to what?"

"The satellite," he said. Surprised that he even knew about the trip, I felt annoyance at the temerity of the question.

"The matter was private, I'm afraid. Certainly, it doesn't concern you," I said.

"It very much concerns me. I'm counsel on the satellite project for Howard," Nixon returned. I stared at him.

"No one said anything to me about that."

"It's not general information," he said. "You can believe me," he added.

One more tentacle of the octopus. Nixon's long secret history of association with Hughes, plus Hughes's circuitous methods, made his claim quite believable. But I had no proper authorization to discuss the matter with him and absolutely no desire to do so.

"Now I want to know what happened in Rome," Richard Nixon asked again.

"I'll only talk to Hughes about it," I answered.

"That's nonsense. I've every right to know," Nixon said.

"Sorry, only Hughes."

"You're being unreasonable. As counsel on this project, it's necessary that I know."

"I'm sorry. I won't talk about it. The trip was a private one. I'll discuss it only with Hughes."

"Completely improper," Nixon snapped and lectured me on the importance of his position in the project. I felt for a moment that the clock had been turned back to the days of the

Trujillo pursuit when he had insisted on playing Mr. Vice President.

"Sorry," I said, cutting him off and getting to my feet.

He was furious when I walked out of his office. And I was more grateful than ever that the venture hadn't succeeded.

A day later Robert Maheu called. He too wanted to know about the trip to Rome, and asked for a written report to "give to the boss." Once again I refused. When Howard Hughes had wanted to enlist my assistance in his grand plan, he had made himself available. When he had wanted to make me a party to his schemes, he had arranged to see me. He would have to do so again if he wanted answers.

He never did. Perhaps he sensed that his grand design had been turned down. Perhaps he realized that others had seen through it. Or perhaps he had already turned his attention to other plans. Whatever the reason, I never met again with Howard Hughes.

I later heard that he tried to interest still other countries in the satellite project, but as far as I know, Howard Hughes's satellite never orbited. Like the man without a country, he wandered from place to place and was refused at each. Howard Hughes found that the keys to the kingdom are not always for sale.

7

IN THE
SHADOW OF Z

In 1969 the motion picture Z was released around the world. A semidocumentary exposé, it cast a harsh light on the political situation in Greece, focusing on national corruption and the involvement of the CIA with the Greek military junta.

Z was a strong indictment of U.S. interference in the internal affairs of another nation. It depicted real people and real events, and was for most Americans the first revelation of the highly questionable activities of the CIA. The repercussions were tremendous.

The glare of publicity forced some of the players out of the arena and into the shadows, but the ruthless game still goes on. Recently a man named Richard Welch was assassinated in Athens. He proved to be the CIA station chief in that city, and his murder has resulted in a strange alliance: The hunt for the killers of Richard Welch is being conducted by the CIA *and* the Soviet KGB. This cooperation does not reflect the spirit of detente. It signifies, rather, that both the CIA and the KGB are upset by unexplained, unauthorized assassinations and are afraid of wheels within wheels. Both agencies are busy searching inside as well as outside their own structures for the answers.

My involvement with the film Z, which led to a murky entanglement with the Greek junta, the CIA, and the U.S. Department of State, began with a totally unrelated combination of events. In 1967 I was spending a good deal of time in Palm Beach, Florida, on doctor's orders. Negotiations were under way for a film entitled *The Fabulous Rothschilds.* Some of the financing for the film was to be handled through the Rothschild banking houses in Paris and London. Because I had to make frequent trips between California and Paris and London, I decided to make California my base of operations.

I had hoped to sublet my New York apartment to the actress Jean Arthur, but the landlord refused to allow a sublease so I found myself dismantling custom-built bookcases, wall dividers, stereo equipment units, and all the other special features I had paid good money to have installed. This, and the moving itself, was a time-consuming task, enormously aggravated by the fact that I had to make most of the arrangements by telephone, often from London or Paris. On-the-spot supervision had to be left to a man I hired to oversee the work. I put particular stress on the handling of two paintings, a large portrait canvas by Thomas Gainsborough and a priceless still-life by Rubens.

At this time Jimmy Hoffa, desperately seeking a way out of prison, still thought I might work magic for him. His messages, delivered through Jacques Schiffer, one of his attorneys, pleaded for some plan that might help him. His own legal staff hadn't come up with anything and he was frustrated beyond belief. Needless to say, I wasn't interested in devoting any more time to Hoffa unless I was paid my bonding fee.

Meanwhile, work on the Rothschild film was progressing with a cast that tentatively included Maurice Chevalier, Audrey Hepburn, and Rex Harrison. However, problems developed within the Rothschild family and a great deal of bitterness surfaced. During one trip to London my coronary condition flared up again and I had to curtail my activities. By the time I returned to business full time, the acrimony between the branches of the Rothschild family had reached such a pitch that it was decided to shift the film work from London to Hollywood. Upon finally returning to California, I was shattered to find the Rubens was missing from the things shipped from New York. Apparently it had been stolen and I began a frantic search for its recovery. When one day Jacques Schiffer phoned with still another plea from Hoffa, I asked him to have Hoffa use his influence to help track down the missing Rubens, which had been shipped in trucks operated by the Teamsters. He launched an independent investigation, but it brought no results. The priceless painting stayed missing, and I brought suit against the three moving and storage companies involved.

During a trip to New York I received a call from Rose Mary Woods. Richard Nixon wanted me to pay him another visit at the offices of Mudge, Rose. I would have declined had not Rose Mary Woods remarked, "Clifford Folger suggested Mr. Nixon call you."

Ever since the Eisenhower presidency, when Clifford Folger had been chairman of the Republican Finance Committee and a close confidant of General Eisenhower, I had had a great deal of respect for him. Furthermore, Folger had been instrumental in a number of far-reaching ventures in which I had had an interest. Reluctantly I agreed to see Nixon.

It was a very different Nixon whom I now met. He was full of confidence, "grateful" for my visit, and although real warmth and charm were simply beyond him, he tried hard to be gracious. The purpose of his call was not long in coming.

"I'm going to run for President again," he announced. "We're in the process of forming the finance committee for my nomination. Of course we'd like you to be in on it. I just wanted to tell you the news personally."

"I'm honored," I said.

"I know you served on President Eisenhower's finance committee and were a great help to him," he went on. "I'm hoping we can count on you for more of the same."

"Thank you for asking me. I'll have to think about it," I answered carefully. "There are only so many hours in a day and mine are pretty full."

"I'm sure you'll make this the number-one priority in your considerations," Nixon said, a trace of vice presidential imperiousness creeping into his voice.

When I left the Mudge, Rose offices, I did so with no desire to serve on any finance committee for Richard Nixon. Although Clifford Folger later suggested it might be a good thing for me to do, my negative feelings persisted. I put aside further thoughts about it as one crowded week impinged upon the next. Early in the summer, when I was back in California, I received a call from John Alexander of Mudge, Rose, who, after inquiring about the state of my health, general well-being, and overall happiness, invited me to a public kickoff for the Nixon campaign that was to be held at the Century-Plaza Hotel in Los Angeles on June 23. I was also invited to a breakfast, a private affair for select guests that would be held before the kickoff.

I agreed to attend, and arrived at the Century-Plaza to find a small welcoming committee and Richard Nixon. It was emphasized that a place on the finance comittee had been held open for me. Evidently my work for many of the Middle Eastern oil-producing countries, particularly my involvement in the Shah of Iran's dispute with England during the Truman administration, had been carefully researched. With only a nod toward subtlety, I was asked about the possibility of obtaining sizable unmarked cash contributions from my Mideast sources, a harbinger of future preoccupation with untraceable cash donations.

I maintained an uncommitted interest until later in the day, after the public announcement at which Pat and Julie Nixon appeared. Then I dropped all pretense of interest. Listening, observing, but mostly remembering, I decided I wanted no part in helping Richard Nixon become President. Dwight D. Eisenhower's words kept returning to me: *I wouldn't want to leave the presidency in that man's hands.* Uncertain health was my formal reason for not accepting a place on the Nixon finance committee, and the finality of the decision was made clear.

From the sidelines I watched Nixon's familiar tactics gaining the nomination, and eventually the presidency. These echoes of the past made me glad all over again that I'd stayed out of the proceedings. But other events were gathering momentum and pointing me in the direction of *Z*.

Jacques Schiffer called to say Hoffa had agreed to a resolution of the bonding fees but wanted to know if I had any ideas about getting him out of jail. In truth, I had toyed with a plan that appeared legally valid, and I had discussed it briefly with Schiffer.

It revolved around a habeas corpus action to be brought in

the federal court in Pennsylvania against the government. When we discussed the legal technicalities, Schiffer agreed the plan had merit and said he would get back to me on it. He did call back a few days later, an upset and puzzled man. Morris Shenker, Hoffa's chief attorney, opposed the plan. Allen Dorfman and Frank Fitzsimmons, who were then in charge of the Teamsters and supposedly figureheads for Hoffa, also opposed the idea.

Schiffer then talked with Hoffa about the idea and Hoffa wanted me to come to Pennsylvania and discuss it with him at the prison. I refused emphatically. Every one of Hoffa's visitors was monitored by the Justice Department. Bob Kennedy, now a Senator from New York, was being pushed as the Democratic candidate for the presidency. I wanted no more head-on collisions with Robert F. Kennedy. Besides, there was no reason for me to journey to see Hoffa. Schiffer was capable of discussing the plan with him. Since some of Hoffa's associates and confidants were strongly opposed to the plan, nothing ever came of it, although I am convinced it would have secured his release from prison. Then an assassin's bullet cut down Bobby Kennedy. Jimmy Hoffa lost an implacable enemy and Richard Nixon achieved the presidency.

I was having legal problems of my own at this time over the stolen Rubens. The court insisted I offer authentication of ownership. This posed certain problems. Both the Rubens and the Gainsborough had been brought from Rome to New York by Cardinal Ottaviani when he paid a visit to Cardinal Spellman. I bought the Gainsborough in Rome, but at a luncheon reception given by Cardinal Spellman for Cardinal Ottaviani, I was presented the Rubens in appreciation for providing free films to the boys' orphanage in Rome. Insofar as the Supreme Court of the State of New York was concerned, I had no sales slip and no commercial record of ownership of the Rubens. I was given time to provide authentication of ownership.

The complexities of the matter did not lend themselves to a long-distance resolution, and I decided a personal visit to Cardinal Ottaviani was in order. Besides, it was time for a visit with old friends and associates at the Vatican.

In Rome I obtained a letter, signed by Cardinal Ottaviani, which read in part: "I also recall very well and do certify you legally acquired two original paintings; one, an original and authentic Rubens, entitled 'A Bowl of Fruit' and signed by the artist." The letter of authentication was dispatched to my attorney in New York and I went to the film festival at Cannes. After a few days of screenings, I took the night train to Paris for a conference on a film I owned starring Brigitte Bardot. After the meeting I went to dinner with a group of friends and was introduced to Eric Schlumberger, the producer of *Z*.

Schlumberger, a dark-haired man about six feet tall, was terribly excited over the success of *Z* in Paris and insisted I go with him to view the lines outside the theater where the film was playing. I had been to a screening of *Z* and had rejected it for American audiences, proof that it's impossible to be right all the time. However, Schlumberger's enthusiasm was contagious, and I accompanied him to a theater on the Champs Élysées. He had not been exaggerating. The crowds were astonishing, inside the theater and out. Pulling me along with him, he insisted I take another look at the film. When it was over, I still felt it wouldn't appeal to American audiences, but the size and enthusiasm of the crowds were impressive. Eric Schlumberger spent the better part of the week trying to convince me to buy the film rights of *Z* for American exhibition.

The continued size of the crowds at the theaters was more convincing than his salesmanship, and I had second thoughts about buying the film. However, I still had a major reservation. It concerned the star of the film, Yves Montand. Having represented Montand, I was very familiar with his left-wing image in the United States, particularly with American officials. I gave little thought at the time to what the reaction would be in certain circles to the message of the film.

The crowds continued to besiege the Paris theaters and Schlumberger continued to besiege me. Box-office reports from theaters in other French cities, and throughout Europe, convinced me I'd been wrong in my original estimation. When I finally agreed to deal with Schlumberger, though, it was as much because of his creative strength and potential as a film-maker as anything else. An understanding was reached wherein I agreed to be the American representative of Régane Films, and Eric Schlumberger and I agreed to negotiate the sale of the film for exhibition in the United States.

Immediately we ran into unusual difficulties. The distribution rights were offered to a number of major American motion picture companies—Metro-Goldwyn-Mayer, Columbia Pictures, Paramount, 20th Century–Fox, and Universal Studios—and all turned them down flat. This unanimity was puzzling. The picture was a box-office success all over Europe, and nothing convinces a motion picture executive like box-office statistics. Those figures take precedence over personal judgments. Yet each of these major companies seemed to be ignoring the figures by which they normally swore. All my inquiries as to why the film was being refused were met by platitudes that didn't make any sense.

Schlumberger very much wanted the film to be shown in the United States, and now so did I. I had become irritated by the strange and unfathomable resistance of the major Hollywood companies. Finally, a small distributor, Cinema Five, reacted positively. This company, owned by Donald Rugoff, was in financial straits at the time and proposed a very low figure for a national distributorship, $350,000. But Rugoff was the only one offering anything, so it was decided to conclude with him.

By now, I was quite optimistic about the film's prospects in America. It came as a shock when, after everything had been signed and sealed, publicity work begun, and prints shipped, Rugoff phoned to say he wanted to back out. He claimed he had fears about Yves Montand's presence in the film, something he had certainly known about from the onset. His behavior seemed as enigmatic as the unanimous refusal of the film by the major Hollywood companies.

While on vacation in France, I received a cable from Donald Rugoff. He wanted to meet me in the south of France to discuss his backing out of the contract. I agreed to meet him, only to receive another wire a few days later in which he canceled the meeting. Strange and mysterious behavior, but I had other business matters to think about. I returned to New York just in time to read the reviews of the film. They were wildly enthusiastic, and Z was on its way to becoming a major box-office success as well as the center of a political hurricane.

I was curious to hear how Donald Rugoff felt about the film's success, but when I tried to reach him, I was told he was away on a two-week cruise. It seemed an odd time to choose for a cruise. It was almost as if he didn't want to be anywhere near the film when it opened. I felt exactly the opposite. I had no desire to dissociate myself from Z. Obviously it was going to be a major income-producing venture, and I happily redoubled my efforts to promote it.

Those efforts took an unexpected turn when the Columbia Broadcasting System contacted me. Columbia was issuing an album of the musical score of the film, which had been written by the Greek composer Mikis Theodorakis. Since writing the score, Theodorakis had been imprisoned in Greece for anti-government activities. My involvement with Z and my association with a number of well-known Greek businessmen had convinced CBS that I was the person to go to Greece and try to effect the release of Theodorakis. Columbia hoped he could be freed in time to appear at the Academy Award ceremonies in Hollywood, where there was talk that Z might receive an Oscar. Z had so exacerbated political sensitivities in Greece that I didn't see how this could be accomplished.

Still, the idea intrigued me and I agreed to see what could be done. The first requisite was to find someone in Greece who had good contacts and knew his way around the sandbars and shoals of the political waters. I decided on a young man I had known for several years, Achilles Vlachopoulos, whom I had met through Aristotle Onassis. A suave, wavy-haired young man with an excess of Mediterranean charm, Vlachopoulos was treated almost like a member of the Onassis family. He was especially close to Onassis's children, Alexander and Christina, and it was felt that with a little grooming and schooling, he could someday become a trusted family financial adviser. Vlachopoulos's job then was tending to the desires of the VIP travelers on Onassis's Olympic Airlines. He was also an aspiring singer who had had some small success in the local Greek cabarets.

Vlachopoulos seemed the perfect choice. I reached him in Athens and had him fly to New York for detailed discussions on what might be done to free Theodorakis.

Armed with instructions, Vlachopoulos returned to Greece and called me from there soon afterward. His words were hardly encouraging. It was a dangerous business, I was told. The Greek colonels had increased civil restrictions since Z had been released. Everyone was on edge. Despite vehement denials of CIA influence in Greek affairs, that influence was stronger than ever. Only Washington, I was told, could exert enough pressure to obtain the release of Theodorakis. All other avenues were closed.

Nevertheless, I decided to go to Greece myself. First I met with William Rogers, then Secretary of State under Richard Nixon. At the time Washington was steadfastly denying all charges of interfering in Greek affairs. Various spokesmen termed the kind of covert operation detailed in Z "unthinkable" and "ludicrous." I informed Rogers I intended to try to persuade the Greek junta to free Theodorakis, and pointed out that his release could only improve the image of the Greek regime, which was currently pretty distasteful all around the world. He listened without significant comment, but had a coded cable dispatched to the American Ambassador in Athens, instructing him to give me as much assistance as possible.

Not exactly sure what Rogers's gesture meant, I flew to Athens the next day. There, acting under instructions previously given him, Vlachopoulos had contacted Theodorakis's wife and attorney and had arranged for me to meet them. I wanted to gather whatever ammunition they could provide to use in my plea for Theodorakis's release.

The attorney called first and we met in secret in a room at the Hotel Grand-Bretagne. Then he drove me to a house where Mrs. Theodorakis was staying. A second man, who appeared to be a guard, was also present. I could not help thinking all this furtiveness was unnecessary if the Greek secret police were as efficient as I had heard. The attorney spoke English well and served as interpreter. Mrs. Theodorakis wore the black dress affected by so many Greek women. Short, rather heavy, and colorless, she alternated between tearful outbursts and almost phlegmatic calm. I was given an impassioned briefing on the political and personal injustice of keeping Theodorakis in prison. He was, I was told, a very sick man with advanced tuberculosis and a host of other ailments. Beyond that, they revealed no new information that would help me argue for his release. Somewhat disappointed, but alarmed over the information about his health, I went to the American Embassy and, in accordance with the coded cable sent from Secretary Rogers, found the embassy people cooperative.

An appointment was made for me to see Colonel Patakos, a member of the ruling junta who was also Deputy Prime Minister in Command of the KYP, the Greek secret police. It would have been absolutely impossible for me to have seen Colonel Patakos, I learned later, had the American Embassy not asked for the meeting.

The Colonel was just under six feet tall, balding, with sharp direct eyes and a countenance as rugged as the Greek mountains. He listened as I catalogued the reasons why Theodorakis ought to be released and allowed to leave Greece. It would be the humane thing to do, I emphasized, noting how terrible it would look if he were to die in a Greek prison. I ended the plea with the suggestion that perhaps the Colonel did not know about Theodorakis's precarious health.

The Colonel gave me a chilly smile. "Would you step into the next room with me?" he asked. I followed him into a small anteroom with a modest motion picture screen. The Colonel barked some orders, the lights were lowered, and the screen came alive. I saw scenes of Theodorakis playing basketball, Theodorakis swimming, Theodorakis playing handball. I saw pictures of him enjoying his food, playing cards, relaxing, then still more scenes of him jogging and exercising. I watched until the screen went blank and the lights came on.

I looked at the Colonel. The rugged face showed mild, condescending amusement.

"Does that appear to be a man on the brink of death?" he said. "Does that appear to you to be a man in the last stages of tuberculosis?"

I made no comment and followed him back into the main office. "I am not in a position to grant any release," he said, leaning back in his chair. "However, life is full of surprises. One never knows what tomorrow brings. In thirty days from now, Mikis Theodorakis might be someplace else entirely. But for now he is in prison and for now he will stay there."

The interview was ended and I left, feeling a little like Alice in Wonderland. I had learned both ends of the Greek political spectrum could be devious. I went back to the American Embassy because I had promised to report on the results of the interview. I did, without holding anything back. The following morning I was happy to leave Greece for Paris. Two days after my arrival the Paris edition of the *Herald Tribune* reported Theodorakis was to be released. Immediately I called the *Tribune* and had them retract the story.

Shortly afterward I returned to the United States, having closed the Theodorakis chapter, I thought. But in a little over two weeks Mikis Theodorakis was released. The French journalist Jacques Servan-Schreiber flew him from Athens to Paris via helicopter. Moreover, Servan-Schreiber claimed total credit for the release. I was furious to read it was he who had met with the colonels and he who had convinced the regime to release Theodorakis because of his poor health.

I had to put aside my fury that morning to attend a screening, but I was seething and inwardly debating how to tell the truth about what had happened. During the screening I was called outside. Two phone calls for me had come in almost simultaneously, one from *The New York Times,* the other from the office of the Secretary of State. Something told me to take the Washington call first. A spokesman for Secretary Rogers was at the other end. The State Department, I was told, wanted the story of Theodorakis's release to stand just as it was. I was to say nothing to change it. The message was close to an order.

I hung up and took the call from the *Times.* It didn't take me long to realize the *Times* had found out what had actually happened and wanted me to give a confirmation and an interview. I refused. The story remained as it had first appeared.

Perhaps I should not have agreed to the request from Washington. I still wonder about that. By acceding, I became a party to the CIA's continued covert influence in Greek affairs. The CIA had seen that releasing Theodorakis would soften criticism of the Greek regime. At the same time my government did not want the extent of American influence in Greece known. Consequently, the release had been credited to Servan-Schreiber and the French, perhaps by arrangement, perhaps by more subtle means. It was a corroboration of the charges made in *Z.*

When I acceded to the request from Rogers's office, I did more than help maintain the CIA's cover. I also unwittingly placed myself in the position of knowing truths powerful circles did not want revealed. The political impact of *Z* in this country had been made possible only because I had managed to get the film distributed after all the major Hollywood studios had turned it down. Now I knew that the film's composer had been released at the behest of the U.S. government. These two bits of knowledge put me in a kind of double jeopardy, though I did not concern myself with that kind of thinking at the time. *Z* was becoming a problem in other ways.

My contract for the film called for a percentage of every box-office dollar, and although there were a lot of dollars to share, the proper sharing of them had begun to be a problem. Rugoff and I had increasing disagreements over the returns of the film and the stipulations of the contract. The disagreements became known to many inside and outside the motion picture industry. A considerable amount of money was involved, and it seemed the courts would have to settle it. However, I hoped to keep out of litigation then, for other affairs were keeping me busy.

All through the *Z* affair Jacques Schiffer had continued to call in Hoffa's behalf. Hoffa wondered if I thought his chances for release were any better under the Nixon administration. The answer was I had no idea and certainly no special entrée to offer. Jacques Schiffer told me Hoffa was having problems freeing the bonding monies but had promised to "make it up to you if you can come up with something." Schiffer assured me in all sincerity that he believed in Hoffa's promise, and I have no reason to doubt he did. However, I had nothing to offer and little time to think about Hoffa. I had become involved in a new proposition with tremendous potential.

Through a friend, Peter Smillie, then vice president of the Technical Tape Corporation, I had been introduced to a man named Ernest Keiser. The introduction took place when I visited Peter Smillie in Nassau in the Bahamas. Keiser, over six feet and slender, had the never-quite-relaxed mien of a Prussian officer out of uniform for the day. I was told he was a gem and old coin merchant, but his real interest when I met him was the development of the island of Belize in the British Honduras. He wanted to transform the island into another Freeport, Bahamas, replete with hotels, resorts, gambling casinos—in short, an oasis for pleasure.

The plan had been worked out in some detail, and it offered many interesting possibilities. Keiser needed financing, of course, and wanted help finding investors. As I was to see Flor Trujillo when she came to Miami on other business, I arranged to bring him to meet her. I advised Flor that the idea was sound and worth her consideration. Keiser estimated the development of Belize would require approximately $5 million. Later, when Flor and I were alone, we discussed other Trujillo matters in Geneva and the possibility of interesting the Spanish banker Francisco Paesa in the Belize project. Paesa, who lived in Geneva, was young, separated from his wife, and looking for new ventures. It was decided that since I had to go to Geneva on Trujillo affairs, I would discuss the matter with Paesa. Paesa was very interested and he agreed to come to a meeting of all concerned in Miami.

While in Athens on another matter, I received a call from Achilles Vlachopoulos. He was tired of working for Olympic Airlines and aspired to be a full-time singer and entertainer. He desperately wanted to break into show business in America. Before agreeing to help him, I telephoned Onassis, who urged me to do whatever I could for Vlachopoulos. It was arranged the young man would come to the United States where I would put him in touch with the proper people at MGM and other studios, smooth his way with the American Guild of Variety Artists and Immigration, and generally try to aid his career. Unfortunately, Achilles Vlachopoulos's career did not go anywhere. The magic just wasn't there, but he did try hard and he became a frequent visitor to my place in Miami. He was a pleasant young man, and I didn't hesitate to introduce him to my friends and associates.

When I returned to Florida, Ernest Keiser introduced me to a "friend and aide," a young man named Brian Wise. London-born, Wise was something of a cross between David Niven and James Bond—smooth, assured, a surface person.

Instinctively I distrusted him, but I had not yet learned how important it is to pay attention to instinct. I told myself the world was full of surface people. In any case, as Keiser's assistant, he took part in most of our conferences and negotiations.

When Francisco Paesa arrived for the Miami meeting, the plans for developing the island were discussed in great detail. Everyone agreed it was worth undertaking, and Paesa was confident his bank in Geneva could finance a large part of the necessary capital. With a commitment from Flor Trujillo, the mathematics seemed to work out, although there were many financial arrangements still to be completed. After the meeting Paesa, Flor, and I were treated to an air tour of Belize conducted by Brian Wise. On the chartered plane everything seemed to be coming together and I looked forward to working out the details of the plan. However, I was interrupted by Achilles Vlachopoulos.

He appeared one day in a state of agitation. His career as a vocalist had been going nowhere, a fact I was aware of through other sources. Now he was in some kind of trouble— the old story of new friends and bad company. Some of these new friends were apparently involved in narcotics traffic and had been apprehended. The Narcotics Division of the Treasury Department had already questioned Vlachopoulos, and he had learned they wanted to bring him in for more questioning.

He almost tearfully assured me he was innocent. Conditioned by living in the Greek semi-police state, he was terribly frightened at the prospect of being taken into custody by federal agents. He wanted to leave the country as fast as possible. I argued flight would hardly make him look innocent, but he was adamant and there was little I could do to persuade him to stay. It all happened rather suddenly, and his haste seemed unnecessary. Yet he promised he would return as soon as it became clear he wasn't involved.

After this interruption, I resumed the task of putting together a detailed financial arrangement for the Belize plans. At last, after countless transatlantic telephone calls and cables, plus numerous trips to Geneva and Paris, the time came for concluding the arrangements. It was then that Ernest Keiser seemed to hang back. He said or did nothing definite, yet I became aware of a slowdown in his moves. He was still enthusiastic, but he seemed unwilling to advance his portion of the finances.

It was an entirely unexpected turn and Keiser's explanations were unsatisfactory. He was, among other things, to advance money for certain cash deposits and letters of credit. This money was suddenly unavailable to him, and I became annoyed and concerned. All the plans had been brought to the point of conclusion. It was hardly the time to delay or entertain second thoughts. With everyone else waiting, I decided to advance part of the cash myself and use my own sources to obtain the necessary credit. I had scheduled appointments in Geneva that were too important to cancel and that affected other significant relationships.

I left for Geneva with the clear understanding Keiser would join me there with the funds he was to furnish. I also left with the distinct feeling something was wrong someplace.

In Geneva I met with Jean François of the Banque Romande. His bank required an advance security deposit of $25,000, then delivered to me personally a letter of credit for $2.5 million. François, a personal friend of mine, had been the financial genius in settling the Trujillo money matters in Switzerland. I telephoned Ernest Keiser and told him he had to meet me in Geneva the following Friday with the funds he was to supply. He agreed but there was something in his manner that still bothered me.

Vlachopoulos had been quite friendly with Keiser in Miami, and it occurred to me I might get some information about Keiser's change in attitude from him. I put in a call to Vlachopoulos in Athens and was told his phone had been disconnected. It was another unexpected turn that added to my gnawing apprehension. One day later, when I received a cable from Keiser asking me to return to Miami, I knew there was something definitely wrong.

I telephoned Miami and told Keiser to appear in Geneva as agreed or the entire deal was off. I said I was going to Athens and would be back in Geneva on Thursday. Keiser promised he would be there and asked me to reserve two rooms at the Hotel Richemond for him and Brian Wise.

It was a positive sign at last and I made the reservations. Then I prepared to go to Athens, where there were a number of people I wanted to see in addition to satisfying my curiosity about Vlachopoulos. I made some calls, arranged the appointments, and reserved a hotel room for twenty-four hours. When the plane landed, I went straight to my hotel and, after verifying my appointments, tried to reach Vlachopoulos once more. His telephone was still disconnected. Since I was concerned about him and had time to spare, I decided to call on him at the address he'd once given me.

Within the hour I had found his apartment and was knocking on his door. I could hear someone inside. Finally I heard steps approaching. The door opened and Vlachopoulos was standing before me, a look of abject terror in his eyes. "I don't want to talk to you," he said, actually trying to close the door on me.

"Why, for God's sake," I implored. "Why did you have your telephone disconnected?"

"I wanted it so. Now please go away. You're the last person I want to be seen with."

"You've got to tell me what's wrong and I'm not leaving until you do," I said.

"They've been hounding me."

"Who?" I said, thinking of his troubles with the narcotics agents when he left the United States.

"The KYP," he said. "They know I helped you when you were trying to get Theodorakis out of prison. Please go away," he whimpered.

"You had to go into hiding because of that? I don't believe you."

Then he became defensive, almost belligerent. "You'd better believe me. Just believe me."

"I do, Achilles. I'm sorry this happened to you."

I did feel terribly concerned for him. He was obviously highly nervous, a very different young man from the one I had known in Miami. His attitude vacillated between hostility and warmth. It was as if he were checking a desire to open up to me. Strangest of all, he seemed very embarrassed. I didn't press him further. I decided it would be best if I left, and I did, more troubled than I had been in a long time.

The next morning I woke early for my last appointment in Athens. I was about to check out of the hotel when the telephone rang in my room. It was Vlachopoulos, his voice quavering with nervousness.

"Are you going back to Geneva now?" he said, and not waiting for my answer, "You should be careful. Be very careful."

"Careful about what?"

"Just be careful," he repeated and the telephone went dead. I stared at the receiver, then put it down. It had been a strange call, yet entirely in keeping with Vlachopoulos's behavior on the previous day. But this time he had done something in spite of his fear. He had risked calling me to warn me of something, then refused to tell me of what, or whom.

I thought about what kind of danger I could be in, and the only thing I could come up with was Vlachopoulos's reference to the Greek secret police. Either that, or his message was merely the product of an overwrought mind. Certainly he was not himself. In any case, the abruptly ended call did not add to my peace of mind. The trip was not going well at all. First there were Keiser's delaying tactics, and now Vlachopoulos's bizarre behavior.

I pushed all this into a corner of my mind where it continued to simmer through the remainder of the morning as I finished the last of my scheduled meetings. Finally, briefcase in hand, I reached the airport and boarded the big Swissair jet that would fly me to Geneva.

The plane touched down into the cold gray dusk, and I was one of the first passengers off it and into Swiss customs. Through a huge pair of double glass doors I saw someone waving to me. It was Brian Wise. I looked for Ernest Keiser but he wasn't to be seen. Another man stood beside Wise. He was tall, about thirty, with a shock of red-blond hair. I had never seen him before.

The customs people finished with me quickly and I pushed through the glass doors.

"Hello, Bill." Wise greeted me with a broad smile, full of his usual transparent charm. "This is Randy Morrison." Morrison, in spite of the red-blond hair, had Latin features, dark eyes, and a light-olive skin.

"Where's Ernest?" I demanded.

"He was delayed. He'll be along later," Wise said. "I've got a car outside."

I pushed down my annoyance at Keiser for not being there and followed Brian Wise from the terminal.

"I understand you've come to conclude Ernest's package for Belize," Randy Morrison said, and I nodded. I wasn't in the mood for small talk. We crossed a street to where a small car waited. Randy Morrison leaned forward and opened the front door.

"We've got everything at my room at the Devon," Wise said.

"The Devon?" I said. "I reserved rooms for Ernest and you at the Richemond." Wise and Morrison exchanged quick glances and suddenly the very air seemed to change. I don't know where the warning came from, but I felt real danger. Automatically I took a step backward.

"I'll take a cab," I said. "You bring everything to my room at the Richemond."

"Get in the car. You're going with us," Morrison said, his voice suddenly harsh. I was about to protest when my arm was seized from behind in a half-twist and I was propelled into the front seat of the car as Brian Wise slid behind the wheel. Morrison slammed the door shut and leaped into the rear seat as we roared away from the curb.

"What the hell is this?" I asked.

"There are some things that we have to talk about," Wise snapped.

"Such as Ernest not being here?" I said. "He isn't in Geneva, is he? He didn't come with the twenty-nine thousand, did he?" I was referring to the $25,000 I had advanced, plus another $4,000 Keiser was to bring for assorted fees.

Wise didn't answer and I was certain I had zeroed in on the core of it. Unable to meet his part of the bargain, Ernest Keiser had apparently grown desperate. Somebody thought a touch of intimidation would make me agree to wait for the answer or effect some compromise. Somebody thought wrong, I told myself.

"You're wasting your time," I told Wise. He still said nothing as we sped around sharp curves. I sat back, fed up with the whole project. If Keiser was this crude, I wanted no part of him. Dusk was thickening into darkness as the car raced away from the Richemond. I remained silent. Perhaps their plan was merely to drive me around for a few hours to see whether I could be frightened into agreeing to whatever it was they wanted. When the car slowed, I saw we were approaching the French border at Gex. We came to a halt and the border guards examined our passports.

I considered bolting and accusing Wise and his friend of abduction, then changed my mind because of what was in my briefcase. Besides the letter of credit for $2.5 million, a very private transaction, it contained a sheaf of documents relating to the finances of Flor Trujillo and her father, as well as papers on sensitive matters involving the Swiss banking establishment. I knew the ways of the French police. They would hold on to such material for ages, probe and investigate a thousand paths and byways. The papers in my briefcase would have embarrassed a number of valuable and highly placed associates.

Sitting quietly was the best course, I decided. It was still my feeling that Wise and his friend Morrison were playing a bluffing game for Keiser, a crude piece of business. When the border guards finished their check, the car roared on to the French Alps. It was night. The road curved almost as soon as it left the border and Brian Wise turned sharply onto a side road thickly grown with trees and brush on both sides. This side road climbed higher into the mountains and was known locally as the Chemin de la Lechere, one of the local roadways that do not appear on ordinary maps. The Swiss police, I was to learn, refer to it by another name. They call it Murderer's Row.

Now Wise began to throw questions at me and Morrison joined in. They were far from what I expected. Neither man made any reference to Ernest Keiser, to the money he was to bring, or to the Belize transaction.

"You've been working for the leftists, haven't you?" Wise said.

"What leftists? What are you talking about?"

"You know," he snapped. "You had the picture brought to America. You got the financing for it."

"For *Z*? Yes, but so what? That was a business venture, not politics."

"Shit." Morrison laughed. "You're deep into it."

"I'm not into anything," I protested. "What is all of this?"

"You're into it, all right," Morrison repeated. "They sent you to get Theodorakis out."

"That was for the album and the film," I said.

"Sure," Wise said. "And you're close to Onassis, too. You like to work both sides of the street, don't you? Only this time you made a mistake."

"You're funneling Trujillo money into it, too," Brian Wise said and I stared at him in disbelief.

"I'm not funneling money into anything. I don't understand any of this." It was true. There had been not one word about Keiser or the $29,000 due me or any of the things I had come to Geneva for. "Where's Keiser?" I asked.

"Forget Keiser. What else do you know?"

"Know about what?"

"Don't play games with us," Morrison threatened. "You know who got Theodorakis out. Who else did you tell?"

"Look, this has gone far enough. I don't know what this is all about, but I'm getting out. I came here to conclude the Belize deal and that's all."

"Forget Belize," Wise said and suddenly I realized Belize had been nothing but an elaborate camouflage from the beginning, a meticulously constructed scheme to bring me to Geneva at the right time. But for what?

"What do you want with me?" I said. Neither man answered. Then Wise slowed the car. The headlights picked up the line of a curve we slowly rounded, and then the road became little more than a path through the rough terrain in the snow-capped French Alps. Tree branches brushed the car from both sides.

"Where are we going?" I demanded. Still no answer.

"What's all this? You know, if you're trying to frighten me, forget it. I don't frighten easily."

I said it more for my benefit than theirs, for the truth was I could feel my fear was about to immobilize me. I turned to glance back at Morrison and my breath escaped in a sharp gasp. He had pulled a rubber mask over his face.

"For God's sake, what are you doing?"

"We're going to kill you," Wise said.

I turned to stare at the handsome face beside me and wondered whether I had heard right. The words had been uttered coldly, calmly, as if they had been uttered many times before. Close to panic now, I realized they had not been said to frighten me.

The car slowed nearly to a stop and I was aware of movements in the back seat. I didn't turn to look. Perhaps I should have. I doubt it would have made any difference. My hand stole to the door handle and I waited for my chance. Suddenly Wise put on the brakes, and what happened next was a blur of automatic reactions as I yanked the door open and leaped from the car. It was too late. I felt the cord snap around my neck from behind. My hands reached up and clawed at the garrote as I choked and fought for breath. Out of the corner of my eye I saw Brian Wise's hand rise and then something hard and heavy smashed into the left side of my face.

I couldn't see. My breath came in a rasp. I tried to fight off losing consciousness, but the garrote tightened and another blow to my head sent me reeling and everything swirled into a void. Wise and Morrison threw me from the car and I rolled down the roadside into the underbrush.

I came to rest against the base of an alpine tree. For all their expertise, Wise and Morrison had botched their job. I had no idea how long I lay there before I felt the first glimmering of life. Perhaps it was the wetness of the falling snow that brought me to my senses, or maybe it was an awareness of pain, but slowly I began to realize I was not dead. For some reason the killers had been in too much of a hurry.

In spite of the searing pain in my left eye and a throat so sore and swollen I could barely breathe or swallow, I felt I was the luckiest man alive. Albeit barely. My face was swollen out of shape and I couldn't see and I was bruised all over from the rocks I had rolled over and the tree I had crashed into, but I was alive, bloody from head to toe.

I forced my good eye to open and blinked away the blurriness. It was pitch dark and I couldn't see anything but the snow, which was now falling heavily. I was grateful, for it cooled my burning face. For a long time I lay still, slowly gathering the strength to move, slipping from dreamlike state into consciousness and back to dreaming again until I had great trouble distinguishing between them. I felt detached, as if I were watching a movie run in slow motion, a badly edited film that made no sense at all, for none of the frames fit together.

The snow was now blanketing me and I knew I had to move. I pulled myself half upright and blacked out instantly from a pounding wave of pain. I was wedged against a tree trunk, and raising myself up again, I used the tree for support as I began to inch myself upward.

The edge of the road above was not that far away but it seemed unattainable. I pulled myself along the snow-covered mountainside, grabbing hold of rocks and brush to propel myself forward, stopping every few inches to catch my breath. My neck seemed on fire where the garrote had cut into it and my left eye hurt with terrible intensity. When I finally reached the road, I crawled to the center and lay face down, afraid I would go unnoticed if I remained on the side of the road. The headlights of an approaching car would have to find me, and I would have to depend on the dangerous mountain curves to slow the car down in time.

I passed out again and woke once more, still alone in the snowy dark. The road had been well chosen. It was a deserted stretch and I don't know how many hours passed before a carful of *forestiers* came along and took me to the local police station. From there I was rushed to a hospital, the Catholic St. Julien-en-Genevoise in France, where I was given emergency treatment to prevent the loss of my left eye. A few days later I was moved to the Swiss Cantonal Hospital in Geneva.

In between, the police came to question me. The briefcase I had jeopardized my life to keep out of their hands was now in their possession. However, they were more concerned with the murder attempt. I told them what had happened, naming Wise and Morrison. I also had a call placed to my lawyer in Paris, Claire Jourdan, and she came at once. The French police ascertained a number of things quickly. They traced the alpine road where I had been taken and found the tire marks and the spot where I had rolled down the incline. They also found the garrote Morrison had thrown from the car. The car itself was found abandoned, but inside was a document that bore the name of Brian Wise. The car had been rented in Geneva, and the agency there identified Wise as the man who had rented it. A police alarm was issued for him and Morrison.

During those first days following the murder attempt I was awake only for short periods, and each questioning session fatigued me terribly. As I slept and half dozed, little vignettes kept flaring up and fading away. The feel of the garrote around my neck. The terrible look of Morrison in the face mask he put on to conceal his identity should another car have passed by. But most of all I pondered the total unexpectedness of it all, for it still made no sense whatsoever to me. I slept, dreamed, thought, slept again, each time waking to murmur a grateful prayer I was alive.

When the police questioned me about motives, I was unable to give any. Brian Wise was an associate of Ernest Keiser,

I told them, yet I couldn't implicate Keiser through anything Wise or Morrison had said. They had never mentioned the monies owed by Keiser or even confirmed he was in Switzerland. When contacted by the police at his home in the Bahamas, Keiser denied any knowledge of what had happened, of course. He said he had no idea what would make his associate Brian Wise do such a thing.

But the police were intrigued by a fact they uncovered in the course of their investigation. Keiser had asked me to reserve two rooms, one for himself and one for Brian Wise. He had, however, made three reservations for the flight from Geneva back to Miami. Obviously, Wise and Morrison had arrived with a third person. As there was no extradition agreement between France and the Bahamas, the police had no way of forcing Keiser to appear for questioning, and he declined to appear voluntarily.

Wise and Morrison fled France and dropped from sight. The investigation pointed to Ernest Keiser's involvement, although the specifics were far from clear. The episode was wrapped in mystery.

Added to all the obfuscation about the kidnap-murder attempt was a strange sequence of events that defied explanation. Or perhaps a sequence of nonevents would be a more appropriate term, for they were notable only because they didn't occur.

When I was first brought to the hospital in France, the doctors seriously doubted I would survive. My left eye was virtually severed from its tendons and I was in severe post-trauma shock. Because I was an American citizen, the American Embassy in Berne was notified. I had been moved back to Switzerland because I was registered in Geneva and the Cantonal Hospital had more extensive facilities for treatment of the eye injury.

During those days as I lay fighting for life I had trouble distinguishing my dreams from reality. I dreamed often of my father, Samuel Taub. When I had regained consciousness on the night of the garroting, I had looked up toward the road, despairing I would ever make the climb, and saw my father standing on the roadside with his hand out to me. Although it was snowing hard and my vision was greatly blurred, I saw him as clearly as if he were alive and greeting me at his door. It was my dead father's very real presence at the top of my climb that gave me the will to make it.

My father was paralyzed from the neck down for the last ten years of his life, the result of a fall. At first his doctors didn't think he would live and had told me to summon the family. I had a desperate hope that a neurosurgeon might save him, and thought of President Roosevelt at once. I had had many meetings with him and a good relationship with the family. I called Missy LeHand, his secretary, and she put me through to Eleanor, who arranged for a neurosurgeon to be rushed to my father's hospital. His name was Dr. Temple Fay, an eminent neurosurgeon and doctor for President Roosevelt, and he saved my father's life. Later, when I called the hospital inquiring about his bill, which I hadn't received, I was told there would be no charge, "at the request of President Roosevelt."

One day, as I lay dreaming about my father and the Roosevelts, I opened my unbandaged eye and focused on a blurred figure standing by my bed. It was Jimmy Roosevelt. I had known Jimmy for many years, and we had had recent business discussions. He was staying in Geneva and had given me his telephone number there. The hospital had found the number in my jacket and had called him. Later Jimmy Roosevelt was to say two different things. One, that the American Embassy in Berne had called to ask him to look in on an injured American citizen, which he did. And two, that he didn't really know me but had come only because of the embassy call.

Not one other soul came from any official American agency after that. Although the hospital was conscientious and efficient, the eye injury was a concern for specialists. There were fine surgeons skilled in treating injuries like mine at the nearby American Military Hospital. Their skills would have been of inestimable help—perhaps they could have prevented the extensive work that later had to be done back in America.

But no one came from the American hospital. No one came in any official capacity. It was as if my government were waiting to see whether I would live or die. After all, I had had a coronary. Perhaps the murder attempt would prove successful after all, if a little delayed.

The absence of visitors could not be blamed on the obscurity of the event. The kidnap-murder attempt was a story of headline proportions throughout Europe. *France-Soir, Le Figaro,* and *Le Monde* in France; *La Suisse, Le Genoise,* and the *Neue Zürcher Zeitung* in Switzerland all ran banner headlines about it, with pictures taken by the police of the area and of my battered self. Radio Luxembourg, perhaps the most powerful European communications medium, featured the story. Many of the newspapers referred in their lead captions to the attempted murder of an "associate of President Nixon." Reporters came in hordes to the hospital and later to the hotel where I was convalescing, but I was not available to the press. No visit was ever made by any official representative of the American government.

The other strange nonevent was not one word of the attempt ever reached the American press. The major wire services, which normally pick up even the most minor stories and send them around the world, somehow did not wire this headline event to the United States.

Possibly the story was sent but never printed by an American newspaper, though I think that implausible. I was amazed to discover upon my return to the United States that as far as the home press was concerned, the murder attempt had never happened.

Claire Jourdan gave generously of her time. After she left to attend to business in Paris, I found myself in great need of someone who could fend off reporters and deal with French and Swiss officials in retrieving the documents and valuables in my briefcase. Achilles Vlachopoulos had been in my thoughts since I had recovered enough to try to fit together what had happened. Had he been warning me that last morning in Athens about the murder attempt? Certainly he knew Brian Wise and Keiser. In fact, he had become quite friendly with Wise in Miami. Had he heard something that had unnerved him, but not enough to make accusations? If so, his strange behavior might have been the result of his dilemma.

The questions bothered me so much I decided to call him. His telephone was working again, and I quickly reached him.

"I'd like to talk to you," I said. "And I also need someone here to help me."

"No, no. I can't come," he said.

"You're not working, are you?"

"No," he admitted. He was plainly nervous at hearing from me again. I thought of reminding him of the substantial help I had given him when he was trying to break into show business but decided not to press. Achilles Vlachopoulos once again wanted nothing to do with me. Perhaps it really was because of the Theodorakis business. Perhaps. It was just one more maddening puzzle piece that fit nowhere.

Before I left Switzerland I made an official complaint to the American Embassy about its neglect of an American citizen. It was for the record only. I had already decided to pursue the matter when I returned to the United States.

Later, while recovering from the special eye treatments in Miami, I learned another piece of information that sent shock waves through me. Only a day before I had gone to Geneva, Brian Wise had made a call to Vlachopoulos in Athens. The call, placed through a friend of Vlachopoulos, was on record with the telephone company. This significant piece of information was turned over to the authorities, and because the people involved had traveled across several borders, the investigation widened to include Interpol.

When I informed them of the Vlachopoulos call they immediately went into action. Vlachopoulos was arrested by the Greek police at the request of Interpol, acting on an order by the French courts.

Once arrested, Vlachopoulos talked freely, giving depositions that were recorded in the Greek, French, and Swiss courts. He claimed the kidnaping had to do with the large amount of money in dispute over the returns of Z. Vlachopoulos said he had been drawn into the affair by the promise of money, which he said he needed desperately, and his role was to keep the plotters informed of my plans and movements. The Belize plans looked more and more like an elaborate cover, a means of drawing me in to the eventual moment of truth.

Arrest warrants were issued for Morrison, Wise, and Keiser, and Interpol intensified its efforts to find the first two. Ernest Keiser stayed in the comparative safety of the Bahamas. I read and reread the Vlachopoulos statements, which were sent to me. He gave names, places, times, and that ancient and dishonorable motive, money. On the surface his reasoning could not be faulted. Yet something was not right and other interpretations of his testimony kept intruding.

Sometime later, tired of being confined to the Bahamas, Ernest Keiser contacted me with the news that he wanted to make a deposition to "clear his name" and tell the truth about the real plotters. I agreed to meet him. He came to New York and his deposition was taken on February 24, 1972, and filed in the criminal courts of Geneva, Switzerland; Athens, Greece; and Bourg-en-Bresse, France, as well as with the U.S. Department of Justice and the Commercial Court of Paris.

In his deposition Ernest Keiser swore Donald Rugoff was one of the plotters. His long list of other conspirators included almost everyone who had been a part of the Belize negotiations and involved in the film *Z*. He claimed the reason for the murder attempt was the *Z* money dispute.

From his deposition:

> *Question:* Did Rugoff propose to do something?
> *Keiser:* Rugoff proposed to Vlachopoulos somehow to dispose of William L. Taub.
>
> *Question:* What do you mean by "dispose of"? What did they talk of? What was the clear language?
> *Keiser:* Well, they said they wanted to get rid of him.
>
> *Question:* Did they mean physical harm and violence?
> *Keiser:* Physical harm; and dispose of his body.
>
> *Question:* Was this to be for a financial consideration to those parties?
> *Keiser:* Yes; it was financial gain.

In the deposition Keiser exonerated himself, naturally, claiming he was not truly a participant in the kidnap-murder attempt. This contradicted statements given by Vlachopoulos. When the deposition was filed in all the places named, Donald Rugoff stated the testimony was a lie. My dispute with Rugoff had entered the courts, and he wanted to make his denial of the charges a part of the court record. This was disallowed. At a hearing before the Supreme Court of the State of New York, it was ruled that because there had been no trial, there could be no formal denial.

As I had with the Vlachopoulos depositions, I scanned

Ernest Keiser's again and again. It, too, did not ring with the sound of unalloyed truth. Keiser claimed he had been only an observer, just as Vlachopoulos had claimed. I knew better in Keiser's case. He had involved himself too deeply in the Belize negotiations, and his withdrawal as they neared completion had been too sudden. That his statements were self-serving was to be expected. But they seemed too glib, the confession too neatly packaged to take in almost everyone. Most disturbing of all, I kept remembering Morrison and Wise in the car that night. Their questions did not concern Belize, or money. They wanted to know about my political involvements. They talked of Z and its impact, of the Greek regime and of what I had done, of what secrets I carried and in whom I might have confided.

Possibly Belize began as a legitimate enough proposition, and was then seized on as a perfect cloak for other objectives. But who was really behind it? Keiser's statements were unsatisfying, the motives he gave too simplistic. I had a growing conviction that he and Vlachopoulos were telling half-truths and that Belize had been part of a multiple cover.

Interpol had continued a close surveillance of all those under warrant for arrest. Ernest Keiser made the mistake of going to Monte Carlo with his girlfriend and her father soon after he gave his deposition. He was arrested there. The others were released when it became clear they had no connection with the crime. Keiser was taken in chains to France and imprisoned.

In 1973 Randy Morrison was caught and jailed in Holland, where he made statements accusing Keiser of complicity in the plot. Brian Wise was arrested in September 1975 in Cologne, Germany, and also made statements that implicated Keiser.

The trio had a distinct professionalism. Only Vlachopoulos seemed to be an amateur, drawn in and used, too weak to extricate himself, and undoubtedly held in line by threats.

But even these facts were unsatisfying. I came to the conclusion that I had been given facts but not truths. The facts did not quite fit.

There finally came a time when I had to recall the conclusion of the film Z, when the narrator speaks of what did *not* happen to certain prominent individuals in the story. In 1972 Ernest Keiser was released on $50,000 "caution money," which (in France) is what the French quaintly call bail. Inquiries as to who put up the bail money were firmly refused by the French courts, which are not legally required to provide such information.

Morrison, after his arrest in Holland and while awaiting deportation to France to stand trial, managed to "escape" from an ancient high-security and supposedly escape-proof moated prison from which no one had ever escaped before.

Brian Wise, after his imprisonment in Cologne in 1975, was held in jail until the French asked for his extradition. He fought extradition for months before he finally appeared in Bourg-en-Bresse for a preliminary hearing. Later, he too was released on bail and again the French courts would not reveal who furnished the bail money. Eventually, both Morrison and Wise were convicted and received, respectively, three- and two-year sentences.

There was no real explanation for what had happened until one day, much later and with shattering unexpectedness, I was given answers that revealed how clever and careful and deep were the layers of deception. But before that moment came, other wheels within wheels had been set in motion. *Z* was almost an end that became a beginning.

8

HOFFA'S PARDON AND THE CHINESE GOLD

That snowy night in the French Alps would leave with me a constant and unwelcome condition. My left eye was badly in need of further treatment, and the Geneva specialist had recommended surgery. With most of my belongings still in the hands of the French police and my mind filled with unanswered questions, I decided to return home. The press was still encamped in the hotel lobby, eager for more details, so I slipped out a side door in disguise.

When I reached the airport and checked in for my flight, two men approached me and asked, "Are you William L. Taub?" I ignored them and hurried onto the plane, where I spent the first part of the flight searching my memory for their faces. My nerves were as shattered as my eye, I decided, and I never did find out who they were or what they wanted.

In Brussels, during a short stopover to change planes, I called New York where Flor Trujillo's housekeeper, Margarita, was temporarily on loan to me. I had her meet the plane at Kennedy International the following day. Safely home in the care of the personable and efficient Margarita, I immediately made an appointment to see an eye surgeon. His examination resulted in another recommendation for surgery. I was told the

Bascomb Clinic in Miami was one of the best places available, and decided it would be a good idea to follow my hospital stay with a Florida recuperation.

I had no way of knowing a season of apologies and bargains was about to begin. Before my first day in New York was over, another series of curious events began to unfold. Still seething over what had happened and not happened in Geneva, I called Rose Mary Woods at the White House, knowing her to be the best route to Richard Nixon. I was told she was unavailable but would return my call.

Hardly three minutes passed before she did. She was delighted to hear I had returned "well enough to travel." Speaking for President Nixon, she continued, she wanted to convey his regrets at not having been in "a position to offer more assistance" in the Geneva affair.

Honest anger taking precedence over discretion, I told her Nixon's "regrets" were neither adequate nor understandable. They did not in any way explain why a cloak of official silence and disregard has been thrown over the attempt on my life.

"You're jumping to hasty conclusions," Rose Mary Woods soothed. "The entire matter has been assigned to the Attorney General."

"If it takes as long as it did in Geneva, I'll not be hearing from anyone at all," I said.

"You'll be hearing," she said.

The following day I did hear from the Attorney General's office. The promptness may have been designed to placate me, but it only highlighted the total lack of interest that had been shown in Geneva.

The Attorney General's office informed me my case had been assigned to the FBI. The United States attorney in the district of Philadelphia would also be in touch with me. In another display of impressive promptness, a letter came from Philadelphia in which I was given the names of the two agents who had been assigned to my case. I was asked to meet with them as soon as I was able to travel, a visit that would have to be postponed until after my eye surgery.

The very next day I had another telephone call from Rose Mary Woods. She said I would soon be hearing from a friend of President Nixon who lived in Paris. I remembered him from the days of the Trujillo monies pursuit.

"I don't understand this at all," I exclaimed. "When I was in the hospital in Geneva he was a lot closer. Why is he being brought all the way from Paris to see me now that I'm back in New York?"

"I wouldn't know about that," she said. "However, you will soon be hearing from him."

Curiouser and curiouser, I thought, putting down the telephone. What a circuitous approach they were taking. The following Saturday morning the man from Paris called. I recognized his voice at once.

We agreed to meet that evening at six, and he arrived promptly. "I have come from Paris to visit you because President Nixon felt it would be more confidential this way."

"Confidential? Why?"

"Well, you know the President is always very conscious of the press and their rumors," he said. "He doesn't want any word about what happened in Geneva to leak out until the Justice Department has had more time on the case."

Richard Nixon's wariness of the press was well known, yet the answer failed to satisfy me any more than had my thrust-and-parry conversations with Rose Mary Woods.

"I'd like to ask you something. Don't you think it's unusual, sending you all the way over here from Paris, when Mr. Nixon has so many people right here who could have seen me?"

My guest shrugged. "Most unusual, I agree. But here I am and I have been told to offer you whatever assistance I can."

"I'm afraid the only assistance I need now will have to come from my doctors," I said.

"Ah well," he said, rising to leave. "I am returning to Paris tomorrow. Please call me in Paris for anything—anything at all. The President wants me to emphasize that."

One fact was clear. The purpose of his visit was to establish himself as my contact, one that bypassed much closer contacts. Why I had suddenly become the object of a rush of concern remained an enigma.

I had other problems to think about, however. I took Margarita to Miami with me the following day and was hospitalized almost immediately by the examining surgeon there to prevent the loss of sight in my left eye. For three days I stayed at the hospital in a room with provisions for Margarita to stay also. After my release I rented a house in Miami, had an unlisted telephone installed, and began a long recuperation. It was interrupted by the first of many trips to Geneva and the French courts regarding the kidnap-murder attempt.

My nerves were still taut and, fearful of traveling alone, I decided to hire a bodyguard to accompany me to Europe and back to Miami. Upon my return I got in touch with Jacques Schiffer, who had made numerous calls to my New York apartment. Schiffer wanted a meeting to discuss still another plea from Hoffa and a rather weak new idea for his release. Hoffa's people, I saw, continued to pursue the wrong paths. I refused to tell Schiffer where I was mending and he reluctantly agreed to wait until my return to New York to explore the matter.

By October 1971 I felt well enough to get back to work and flew to Europe on a trip that combined business and court hearings. While I was in Paris I entered into final negotiations on a film that was to be called *Mao's China*. The film was part of an adventure that had begun the year before with an introduction to an incredible woman I shall call Dorothy Ho-chan. If anyone deserves to be described as a woman of mystery from the inscrutable Orient, it is she. Handsome, well educated, fluent in English, French, and her native Chinese, and conversant in a handful of other languages, Dorothy Ho-chan was also obviously a woman of substantial means. She traveled in two worlds, East and West, with no apparent difficulty. She also maneuvered in and out of many different social circles with ease, and was an intimate friend of many people in high places. I came to know she was a close friend of Mrs. Claire Chennault, also known as the "Flying Tigress." Both were generous contributors to Richard Nixon's campaigns.

Ernest Keiser first mentioned Dorothy Ho-chan to me when he was beginning his campaign to involve me in the grand Belize masquerade. He told me one afternoon of a woman he knew who possessed "several millions in gold bullion."

"Where is this fortune?" I said, not certain of the reliability of his information.

"It's stored here in New York, in a major bank down on Wall Street."

"If it's stored here, then I take it it was brought in from

somewhere else," I conjectured. "Do you know how it came into the country?"

Keiser didn't know, he said, but convinced me the story had substance. Gold was then valued at $35 an ounce in the United States. Keiser said, "The woman I'm telling you about wants to get the gold out of the country and into Canada or anywhere else she can make transactions on it."

I told Keiser surely he must know it was against the law to deal in gold or move it in or out of the country without special permission from the Treasury Department.

"I know," Keiser said. "But she wants to find a way around those restrictions, and I told her you might be able to help her." He added it would be most rewarding to me if I agreed to help. However, he would tell me no more about the mysterious lady who owned all those gold bars in the Wall Street vault.

On my next trip to Washington I stopped by the Department of the Treasury and talked to Miklos Lonkay in the office of general counsel. He told me the Treasury Department's Gold Regulation Form was very complex, and any traffic in gold must comply with the terms of those regulations without exception. Later he sent me a letter enclosing a set of regulations and application forms for a gold license, all of which had to be filed before gold could be transported.

I checked with gold dealers and learned no one would touch any gold not cleared by Treasury. Then I met Keiser and told him what I had learned. "I don't think you understand the magnitude of this thing," he said rather loftily. "We're talking from fifty to a hundred million dollars' worth of gold."

"Regardless of the magnitude," I said, "I've been to Washington and I've told you what I've found out so far. If I can't meet this woman and learn all the details, then I'm not interested. I can't represent somebody I don't know, especially in something of this magnitude."

Keiser backed away from identifying her and shifted his approach. "Do you think there's any way to have the gold taken out of the bank without a license, put into a private plane, and flown to Canada?"

"I wouldn't know and I'm not about to find out," I said. "If this woman wants the gold moved legally and under license from the Treasury Department, then I think I can find the best way to do it. Otherwise I'm not interested."

I thought my response had been clear enough, but soon Keiser called again. This time I agreed to accompany him to Inglehard Company in Newark, New Jersey, a prestigious firm that assayed and purchased gold.

The Inglehard people pointed out the gold couldn't be moved without a gold license from the Department of Treasury. Then, apropos of nothing, they asked, "Could this gold have come from China?" Keiser said he didn't know, and I surmised that since the Inglehard specialists were undoubtedly familiar with the probable source of any sizable undeclared gold caches around the world, China must be one such source.

I thought I had heard the last of the strange story of the gold bullion and its mysterious owner, but when I was in Paris not long afterward, I heard again from Keiser. He was also in Paris and wanted to arrange a meeting with the woman connected with the gold. Shortly after I met Dorothy Ho-chan. She revealed that the value of the gold bullion at 1970 rates was over $100 million. She also admitted the gold had come from China at the close of World War II, when, she said, she had brought it into the United States by ship under diplomatic immunity.

Dorothy and I quickly became good friends. She was intelligent, mercurial, amusing, flamboyant—all qualities I enjoy. She asked me to continue to think about how the fortune might be moved under American law, but without revealing the extent of its worth. It was perhaps an impossible problem to resolve, I warned her, but she said she'd be patient. Dorothy Ho-chan never revealed the exact source of her personal wealth, but I gathered it came from family ties to the great Philippine sugar plantations. She said she was a close friend of Imelda Marcos, wife of the President of the Philippines, and I also assumed she had had ties with the Chinese hierarchy before the revolutionary government of Mao Tse-tung ascended to power.

She maintained an apartment on Fifth Avenue and a residence in Tangiers. "I'm going to give you my card," she said. "This card in the other part of the world is an open sesame to anywhere you may want to go, to anyone you may want to meet." The card, a brilliant Chinese red with her name imprinted on it, proved to be all she promised.

During dinner that week I mentioned I had a birthday on the horizon. "I'm supposed to be in Tangiers then," Dorothy said, "but I'll change my plans and come to New York to celebrate your birthday with you." It was a nice gesture but hardly one I expected her to carry out.

Only a short while later, when I was in the Dominican Republic on business affairs for Flor Trujillo, I received a cable from Dorothy reminding me she would be in New York for my birthday. I was delighted. Dorothy Ho-chan, whom I had known only a few weeks, was that kind of person: impetuous, warm, generous . . . or so I thought.

I was flabbergasted when she presented me with a very expensive gold watch at the end of my birthday celebration. Afterward, during a 3 A.M. walk from my apartment at Sixtieth and Park Avenue to hers at Fifth Avenue in the Eighties, she revealed she came from a family with huge investments in mainland China, and said she was well regarded in that country.

"You must visit China," she told me. "When you do, I shall introduce you to one of the most brilliant and charming women you will ever meet. Her name is Chiang Ch'ing but you know her as Madame Mao Tse-tung."

Dorothy Ho-chan also revealed she knew Richard Nixon quite well. She told me the Chinese Embassy in Tangiers was the focal point for Chinese affairs relating to the outside world. China at that time was still a very closed society, not yet a member of the United Nations nor part of any major world organization. But even a closed society needs a channel to the outside.

Dorothy didn't want to leave New York without meeting Flor Trujillo. When I introduced them I expected these two women who were both so successful at maintaining their autonomy irrespective of husbands or family would enjoy each other. To my surprise, Dorothy was jealous of Flor and had trouble concealing it. She left for Tangiers almost immediately. We soon learned to adjust to Dorothy's unannounced arrivals and departures.

Three weeks later Flor and I were invited by Aristotle Onassis to fly on Olympic Airways to the south of France, where a mutual friend and business associate from Saudi Arabia would entertain us. Our flight was delayed three hours, during which time Flor decided to get a head start on the partying. By the time we arrived at the Riviera she had drunk three or four bottles of champagne and told me, "Bill, I'm going to sleep. I'll see you in about two days."

One night we went to an elaborate party, given by Juliette Greco, at St. Raphael, on the Riviera and one and a half hours from the Carlton Hotel in Cannes, where we were staying. We returned to our hotel exhausted to find a garbled message from someone in Tangiers, asking me to get accommodations at our hotel, which I knew to be full.

"Oh, oh," Flor said. "That could mean only one person."

"She's staying with you. She's not staying with me," I said, but we were too tired to argue. Friday night at six my telephone rang. Dorothy Ho-chan was in the lobby of the Carlton.

"Surprise!" she cried and greeted me as if our reunion were long overdue. When I told her the best accommodation I had been able to reserve was one tiny room without a bath, she waved aside my concern. "That suits me fine," she said. "I came to go to the casino, not stay in my room."

She wanted to see Flor at once, as she had something for her. Flor was astonished when Dorothy held up a heavily embroidered white silk dress that she had brought from mainland China.

Later she was leading us to the casino. Flor and I were members but Dorothy was not. However, membership simply meant paying a small fee and showing one's passport. Dorothy refused to show hers. She argued and maneuvered and hedged and cajoled until finally I realized it might be our presence that was inhibiting her. Flor and I walked away but not before I managed to get a glimpse of a plastic folder she pulled out of her purse that appeared to contain at least twenty passports. I don't know which one she decided to show, but she quickly received her membership card and joined us inside the casino.

Then she discovered her Moroccan money was not acceptable. She seemed on the verge of tears. Gallantly I offered to go back to the hotel and lend her money I had in the vault there.

"How much do you have?" she said.

"About thirty-five hundred."

"That will get me started. I'm going to win fifty thousand dollars tonight," she announced.

I raised my eyebrows and told her that since I was lending her the money, we would split the winnings down the middle. She laughingly agreed and we shook hands on it. When I came back from the hotel with the money, she was waiting for me at the blackjack table. She never moved from her spot all night, and at 3 A.M. she cashed in the equivalent of $53,000 in French francs.

As she stuffed her earnings into her bag, I said, "Wait a minute. How about my half?"

Her smile vanished. "Oh no you don't," she said. "That was just a silly game. I take my gambling very, very seriously."

I was furious. Dorothy was livid. Either she or I was about to be killed. Flor managed to intervene and lead me back to the hotel. "At least you've got your thirty-five hundred," she said. "So you haven't lost anything except your temper."

The following day Dorothy called. She was in high spirits, as if we hadn't nearly come to blows at the cashier's window the night before. "I'd like to take you all out to dinner tonight," she said. "Will you make the arrangements?"

"I'd be delighted," I said, and immediately set to work. I called the most expensive restaurant on the Riviera, made reservations for eight, and ordered a platter of goose liver pâté with truffles, two cans of their best beluga caviar, and eight bottles of Dom Perignon on ice. We would make a night of it, I vowed, and I would recover a tiny portion of my winnings.

Dorothy hardly noticed the spread. She ordered only soup and fidgeted through the entire dinner. She could hardly wait to get back to the casino. That night she lost. She said she was stone broke and again asked me for my $3,500.

"Not on your life," I told her. "I'm not giving you thirty-five cents until you honor our agreement."

She was angry beyond words, stayed one more day, and then she was gone. I was relieved to find she hadn't charged her room to her good friend Bill. The light was beginning to dawn. Dorothy Ho-chan was a compulsive gambler. She seemed to have an inexhaustible supply of money, but I began to suspect that behind the lighthearted, worldly-wise facade was a desperate woman. Twice I had seen what happened when she was without money and I didn't like what I saw.

It was October before I saw her again. I was at the George

Cinq Hotel in Paris when I was called on the house phone. Dorothy Ho-chan was downstairs, having just taken a room at the hotel. "Are you busy for dinner tomorrow evening?" she said.

"Nothing I can't cancel."

"Good. Then you'll join me. I'm entertaining some very important and interesting people I want you to meet."

"Wonderful," I said. "May I ask who they are?"

"You'll find out when you get there," she teased.

She refused to be drawn out, and I knew her well enough by then to realize this was one of those times she chose to draw a veil around herself. The next evening I joined her party at Laserre, which I consider the most elegant restaurant in the world, tucked into the spot where Avenue F. D. Roosevelt becomes Avenue Montaigne. There were three other women besides Dorothy at the table, and Dorothy rose to make the introductions.

"May I present Madame Mao Tse-tung," she said. I stared down at the most powerful woman in the world. She was clothed in a Chinese kimono-style gown of magnificent blue-green silk with a matching headpiece best described as a chic bandanna. I found my voice and managed the proper amenities. Madame Mao was not strikingly Oriental; her face was more arresting than beautiful, with an alive, contained quality. She wore jade jewelry, her makeup was lightly applied, and on her bare feet she wore sandals. Had she been dressed like Dorothy in the latest Parisian fashions, she might have passed for an elegant Frenchwoman.

The two young women, both in Chinese dress, were her daughters. I was told the silent man sitting next to them was Madame Mao's bodyguard. As we ordered, Dorothy managed to whisper that Madame Mao was on "private business." I looked at the elegant woman sitting next to me, engaged in animated conversation with her daughter Li Na, and was surprised to hear that a member of the Peking government could have "private business." The phrase had a faintly clandestine ring to it.

Madame Mao became increasingly voluble, almost sparkling. She had apparently been told by Dorothy Ho-chan that I had represented many well-known theatrical people and was involved in many aspects of the entertainment industry. "I appeared in films when I was younger," she told me to my surprise. "I also appeared on the stage where I was known as Chiang Ch'ing. Ever since my years in theater and films I have been very much interested in film as a mass communications tool."

I wondered whether she would launch into an ideological explanation, but she did not. Instead, she said almost wistfully, "But my first love has always been the opera. When I was young I wanted a career as an opera singer, but my voice never developed enough for that. I longed very much to do your Western opera, for I find it a fascinating combination of forms."

"You know," Dorothy interjected, "Madame Mao is chairman of the Cultural Commission of the People's Republic of China."

"In your Western opera," she continued, "there is a wonderful combination of music, story, dance—there is nothing quite like it in Chinese theater, but there should be." That was a comment I often remembered in the years to come as she became the leading force in the development of the spectacular opera-music-dance pieces that were such effective propaganda for the vast Chinese audience.

"I should love to visit Hollywood someday," she said. "Perhaps you could show me around."

"I would be honored to do so," I said. She nodded toward Dorothy. "Our good friend here has invited me to visit her in New York."

"When you do, I hope you'll visit me also," I said.

"Of course. I would like to see New York, but this is not the time for it. Not yet at least. There must be a better political climate. But why don't you come to Peking? We are interested in Western visitors to our country."

This was not something I was aware of. In less than six months a group of Ping-Pong players would be invited to China, but at the time of our conversation very few Westerners ever visited mainland China, especially with official invitations. Naturally the idea fascinated me, and I couldn't help wondering whether her remarks were indicative of a shift in Chinese policy or merely polite dinner conversation.

As we continued to talk, it was obvious the invitation was not only sincere but for a reason. "There is something which may be of great interest to you," Madame Mao said over dessert. "We permitted a television crew from Belgrade to come into China this summer. As director of the Cultural Commission, I arranged for their visit. They shot thirty-five thousand feet of film showing Chinese life as it really is. It will be the first real inside look for Western television viewers of what it is like to live in our country."

She seemed to be choosing her words carefully. "Such a film would be wasted on a small audience," she went on. "But it would be very worthwhile for American and European audiences to see in large numbers. It would increase the mutual understanding of people everywhere. I think you should first see the film yourself. I can arrange this for you."

"Yes, I would like that," was about all I could muster.

"Good. If you are interested in what you see, perhaps you would like to be the one to bring it to the Americans. You Americans should know more about the People's Republic of China."

I was awed by her exquisite orchestration of the conversation. The general discussion on the arts had been the prelude to her specific proposal, that I become the liaison between her government and the American people. And I had caught her distinction between Americans and their government. She intended to reach out to the people, not their official representatives, and I was to be her instrument. She knew it was through the arts that people understand each other most readily, and she had chosen film, a medium she knew well, to reach the largest potential audience.

Before dinner was over, she gave me the name of the Belgrade television man and his Paris telephone number. I promised to call him first thing the following morning.

"Good." She smiled. "And don't forget. You have my personal invitation to visit China, which I hope you will do soon."

I tried to find out where she was staying in Paris, as I wanted to send her flowers. The question was turned aside with a charming smile. "I'll be leaving tomorrow, early," she said.

Dorothy Ho-chan returned to Geneva in the morning and I met with the man from Belgrade television. He was under the impression a representative portion of the film was available for viewing in New York, but upon my return I found this was not so. It was impossible to move further on Madame Mao's proposal without returning to Paris to see the film.

Dorothy had dropped out of sight, and for several months I was preoccupied with the Belize proposition, among other things. But I did hear from Dorothy in a roundabout way through a totally unexpected source: Ron Ziegler, Nixon's press secretary. He called to ask whether he could do anything for me in behalf of Dorothy Ho-chan. I said there was nothing to do. Dorothy and I were just friends.

"Are you appearing for her at Treasury?" he asked.

"No, I am not," I said and Ziegler abruptly ended the call.

I added this call to the growing stack of bizarre incidents connected with the elusive Dorothy Ho-chan. Not only had my inquiries about the gold bullion been most discreet, but I hadn't even known Dorothy's name when I made them. It was clear she had been in touch with the Oval Office. Ron Ziegler's phone calls originated from only one place.

Soon after I became totally involved in the events that eventually led to that shattering night on the mountainside. When I learned I had to be in Paris for court hearings, I was glad to resume my pursuit of the China film offer. Again I met with the Belgrade television man and viewed the footage he had ready. It proved to be far better than I had dared hope.

During one of our meetings the Belgrade television man gave me three of Chairman Mao's Little Red Books, which he had brought from Peking. These small "bibles" of Mao's practical and philosophical doctrines had not yet been widely circulated outside China, and authentic editions were highly prized. I gave one to my attorney in Paris, Claire Jourdan, and kept the other two.

Before leaving I received a call from Nixon's Paris intermediary suggesting I visit his office. Still intensely curious about his role in the official burst of concern, I met him and told him of my interest in the China film. He deftly, almost idly, turned the conversation around to Nixon, recalling our early adventures in pursuit of the Trujillo settlement.

"You know, it is an error for you to think President Nixon is not a man of gratitude," he remarked. "He is concerned over the unfortunate things that happened to you and he is very much aware of all those who have valued your talents and friendship—all the way back to President Eisenhower.

"I am sending a coded cable to the White House informing the President of our meeting. I can assure you someone on his staff will be contacting you when you get back to America."

He offered no explanation for the establishment of this rather mysterious channel of communication, but his careful choice of words was reminiscent of his conversation with me during his visit while I was recuperating in New York. Since the purpose of the new communications channel would undoubtedly be revealed in due time, I flew back to New York thinking of other things, like the two Little Red Books in my suitcase.

Upon my return I had to make an urgent trip to Baltimore on family affairs, and when I came back I found an envelope from the White House in the pile of mail awaiting me. It contained a letter from presidential staff assistant Michael B. Smith informing me that a Brigadier General W. C. Lemly, USMC Retired, had written to the President in an attempt to reach me. The letter enclosed General Lemly's address in Coronado, California.

Since I had never heard of General Lemly, I was intrigued to learn he had been asking Richard Nixon about me. I decided to call him rather than write. He was astonished to hear from me and had a lot to say.

"I know about what happened to you in Geneva," the general said. "I'm a neighbor and long-time friend of the President here in California. I was having dinner with him in San Clemente recently and I brought up what happened to you in Geneva. I had all the clippings from the European newspapers in front of me. I asked Mr. Nixon why none of them mentioned a word about anything having been done for you by any American officials, and he said there had been some sort of foul-up all down the line. Frankly, I let him know I didn't think much of that answer and I thought you'd been treated in a shabby way."

"Thank you for that," I said.

The indignation General Lemly had felt was still in his voice. "Are you going to let them get away with that?" he said, and I had no answer. It was plain he found the official silence disturbing. He was obviously a well-informed man who maintained a deep interest in world affairs, particularly those relating to America's image abroad. I thanked him again for his concern, and reluctantly turned down his gracious invitation to join him for a trip aboard his boat. We did agree to keep in touch, however.

I immediately wrote a reply to the White House letter from Michael Smith. I thought about the assurance I had just received that Richard Nixon was a man of gratitude. Perhaps I had been overly cynical, I thought, or perhaps leopards do change their spots.

Because the newspapers were filled with articles about Nixon's intended visit to China, I decided to add a final paragraph: "During a recent visit to Paris I received three copies of Chairman Mao Tse-tung's Little Red Book that were brought directly from Peking. I enclose one for the President in view of his possible trip to China." I sent the letter and the book the following morning and with lightning speed a reply arrived from a White House staff member in behalf of President Nixon, thanking me for the Little Red Book. I was told the President was most interested to hear about the film depicting life inside China. It was quickly apparent Nixon knew all about the Paris meeting.

An initial thank-you call was quickly followed by a succession of calls and meetings in New York and Washington. The same theme echoed through them all: the President wanted to do something to make up for the neglect shown in Geneva. The President was a man who valued old friendships. The President believed in the importance of confidence in personal relationships. Rose Mary Woods and a chorus of intermediaries all offered variations on the same theme. My unspoken reply to all of them was, what does the President want from me? I had a long, clear memory and I knew the things Richard Nixon believed in most.

I received my first indication of what it was Nixon really wanted from me in November, at a meeting with an unofficial member of the White House staff, a man Nixon had apparently selected to be our liaison in the sudden and enigmatic resurrection of our friendship.

"You've really had some unexpected disappointments, haven't you?" he remarked sympathetically.

"I'm not sure I follow you," I said.

"Unforeseen things, things not turning out right. Like that Hoffa business back when Bobby Kennedy was trying to nail him. You never were paid those bonding fees, were you?"

"Never," I admitted, wondering what had made him reach back that far.

"Disgraceful, really disgraceful. But I imagine Hoffa was grateful to you nevertheless for saving his neck."

"I think so, but Jimmy Hoffa is a hard man to satisfy."

"But you do still hear from Hoffa and his people, don't you?" he continued.

"From time to time."

"They still think you can come up with something to get him released?"

"Some of them do, yes."

"I understand Allen Dorfman controls the pension fund now, along with Frank Fitzsimmons," he mused aloud. "But they say Hoffa still very much runs the show."

"That's what they say," I said, deciding caution was in order.

"Do you think that's so?"

"Probably is."

"Do you know Dorfman?"

"I've never met the man." The answer was true.

He thought aloud again. "Then your channels are more directly to Hoffa," he said.

"If you can call them channels."

His next remark slid out with disarming casualness. "The Teamsters could stand a better image, particularly relating to the pension fund, don't you think?"

"No doubt they could," I said, wondering where I was being led.

"Do you think Hoffa would be interested in the pension fund business being handled by someone else?" he asked.

"I honestly don't know the answer to that."

"Well, do you think Hoffa still has enough control of the union to make such a decision?"

"I think so," I said. I was quite sure that reply was correct. Jacques Schiffer had expressed many doubts about the loyalty of some of Hoffa's close associates, and had been puzzled by their foot-dragging when it came to doing things that could free him. Yet, I was sure Hoffa still controlled his union.

"An account like the Teamster pension fund." he said, "would be a real challenge. In someone's capable hands I can see the opportunity to make a real contribution while at the same time help improve that image problem they have. Don't you agree?"

I nodded.

"That's the best kind of new business to go after—the challenging kind where you can really do some good."

The meeting ended with some new outlines emerging in my mind. The bland remark about "new business" referred to an account in excess of $2 billion but there was still a lot I didn't know.

My companion saved his bombshell for his parting remark. As I was about to leave his office, he said, "The President would like to have a meeting with you. You'll be hearing from me about that."

Within a few days the meeting was confirmed for Tuesday, November 23, at 6 P.M. Before that day arrived I received another letter from General Lemly in which he thanked me for my phone call and mentioned something very curious. In a letter he had received from the office of the President a most strange contradiction had been raised. The letter said in effect that the President had never heard of me.

"I want to discuss this letter with you personally when the opportunity presents itself," Lemly wrote, "and this rather large discrepancy it has created."

One more bizarre item was added to the mountain in connection to the Geneva affair. That evening I also heard from Dorothy Ho-chan. She was just passing through the city, she said, and had a moment to talk. "I've been in Washington seeing a lot of people, including someone you know," she said. "Do you remember that material in storage I once spoke to you about?" I told her I did remember it, very well. "I may need your help with it—you know, the application and forms and all those documents you said would be necessary."

"Then you're going to move openly," I said.

"I didn't say that," she snapped. "I still want to find another way. When will you be in Paris again?"

"Soon. Within ten days," I said.

"I won't have made a decision by then. I'll probably be in Tangiers. But I want you to proceed with an application for a gold license anyway."

I said I would and we spoke a little longer. Then she had to catch her plane. The fortune in gold sitting in a vault had suddenly taken on fresh importance for Dorothy. Or someone. She had made it plain to me from the beginning that she was acting as an agent for the bullion.

On November 23, as I flew to Washington, I wondered what had prompted my summons to the Oval Office. The questions about Hoffa and the pension that had been posed to me intrigued me. And I wondered whether they were meant to lay the groundwork for my private meeting with the President. On the other hand, maybe he wanted to find out what I had learned about China during my film talks. Or maybe he merely wanted to act in an official capacity regarding Geneva. I simply had no clear idea.

At six o'clock sharp on November 23, 1971, I was ushered into the private office. Richard Nixon was standing as I entered. We shook hands and he gestured to the chair across the desk from him. We were alone. "I'm glad to see you looking so well," he began. "The Justice Department has been in touch with you on that Geneva business, I've been told."

"Yes, they have," I said.

"The whole thing was one damned error on top of another. But I'm glad Jimmy Roosevelt did get to the hospital at any rate." He leaned back in his chair and gave me a tight smile. "I was most interested to hear about that China film. Are you going ahead with it?"

"Yes, I'm going to Paris to conclude negotiations soon. It will be the first one of its kind, maybe an omen pointing to a new era in our relations with China," I suggested.

"I hope so, I certainly hope so. As you know, I have every intention to visit Chairman Mao in February. The world goes around, far away and close at home. Things are always changing," he mused.

I began to wonder what the purpose of my visit was after all.

"I'm going to be looking for a new Attorney General

soon," he said, suddenly changing the subject. "John Mitchell is going to resign. He's had enough of government work. I intend to run for another term, as you know, and John is going to head the committee to reelect me."

"Have you picked a successor to Mitchell?"

"No, not yet. It may be Richard Kleindienst. After the election is over, John is leaving Washington. He's going to be a private citizen again. That's what he wants. You probably know our relationship goes back awhile. We'll both be practicing law, of course, someday . . . this doesn't go on forever, you know," he said with a little deprecating laugh and a gesture that encompassed the room. "Although some days it seems like forever," he concluded.

I nodded, still waiting.

"Now, about Hoffa and the Teamsters, let's get down to business. I understand you've been approached by my people about the pension fund."

"Yes, the matter has come up," I said.

Then Nixon continued. "The Department of Justice keeps getting pleas from Hoffa's people. This Hoffa thing has been going on too long. It's not an ordinary situation and it can't be handled in an ordinary way. We'd like to cooperate and find a way to do something, but of course we would have to reach an understanding first."

"What kind of understanding?"

"I'm told you feel Hoffa still runs the show in the Teamsters Union."

"Yes, I do."

"Do you hear from him often?"

"Yes, but indirectly."

"If an understanding can be reached with him, he can perhaps be released by presidential pardon."

Everything was being carefully spelled out for me, but I wanted to be absolutely certain I understood. "Are we talking about vague possibilities—maybe this in exchange for maybe that—or is this a definite thing?"

"I'm talking about a presidential pardon in exchange for Jimmy Hoffa's cooperation on the pension fund," he said and picked up a single sheet of yellow legal-size paper that had been lying face down on his desk and read from it. What he read were the conditions for Jimmy Hoffa's pardon. He ticked them off one by one, the chief among them being the stipulation that Hoffa could not hold union office or "engage in any direct or indirect management of any labor union prior to March 6, 1980."

I sat back and drew a deep breath. The bargain had been polished down to the practical working details. Nixon had just been waiting for me to say the right words before he read the terms to me.

"Those are the conditions for a presidential pardon?" I said at last.

"That's right. If you can get in touch with Mr. Hoffa immediately, you can propose these conditions. If he accepts them, he can be home for Christmas."

I nodded. Things were to move quickly.

"How long do you think it will be before you can reach Hoffa?" was his next question.

I had to think through the necessary moves before I could answer. Utmost confidentiality was one of the absolutes. "At least twenty-four hours," I said.

"And how long do you think he'll take to reply?"

"I can't answer that. I'm sure it wouldn't take too long."

Then Nixon frowned. "Of course you realize if this goes through, if I pardon Jimmy Hoffa, I'll be accused of God knows what. Everybody will throw a fit, but then the whole thing will just fade away. But I don't care about that. As long as nobody can make any connection between the other thing we've just talked about—that's what's important. That's why I can't approach any of Hoffa's people. They're all too vulnerable. Now, you said you were leaving to go back to Paris on the China film. Will that be soon?"

"I was planning to leave tomorrow."

"Then you'll be in Paris before any final word comes from Mr. Hoffa," Nixon said.

"Most likely. I suppose that might be a problem."

"On the contrary," he said, "Your people will know where to reach you in Paris, I presume. When you hear from them, get in touch with my Paris colleague. Tell him whatever the answer is. He will know exactly what to do."

The final piece was in position. Now I understood why

someone had been brought all the way from Paris to be established as my contact on the Geneva affair. Paris to New York to Washington, D.C., to Detroit—an untraceable route.

"How long do you expect to stay in Paris?" Nixon asked, breaking into my thoughts.

"Ten days, I would guess. I have to conclude negotiations for the film, and the French are very interested in it for French television."

"Why don't you bring it here first—to the White House? We could arrange for a special showing," he said.

It was a thought that had never occurred to me, but one I found instantly intriguing. "Yes, that might be done," I said.

Nixon stood up. "I expect to be hearing from you soon," he said. "I hope something satisfactory can be worked out for everyone."

The meeting was over and the secret service men showed me out. My cab reached the airport in time for me to catch the plane back to New York. I used the air time between Washington and New York to stop my head from spinning. By the time I touched down at La Guardia, I was still having difficulty absorbing what had happened. Was it possible Richard Nixon was using his enormous power to make strictly personal transactions to ensure great wealth for himself after he left office? If there is a quality of naïveté to my musings, it must be remembered this was 1971. Watergate was still only a luxury residence, and few people were entertaining thoughts that the President was committing high crimes and misdemeanors in the Oval Office. Upon reaching my apartment, I immediately put through a call to a man who was not involved in the union's internecine struggles and who was a genuine friend of Hoffa. He could be counted on to work in Jimmy's best interests.

"I have the biggest surprise in the world for you," I told him.

"What are you talking about?"

"I met with President Nixon in Washington. We talked about a lot of things like the pension fund, and Jimmy's influence in the Teamsters, but here's the punch line. Jimmy can be home for Christmas."

"You've got to be kidding," he said, not amused.

"No. I'm absolutely serious. I had it all spelled out." Then

I gave him the conditions for Hoffa's release, those that would be on record as part of the presidential pardon, as well as those that would remain in the shadows.

"I want you to get the message to Jimmy personally," I said. "I'm going to be busy in Paris on a film proposition and I'll be staying at the Intercontinental Hotel. When you get Jimmy's answer, contact me there. The rest of the machinery has already been set up. All I need is his answer."

"It sounds very carefully thought out," my contact said.

"You'd better believe it."

The following night I was in Paris. A series of meetings took place at once, and within two or three days, after viewing some twenty-five thousand feet of the film and conferring with the Belgrade television people, French government officials, representatives of American networks, and others, I contracted to become the producer of *Mao's China*. Because of Nixon's impending visit, the subject matter became one of intense interest in many quarters. The French, because of their longer and more amicable relationship with the People's Republic of China, were especially interested.

But I had become increasingly mindful of that dinner conversation at Laserre the year before, and Dorothy Ho-chan's references to it from time to time. The television film might be only the first step toward a full-length motion picture documentary, and for that I needed Madame Mao's full interest and cooperation. I called a friend in Tangiers and told her my thoughts. She was in accord and, following her instructions, I reached Madame Mao, who personally arranged for special travel documents, issued through the Chinese Embassy in Tangiers, that would permit me to enter China *inter nos*, without using my passport or having the trip recorded there. No one, not even my attorney in Paris, knew I was making the trip.

Before I left, Dorothy sent to Paris an envelope which she said was confidential and was to be delivered directly into Madame Mao's hands. I flew on Air France from Paris to Vientiane, from Vientiane to Peking. At the airport three security men took me in a Chinese-made limousine to a private compound in the heart of Peking. It was early December and under its mantle of snow the city seemed a rather bleak, gray, and uninviting place.

Josephine Baker arriving with the author in Las Vegas in 1952.

With former President Dwight D. Eisenhower in 1968.

With Josephine Baker and Hollywood columnist Cobina Wright (left) at Ciro's Hollywood opening in 1952.

With Sophie Tucker (left) and Hermione Gingold.

Maurice Chevalier
in 1951 after receiving
his U.S. visa.

Marilyn Monroe and
Yves Montand.
Hollywood, 1960.

The author with
Ernest Keiser,
a principal in the
Z incident.
Paris, 1970.

Background, seated left to right: Johnny Weissmuller, Josephine Hoffa, James R. Hoffa, Mrs. Nicholas Tweel, Nicholas Tweel, with unidentified dinner companions. Miami, 1963.

In Paris at a party given by Aristotle Onassis in 1970. At far left: Flor Trujillo and Sheik Abdullah al Khalifa with unidentified dinner companions.

With Flor Trujillo, 1976.

J A M E S R. H O F F A
2420 GUARDIAN BUILDING
DETROIT, MICHIGAN 48226

June 7, 1972

Mr. William L. Taub
118 East 60th Street and Park Avenue
New York, New York   10022

Dear Mr. Taub:

Your wire of June 6, 1972 is acknowledged. You are
authorized to appear in Paris and other places to represent
me regarding securing our discussed meeting, subject to
my being given an unqualified release of my present restrictions. Any action you take is subject to further discussions
and final approval. This does not authorize expenditures of
any monies under our prior agreement.

Sincerely,

James R. Hoffa

JRH:jam

A letter and a series of telegrams arranging a meeting between
James R. Hoffa and North Vietnamese leaders.

5492

NNNN
ZCZC PUA293 SFR166
ITRM HI BGSA Q36
SOFIA 36 15 1335

ELT
WIILRTAUB EXCELLSIORHOTEL ROME

BEFORE DEPARTING TODAY FOR MOSCOU LEDUCTHO DIRECTED YOU
CONTINUE SOFIA MEETING YESTERDAY REGARDING JAMES R HOFFA
IMMEDIATELY WITH DELEGATION LEADER NGUENMUNVI WHO AWAITS YOU
IN PARIS
    PLAMEN VOYNOVSKY CENTRAL COMMITIEE

                                    1540B

61000

21/06 14.04

61000 ACTX2 ⊞1

61232 EXELSIOR

TELEX ROMA

URGENT — NGUENMUNVI   4 AVENUE LEDRUROLLIN   CHOISYLEROI PARIS94
= URGENT OUR MEETING PARIS FRIDAY MORNING JUNE 23 REGARDING
JAMES R HOFFA AS   PREARRANGED BY LEDUCTHO AND MYSELF SOFIA
BULGARIA LAST WEEK STOP ARRIVING INTERCONTINENTALOTEL PARIS
THURSDAY NITE = WILLIAM L TAUB +++

⊕
61000 ACTX2 ⊞1
61232 EXELSIOR

V+
IBOFTCENT STL
WUTLX STL A034 (53)KB722 SSF074
K IKD0181 VIA ITT 0722/28
AWQ147 VIA ITT CWG837 HFH778 NK67A
UINX BU VIHA 051
URGENT HENOI 51 28 1800
URGENT
HAROLD GIBBONS
340 SO GRAND AVENUE ST LOUIS MO 63103
MISSOURI/USA
NO 234
GLADLY INVITE JAMES HOFFA COMMA HAROLD GIBBONS AND WILLIAM
TAUB FOR ONE WEEK VISIT STOP ARRIVAL HANOI JULY
FIRST OR FOURTH DESIRABLE STOP VISAS MAYBE OBTAINED
IN VIENTIANE OR PARIS STOP HOANG QUOC VIET
PRESIDENT VIETNAM TRADEUNIONS
913A+
IBOFTCENT STL

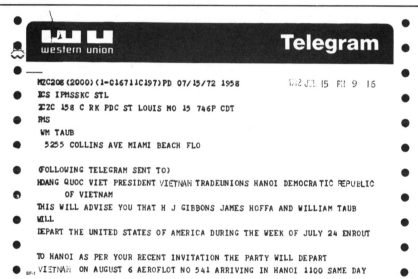

western union   Telegram

MZC206(2000)(1-016711C197)PD 07/15/72 1958   1972 JUL 15 PM 9 16

ICS IPMSSKC STL

IZC 158 C RK PDC ST LOUIS MO 15 746P CDT

PMS

WM TAUB
5255 COLLINS AVE MIAMI BEACH FLO

(FOLLOWING TELEGRAM SENT TO)

HOANG QUOC VIET PRESIDENT VIETNAM TRADEUNIONS HANOI DEMOCRATIC REPUBLIC
    OF VIETNAM

THIS WILL ADVISE YOU THAT H J GIBBONS JAMES HOFFA AND WILLIAM TAUB
WILL

DEPART THE UNITED STATES OF AMERICA DURING THE WEEK OF JULY 24 ENROUT

TO HANOI AS PER YOUR RECENT INVITATION THE PARTY WILL DEPART

SF-1 VIETNAM ON AUGUST 6 AEROFLOT NO 541 ARRIVING IN HANOI 1100 SAME DAY

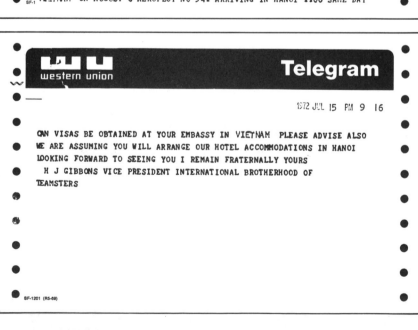

western union   Telegram

1972 JUL 15 PM 9 16

CAN VISAS BE OBTAINED AT YOUR EMBASSY IN VIETNAM PLEASE ADVISE ALSO
WE ARE ASSUMING YOU WILL ARRANGE OUR HOTEL ACCOMMODATIONS IN HANOI
LOOKING FORWARD TO SEEING YOU I REMAIN FRATERNALLY YOURS
H J GIBBONS VICE PRESIDENT INTERNATIONAL BROTHERHOOD OF
TEAMSTERS

SF-1201 (R5-69)

When Madame Mao received me, she was as charming and animated as she had been in Paris. There were differences, however. After I delivered the envelope from Dorothy Ho-chan, she took me to her home where lunch was served and I was introduced to Mao Tse-tung. In the presence of her husband, Madame Mao's conversation became sprinkled with the political rhetoric that had been absent in Paris. The soft, sophisticated gown she wore that night had been replaced by the shapeless peasant tunic that was the uniform of the People's Republic. Chairman Mao listened, nodding as she interpreted for him, and tried unsuccessfully not to appear bored. He was partially paralyzed, and it was obvious to me which of the two was in the ascendancy.

When we talked about the showing of *Mao's China* on American television, however, his interest awakened. As for Madame Mao, her dogmatism gave way to real enthusiasm. She became almost as excited as I was about the full-length motion picture documentary I proposed. The prospect of a film combining propaganda, education, and entertainment really stirred her.

We spent the major part of my second day in Peking exchanging ideas about the television film. She wanted the film to convey definite thoughts as well as an authentic atmosphere. On my part, I was interested in maintaining the integrity of the film as a depiction of life inside China.

At one point she called for tea, then adroitly changed the subject. "I must thank you again for bringing Dorothy's letter," she said. "I understand you are trying to help her with a matter." She paused, waiting for me to fill in the vital missing word.

"Concerning the gold?" I said. "She has asked me to file certain applications, yes."

"It is of no consequence anymore," she said abruptly. "I would hate to see you waste your time. Very soon now the gold will be coming home, you see."

"I'm sorry, but I don't follow you."

"There are ways to move things for important personages. Diplomatic ways we have not been able to take advantage of for a long time, but that will all change soon enough."

I said I still wasn't sure of her meaning. Did she mean by "diplomatic ways" the law of diplomatic immunity?

She evaded a direct reply. "It is just a matter of time now before the gold will be brought home to its rightful owner. It belongs here and nowhere else."

We returned to the main topic. When all the major issues had been resolved and it was time to leave, she said, "Please tell Dorothy I will be in touch with her."

"I'll call her as soon as I arrive back in Paris."

"Thank you. I must advise you, however, it is not a good thing to involve yourself with Dorothy. She is not to be relied upon by you."

On the way to the Peking airport, riding in the same limousine that had picked me up, and accompanied by the same three security men, I mulled over Madame Mao's words. Dorothy had hinted several times that she and Madame Mao were related. I had even wondered whether they might be sisters. Now I wondered whether they were relations or rivals, although there was always the possibility they were both. Dorothy had also made it clear that she and another wealthy Chinese woman, who also contributed heavily to Richard Nixon's campaigns, had often been used as private couriers for Nixon. Is it possible that Nixon was about to become a private courier himself? What else could Madame Mao have meant when she patted the couch beside her and said, "It is just a matter of time now before the gold will be brought home to its rightful owner"? I was baffled. Nevertheless, I decided to heed Madame Mao's warning about the duplicity of our mutual friend.

I was back in Paris. For all public purposes, I had never left. I was still registered at my hotel and they had taken all calls in my absence. One of them was from my Hoffa intermediary.

"You have the blessings of the family," he said when I finally reached him. "All the luck in the world if you can pull it off." No more needed to be said. I took my coat and left for the office of Nixon's man in Paris.

"The conditions proposed by the President have been accepted," I told him at our private meeting. "The other points discussed have also been agreed upon and will be acted on at the proper time."

"I will send a coded cable at once," he said.

"Also please advise the President it is most probable the first showing of the China film could be at the White House, as he suggested," I added. The brief meeting ended. There was no need for more words. All the circuitous and careful moves had come down to this moment.

There were still a number of details to take care of regarding the film, and I stayed in Paris another week, then flew back to New York. Three days after I arrived, Jimmy Hoffa received his presidential pardon. He was released from the Lewisburg Penitentiary in time to spend Christmas at home with his family, as had been promised. The Justice Department announced Hoffa had been freed for "humanitarian reasons."

Two days after Christmas Joe Konowe, a Teamster official and acquaintance, came to my office, and during our meeting asked to use the telephone. "I'm with Bill right now," Konowe said over the wire. Then he handed me the phone. "Jimmy wants to talk to you," he said. I took the telephone.

"Congratulations," Hoffa said. "You did it. I'll be talking to you soon." Thus began and ended the first conversation I had had with Jimmy Hoffa since that afternoon I had talked to him from the phone booth on the corner of Madison and Forty-first Street when Bobby Kennedy was about to bring him down.

Alone later that night, I reflected on all that had happened, and what it meant. Whatever may have happened, I knew that Jimmy Hoffa was once again a free man.

9

MAO'S CHINA

In the argot of intelligence agencies there is a term known as *disinformation.* It means the spreading of false information to create political unrest, to alarm governments, or simply to confuse counterintelligence. Washington also uses disinformation, in its own way and for its own purposes. My involvement in the Hoffa pardon became part of a confusing and often contradictory epidemic of rumors loosed in Washington to deflect attention from the pardon itself. No one seemed to know anything concrete, but everyone seemed to know I had been involved. I was made aware during that fallout period how imperative it is in the Washington game of truth-sifting that all the fringe players touch base constantly to compare rumors. Somewhere, they hope, what really happened will emerge. It hardly ever does.

My daily engagement calendar from that time records calls from a great number of Washington minor league players, as well as many well-known figures, all offering congratulations that were implied rather than direct. I did manage to find out most of the information was coming from the Hoffa camp. Soon, however, the excitement died away, just as Richard Nixon had predicted it would, and the official story of the release of

Jimmy Hoffa remained publicly intact.

Mao's China was then occupying most of my waking hours. Minor and not so minor problems escalated, and it was during those frantic days that I received a visit from one of Nixon's men. It seemed somebody was unhappy with Jimmy Hoffa's elusive behavior regarding his side of the pardon agreement.

"Have you been in touch with Hoffa?" he asked.

"Hardly," I told him. "I'm too involved in other things right now. Anyway, Hoffa's in Florida."

"We know that," he said with some asperity. "Aren't you anxious to get the bonding money? Good God, it's been hanging long enough."

"Of course I am, and I will at the proper time," I assured him, waiting for him to reveal the real reason for his visit. He did.

"It's felt a detailed discussion ought to be held with Mr. Hoffa soon," he said with some urgency. He didn't specify who felt that way, but plainly someone wanted assurances.

"I'll try," I said. "Right now that's as much as I can promise." The emissary left, obviously dissatisfied.

When arrangements to show *Mao's China* at the White House were near completion, I took the time to fly to Miami to see Hoffa at the apartment complex where he was staying. I found him poolside in the hot Florida sun doing push-ups. He had been out of prison a mere month and already he looked in perfect physical condition. Five feet nine, weighing about 160 pounds, he never carried an ounce of loose flesh. He didn't smoke or drink (nor would he allow his wife Josephine to) and he did push-ups every day.

"I came to talk about the bonding money," I said. Hoffa stopped his push-ups, propelled his powerful frame into a patio chair, and took command of the conversation at once.

"Forget about the bonding money," he said. "There are more important things to talk about."

I held my ground. "It's important to me. It's been a long time."

He paused, gave me an imperious look, then said, "Allen Dorfman held that money."

"Dorfman?" I gasped. "Why?"

"It just happened that way. I told you, forget about that.

It's nothing, small change. I've got something better for you."

"But Dorfman didn't have a thing to do with getting the bonding."

"So he didn't, but that's what happened and I can't do anything about it now," he said.

"I don't see why not," I said hotly.

Jimmy struck his hand against the thin arm of the chair. "That's just why I called you down here," he said, totally exasperated. "I can't do anything about anything this way, not with those goddamn conditions around my neck."

"The conditions of the pardon?"

"That's right. I want them wiped out, removed, in the ash can."

"But those conditions were part of the pardon. You agreed to them. If you hadn't agreed to them, you'd still be sitting in Lewisburg," I said, still numb from his revelation about Allen Dorfman.

"I know what I agreed to," he said. "But hell, I didn't think they meant to hold to all that stuff."

"I'd say they intend to hold to it down to the last letter, the last comma."

"Yeah? Well, you know what else was part of the deal," he muttered.

"Right. It was all in the one package. The conditions of the pardon and the pension fund. And you understood it all."

"Sure, but I figured the conditions were window dressing. Shit, I might as well be back in the cooler. I can't move this way. I really got the short end of the deal. Those conditions have got to go."

"I don't see how."

"Look here," he said, lowering his voice and changing his tactics, "it's more important than you think. I don't like a lot of the things I'm hearing. There are things going on I got to look into. While I was away there's been some kind of funny business going on and I can't do anything unless I get back in the driver's seat, all the way in it."

I shook my head. "The conditions were part of the pardon. You know how much screaming went on even with them attached to it. I can't see anyone touching those conditions."

Hoffa narrowed his eyes. "It's worth three hundred and

fifty thousand to you to get them removed."

"That has a familiar ring to it, Jimmy."

"Lay off about that bonding thing for Chrissake, will you? Jesus, man—it just got away from me. I was going to give it to you, but you know all the troubles I had then. Bobby Kennedy was still all over me and then he finally got his conviction. It just got lost in the shuffle. This will be different."

"How?"

"There'll be nobody but you, me, and a man we both trust. You know who I mean." I nodded. "I'll put three hundred and fifty thousand in a vault in any bank you choose. There will be two keys to the vault. You'll have one and the other guy will have the other. As soon as the conditions are lifted, you meet him at the bank and the three hundred and fifty thousand dollars is yours, in cash."

"It sounds fine," I said.

"It *is* fine," he snapped. "If the key doesn't fit, or if something else happens, I always have three hundred and fifty thousand in a suitcase. All you have to do is fly down here and get it." He halted, satisfied with his offer, watching to see my reaction. What he saw was chagrin and anger. "Think about it," he said softly.

"About the conditions? Nobody will touch them. There's no way."

"There's always a way," he said.

I wanted to disagree with him, but the statement was one he had heard from me often enough. There always was a way, but sometimes the way was impossible to find. This certainly seemed one of those times.

Hoffa picked up his beach towel and strode from the pool. The meeting had been adjourned. I walked away slowly. My initial anger had been replaced by numbness. I wanted to reject Hoffa's proposal out of hand, but one fact made me hold back. The cost of acquiring the rights and producing *Mao's China* had far exceeded my original estimates. Three hundred and fifty thousand dollars would indeed be welcome. Perhaps naively, I did not entirely disbelieve Hoffa's story about the original bonding monies having "gotten away" from him. He had at first deliberately held back my fee in an effort to pressure me into contacting Joseph Kennedy about Bobby. He had played

games with the fee and then internal problems in the union—
and Bobby Kennedy—had pushed him into a corner. He had
needed Allen Dorfman badly in those days. He had set up
Dorfman as his alter ego in the union. Perhaps he had been in
no position to cross Dorfman at the time. More likely, he simply did not want to provoke a battle with him over the bonding
money.

I met with Hoffa again the next morning. His sharp, dart-
ing eyes were quick to see my attitude hadn't changed. "You
could come up with something if you think about it enough," he
said. "Why don't you stay down here for a couple of weeks
where it's relaxing?"

I glared at him. "I shouldn't have taken these two days. I
still have a million things to do on *Mao's China*, including a
settlement with the sponsors."

"Who's going to sponsor it?" he said.

"I've been negotiating with Grey Advertising. They're setting up a joint sponsorship with Ford Motor and the Holiday
Inn people."

"Why don't you let the Teamsters sponsor it? You say your
film is a first? Well, that would be a first too."

Most people would have laughed away the idea. I might
have once, too, but during my trip to China, Madame Mao Tse-
tung had made many references to the role of labor in the development of modern China. There had been much talk about
the solidarity of laborers all over the world. It was propaganda,
but it was also strongly, almost religiously, respected. In fact, at
one point in the presence of her husband, when Madame Mao
was waving the proletarian banner most vigorously, the name of
Jimmy Hoffa and his role in the American labor movement had
been mentioned. For these reasons I didn't dismiss Jimmy's suggestion out of hand.

"I'll have to think some more about that," I said. "As of
now, sponsorship seems about lined up."

Hoffa wrote two names on a piece of paper and handed it
to me. "You want Ford, you talk to these two men," he said.
"Those are their private phone numbers. Tell them you just left
me and I told you to get in touch with them. Let them set the
whole thing up for you. Now, what about the conditions?"

"Right now I can't think of any way they could be lifted,"

I told him. By then I had run out of ways to tell him the same thing.

"Somebody better think of a way," he muttered. "I wouldn't have gone along with the deal if I thought they really meant to keep the goddamn conditions on, and you can tell them that for me."

"It won't help you one bit if you try to back out of the other things you agreed to do," I warned him. "You're in no position to make threats."

Hoffa glared. "Then tell them I can't carry through with the deal if the conditions are on."

"I'll try. I don't know that they'll believe that," I said.

Hoffa grunted and turned away. There was little else to say. I left with a last reminder from him that $350,000 waited for me. All I had to do was perform one of my miracles.

Flying back from Miami, I looked at the names Hoffa had written on the slip of paper and decided to call the two men. I might as well get some good out of Jimmy Hoffa, I told myself. Back at my apartment, I tried the Detroit numbers Hoffa had said were private lines. I got through to one of the men and told him I had just left Hoffa in Miami and that Hoffa had suggested I call him.

"I expect to be in Detroit tomorrow—" I began.

"Call me when you arrive," he answered and hung up. I reached Detroit in the late morning and went directly to the Ford Motor Company. At the large reception desk I announced myself and gave the name of the man I had spoken to less than twenty-four hours earlier. The message came back that he was out. The other man whose name Hoffa had given me was also away, I was told, and no one knew when either man would return.

I decided to call my own contacts, who knew about my trip. They, too, were suddenly unavailable. I told the receptionist I wanted to go upstairs to wait but I wasn't permitted into the elevator. Then I asked to call the secretary of one of the people I was supposed to meet and was even refused permission to do that. I had to go outside to a public pay telephone to call the secretary, who seemed to know nothing about what her employer was doing, where he could be reached, or whether he'd ever be back.

The deep frost was rather obvious. Feeling apprehensive, I called Grey Advertising and the Holiday Inn people. It wasn't long before I learned Holiday Inn had changed its mind about sponsoring the film. It became clear Jimmy Hoffa's name was definitely no asset. In corporate boardrooms, especially those of companies that dealt with the Teamsters in any measurable way, nobody wanted anything to do with Hoffa or anyone connected with him.

As work on *Mao's China* continued, the French informed me they wanted to be the first to show the film on television. They felt they had priority because of their close ties to the People's Republic of China. Before I agreed, I wanted assurance of the greatest possible amount of official sponsorship for the showing. I called my attorney in Paris, Claire Jourdan, and told her I felt a meeting with President Pompidou was important.

"He won't see you," she said.

"I'm not so sure of that," I replied. I had met with Michel Rougagnou, Pompidou's press secretary, during my last trip to Paris. I put in a transatlantic call to him, told him what I wanted, and he promised to get back to me. He did within a day. President Pompidou would see me at 10 A.M. on New Year's Day. It seemed a good omen for 1972.

President Pompidou was primarily interested in seeing that the film was shown first to the French public. He was extremely pleased when I told him there would be no scheduling conflict in meeting his wish, and said in an almost proprietary manner, "We have been the first and the oldest friend of China in the West. I have often wondered why your country has been so hostile to China."

I said I thought the climate was changing and noted the forthcoming Nixon visit to Peking.

"Do you think that reflects the feeling of the American people or is it a personal pilgrimage by Mr. Nixon?" he asked.

"I think it may be some of both, but Madame Mao herself is very anxious for the American people to see the film, and she certainly reflects the official view of the Chinese government."

Pompidou ended the interview with a promise to give the showing his personal backing. It had been a most successful trip.

The American television premiere was not arranged with

the same unobstructed speed. At the last minute entirely unexpected developments almost prevented the film from being viewed. But before that, on February 4, 1972, at 3:20 P.M, *Mao's China* was shown to a select audience at the White House.

I was surprised to find the man I'd most expected to see at the screening was not there. The President had sent apologies for his absence and a request that the film be left for a private viewing the following day by the Nixons and the Mitchells. I complied of course, but I had a funny feeling Nixon was at one of his upstairs windows, watching me come in. The film was shown to a gathering mostly chosen by the White House: Pat O'Donnell, a member of the White House staff and one of the President's aides; General Brent Scowcroft, military aide to the President; John Daly, moderator of the television show "What's My Line" and the man who would be the host at the public showing of the film; Dwight Chapin; Herb Klein; Paul Fisher; Richard Kilpatrick; and Connie Stewart, who attended for Mrs. Nixon.

At a tea following the film General Scowcroft asked me whether I would like to accompany Mr. Nixon on his trip to China. I told him I regretted I could not. "Besides, I've just come back from the People's Republic," I said. The General was unable to mask his astonishment. He didn't pursue my remark, but I was certain it was carried to others.

After the tea I headed back to New York to prepare for the WNEW-TV showing of *Mao's China,* set for February 14. Because of an error of omission, the film nearly didn't get aired. I had delegated the job of posting the sizable bond required by the Federal Communications Commission, and four hours before the program was to be scheduled, I discovered the posting had not been done. A frantic series of telephone calls ensued, to Dean Burch, chairman of the FCC, all the way up to the White House, where I reminded Rose Mary Woods that Madame Mao would be affronted if the program was not aired.

Not until the opening frames appeared on the television screen and I saw the words "*Mao's China*, produced by William L. Taub," was I sure the film for which I had made a clandestine, perhaps even illegal, visit to China was going to be seen by the American public.

Relief is too weak a word for what I felt as I sat back and

watched it unreel. The film dealt with many areas of Chinese life: education and political indoctrination, medicine (including the practice of acupuncture, a technique almost unheard of then in America), agriculture, industry, and of course the arts. The depiction was honest in what the film crew had recorded, incomplete in what it had not been allowed to shoot. Nevertheless, it was a breakthrough, for it exposed Americans to a way of life they knew hardly anything about.

Seven days later Richard Nixon arrived in Peking and the film was discussed by him and the Chinese leaders during the eight-day visit. Among the deluge of calls that followed the airing of the film were several from one man on whom *Mao's China* had had little impact. Ironically, Jimmy Hoffa should have paid careful attention to it, for the film and the events surrounding it were to provide him with his last great opportunity. But Hoffa was shortsighted. His calls concerned only one thing: get the conditions removed.

He began to call every day, two or three times a day. I became convinced he was telling the truth when he said his power was eroding as his calls became more urgent, his voice increasingly alarmed.

His unhappiness with the conditions was known at the White House, but there the entire business was considered nonnegotiable, a *fait accompli*. Some viewed his protests as expected but fruitless. "Nobody but nobody in Washington is going to touch those conditions," someone said to me. "Nobody there could come up with anything to justify it." A passing remark, but it triggered a solution to Hoffa's problem.

Nobody there, nobody in Washington. The phrase excited me. *Nobody in Washington* did not preclude somebody far away from Washington. If something emanated from another place, no one in Washington would have to justify it, it would justify itself.

A plan was taking shape in my mind, one so impossible it seized me with fascination. The afternoon edition of the *New York Post* lay on my desk. The front-page article discussed the failure of the Nixon eight-point peace plan for the Vietnam war and the plight of the American prisoners of war in North Vietnam.

My impossible plan consumed me with its possibilities, and

I found myself remembering something one of my mentors had said to me many times: "If they're calling it impossible, it'll happen." His name was J. Howard McGrath, and he had engineered Harry Truman's upset victory over Thomas Dewey in 1948. Over the years McGrath taught me more than anyone else I knew, with the exception of my father. He was a quiet man. As governor, senator, and chairman of his party, he was political up to his eyeballs, and loved it. I was never the quiet type, and I spurned politics in favor of relationships based on personal chemistry, but I kept wondering if Howard McGrath were alive what he would have thought of my plan. The more I thought about it, the more I was sure he would have told me it was an impossible, lunatic idea, so I'd better get to work and make it happen.

10

EMISSARY HOFFA

I had an old friend named Professor Gerasimas Patronikolas, an eminent pathologist who was married to the sister of Aristotle Onassis. He had been feuding with his brother-in-law over money for years, and I had tried many times to intercede for him, never with much success. Dr. Patronikolas was an avid student of Soviet and Chinese affairs and was one of the most knowledgeable people I knew on many subjects, but particularly on anything pertaining to China.

I decided I must see him. On my next trip to Athens I met once more with Onassis to persuade him to release the shares of stock that were in dispute. Once more he refused. The following day I met Dr. Patronikolas in his beautiful villa in Athens. Over lunch we discussed the Vietnam war. I asked him about attitudes in the Soviet Union and Bulgaria, where he had been a frequent visitor, toward the intransigence of the Vietnamese, and about the position of China in the conflict.

"The Vietnamese, and the Chinese even more, are anxious to end the war," he said. "I believe they are desperate to find a way to do so."

"Then they aren't inflexible?"

"By no means. But one cannot overemphasize the importance of keeping face. They will not plead or supplicate or do anything that might appear as acquiescing to Western pressure. I would say this has always been at the very root of the problem in the peace talks. Your Mr. Kissinger simply does not appear to understand what seems so obvious to the rest of the world. One cannot bully them or humiliate them. Yet this is the very tactic Mr. Kissinger seems to have chosen. No one is able, apparently, to find a formula for peace that doesn't demean one side or the other, for of course I understand your government must not lose face either." He sighed and sipped his wine. "Everyone so determined not to lose face while on both sides all those people lose their lives."

"Do you think the North Vietnamese would consider an approach that didn't demean either side? An outside approach?"

"They would consider any avenue," he said, "any avenue at all." I had the distinct feeling he had little hope there were any avenues left to consider.

The talk shifted to his financial problems with Onassis. By the time lunch was over, I felt encouraged. As I had expected, Dr. Patronikolas had given me some valuable information.

I went to Geneva the following day and pursued much the same line of questioning with another old friend, Jean François at the Banque Romande, who had his own international channels. He also led me to believe the Vietnamese were not beyond approaching.

My last discussion during that trip was with my attorney in Paris, Claire Jourdan. I knew her too well to hold to generalities, as I had in my other two discussions. Aware of her excellent connections with international lawyers, especially those in Soviet-dominated countries, my queries were somewhat more specific.

"It is too bad you were not here last week," she said. "I attended a conference in Paris with a group of women attorneys, many on a level in their countries that would correspond to your Attorney General. You would have met a most brilliant and personable group of women."

"My loss," I conceded. "Could you reach some of these people if you wanted their help on something?"

"Oh, yes. That would be entirely possible." She smiled gently. "What would I want their help for?"

"I'm not ready to go into that yet," I said. "But hypothetically for the moment, if I wanted to contact the Vietnamese, would there be a channel there?"

Claire Jourdan thought awhile. "I believe Maria Panova would be the person to talk to on such a matter."

"Who is she?"

"The Minister of Justice of Bulgaria. I don't know what reaction I would get, of course, but I would start with her."

It had been another encouraging session, and I returned to the United States feeling quite hopeful. I realized, however, it was too soon to mention anything to Hoffa. There were still far too many imponderables, and Jimmy would jump all over them.

I saw him in Miami a few days later. He was in a particularly morose frame of mind. The time he had spent in prison had seemed to intensify his pessimism and distrust, and his growling and wailing were getting out of hand. He also seemed utterly ungrateful for the release.

"I didn't really gain a damned thing," he muttered. "I'm all tied up, hand and foot. Do you know what's happening in New York?"

"No."

"Dorfman's gone on trial, that's what. Goddamn, that's bad."

I tried to ignore my involuntary exultation at hearing the man who had collected my bonding fee was in heavy legal trouble. Of course I was well aware of Dorfman's importance as Hoffa's appointed steward of the pension fund. I had also heard Dorfman's attorney at the New York trial was Harvey Silets, a Chicago lawyer who was almost a co-defendant in the action.

"I don't like it, none of it," Hoffa said. My answer did little to cheer him.

"I think coming into New York with a Chicago lawyer who could well become a co-defendant himself is suicide," I said.

Hoffa stared at me. I could tell he was thinking hard.

Dorfman had been indicted in the Southern District of New York on a kickback affair in which he was accused of defrauding the pension fund and violating certain sections of Title 18 of the United States Code, which governs the conduct of loans involving union funds. It was a serious and well-mounted indictment and Hoffa knew he had good reason to worry.

Hoffa next delivered an impassioned speech about how helpless he was under the conditions of the pardon, and then I told him I had to get back to New York. I left him immersed in his bitterness.

Upon returning to New York I was contacted once again by Nixon's liaison man, but this time he did not want to talk about Hoffa. Instead he had a message for me from the White House.

"The President wanted me to tell you that Madame Mao Tse-tung expressly asked about you," he said.

"You sound as if he was surprised."

"I guess he was," he admitted. "He asked if there were any message you might want sent on to her."

"No, but thank Mr. Nixon," I said. I almost told him I had my own avenues for sending messages. I was asked how Hoffa was and I told him Jimmy wasn't terribly happy. His response, more unsaid than specific, was that Hoffa would learn to live with things as they were.

A few days later I called Claire Jourdan in Paris. She was glad to hear from me. "I did a little preliminary investigating on some of the things you asked about," she said.

"Good. I'd like to go into things in greater depth with you," I said, and she cut me off at once.

"Not on the telephone. Anything concerning certain subjects is dangerous. Things are very tense here and there are all kinds of wild stories flying about. Come to Paris if you want to talk more about it."

She intimated her initial explorations had been productive, and while she knew nothing of my basic plan, she had, of course, realized it had to bear in some way on Vietnam. I decided a quick visit was in order, and took a flight the following day. In her office I told her exactly what I had in mind, who would be involved, and what I hoped to accomplish. She listened attentively.

"All right. I'm glad you told me the details," she said. "I will reach out on my own, send out feelers. I will contact a number of people I think could help."

She didn't volunteer any names and I did not press her for any. "But I am a very busy person and there are only so many hours in a day. Do you have anyone else you can rely on to help?"

I gave her the name of Dr. Patronikolas, whom I planned to contact with all the details. I also told her of Jean François, whom she knew from previous business dealings. "The North Vietnamese have a delegation here in Paris," she said. "To interest them, you will need something concrete, a specific proposal that could affect the war. They won't respond to anything hypothetical."

"I think I have something definite," I said. "Meanwhile, you carry on here."

I left Paris, reached Dr. Patronikolas, and informed him of the details of the plan. At first he felt I was tilting at windmills, but when I outlined each of the elements, he decided it was possible, perhaps. "Properly handled, everything falling into place, it might be done," he admitted. "I'll be glad to help in any way I can." Once more I returned to the States, my optimism mounting.

Looming large in my thoughts was the impact of Hoffa's name as a labor leader and the uniqueness of his position. The Soviet, Chinese, and North Vietnamese estimation of Hoffa was nearly the reverse of the American. In fact, the Chinese regarded his imprisonment at the hands of his "corrupt imperialist government" as a badge of honor.

By the time I flew to Miami, I had a vision of my approach. It would emphasize Hoffa's role as a labor figure, as a champion of the rights of the common man.

At my apartment in Miami I fell into bed at once and slept until the phone woke me at 7:30 the following morning. It was Hoffa. "Come over right away," he said. "I've got to talk to you." His voice was strained. "The Dorfman thing's blown up in everybody's face. The bastards convicted him."

"I'm sorry to hear that, but I think I've got something much more important to talk to you about," I began.

"There isn't anything more important. Get the hell over here."

I pulled myself out of bed, dressed, and went to Hoffa's apartment, planning to tell him about my proposal. I found he was interested only in the Dorfman conviction.

"Damnit, do you know what this means?" he thundered.

"He could get up to five years. Five years! That could open up a whole can of worms. If Dorfman goes, I don't know what'll happen. I don't know what I could do tied up this way."

"Maybe I can get you untied," I said.

"When? Tomorrow?"

"No, not tomorrow," I admitted.

"Next week? Next month?" I had to shrug. It wouldn't be next week, I said, but next month was an outside chance.

"I don't want to hear your if's and maybe's. Right now I want one thing and that's Dorfman's conviction reversed. That's got to come first. I've got to keep the lid on things here. He's appealing, of course. I want you to take charge of the appeal."

I stared at him in disbelief. "You must be joking."

"No, goddamnit. I want you to handle it. Seeing as it's New York and you know the track there, you can do it best. Whatever you say we do."

"I think you're asking too much, Jimmy. I don't want to get involved with this Dorfman thing. I think you ought to be able to understand that."

Hoffa shifted his approach at once. "Look, I know what you're getting at. Do it for me, not Dorfman. I'll make the financial arrangements right now for you. It'll be a separate deal, no connection with anything else. Expenses and payment for services rendered."

He turned to the telephone and dialed the chairman of the board of a Miami bank. I listened as he set up a substantial sum, a financing arrangement that would cover anything I needed in my efforts to help Dorfman. It was a very attractive offer but I decided to delay my decision. "It's all set and waiting for you," Hoffa told me as I walked to the door. "All I want you to do is mastermind the appeal."

"I'll call you," I said and walked out without mentioning what I had set in motion for Jimmy Hoffa. He was in no mood to give it proper thought. If time was all-important to the Dorfman appeal, that would be his first concern. I decided to keep him ignorant of the Vietnam plan until I had something more definite to present. Only if the Dorfman thing could be quickly gotten out of the way, could I proceed without interruption and with Hoffa's full attention.

I returned to New York and arranged to see Allen Dorfman. He flew to New York in the private Lear jet he had at his disposal, courtesy of the Teamsters, and he and his pilot were at my apartment door the following morning.

The meeting was concerned primarily with the technical aspects of an appeal and the precise financial arrangements Hoffa had made. I reiterated that my involvement was strictly for services rendered and in no way intruded on anything still pending with Hoffa. Nothing was to be gained by bringing up the bonding fee, so I remained silent about that old wound. Dorfman and I reached an understanding, and now I wanted only to conclude the appeal as fast as possible.

However, it turned out to involve a tremendous amount of work. I was talking to Dorfman by phone anywhere from twice to ten times a day, and found myself flying to and from Detroit, Miami, Chicago, New York, and points in between. The main work was one of delicacy and tact, such as picking out the right set of lawyers to represent Dorfman in his appeal. Many firms did not want to represent the Teamsters at all, and others did not want to go into the court of appeals, particularly the prestigious firms, and I felt Dorfman needed such a firm.

It was during this intense period that I received an entirely unexpected letter from my close friend at the Vatican. He had seen my full-page advertisement for *Mao's China* in *Variety,* the show-business trade paper. His letter, a warm and pleasurable moment in a hectic time, was full of congratulations and reminiscences. He informed me he had brought the advertisement to the attention of the Pope. The letter triggered a new thought. My friend at the Vatican was in such a position that I knew if I wanted something to reach the ears of the Pope, it would within twenty-four hours. Many times the Pope had called for an end to the war in Vietnam. I decided to call my friend at the Vatican and tell him of my plan. He suggested I write him about the details, which I did at once.

Soon after I received a call from Claire Jourdan. She had been in touch with Dr. Patronikolas, and they both felt certain a meeting with the North Vietnamese delegation could be arranged. I also heard from Jean François, and he concurred. All three stressed the need for secrecy. Any leaks to official American sources would scuttle the entire affair.

In less than a week Claire Jourdan called me again with still more encouraging news. A North Vietnamese delegate had been in touch with her. The Deputy Minister of Foreign Affairs had directed him to inform her that a representative of the North Vietnamese was prepared to arrange a meeting with a representative of Mr. Hoffa. Stripping away the circuitous and cautious phrases, it meant the impossible was about to become probable. Events had reached a point where I had to talk to Hoffa.

I appeared at his apartment the following morning at the usual time, 8:30. "I've got some exciting things to talk to you about, Jimmy," I said. His face was set in stone, his mood sour as ever.

"Good. I could use some excitement."

"I think I've found a way, the one way, conditions might be lifted." His attitude changed at once. "The Vietnam war is bogged down. The peace talks are going nowhere. There's no reliable news on the American prisoners of war. If you could meet with the Vietnamese as a special negotiator, break the peace talks deadlock, and see about returning some American prisoners of war, you could write your own ticket."

He started out of his chair, then sat back down again. "Me?" he said finally. "Me, Jimmy Hoffa, meet with the North Vietnamese? You're nuts."

"No, I think it can come about. Listen to me a minute and I'll tell you how—"

"Is this what you wanted to talk to me about?" he yelled. "This crazy idea?"

"I think it can work, Jimmy. I've taken the first steps."

His face grew livid. He lowered his thick eyebrows over his squinting eyes and said, "It's the craziest damn fool idea I've ever heard. You must be out of your skull. You know what? You oughta be in a nuthouse. Why the hell would they come to me? And how could I do a goddamn thing? I can't even run my own union and you want me to go talking to the Vietnamese?"

"That's exactly how you can get back to running your union," I said. "I told you if you'd listen for a minute. I've made inquiries. I've been advised that an exploratory meeting might be arranged."

"You've been advised?" Hoffa snorted. "Yeah—by someone just as crazy as you are. The whole idea is off the wall. The

Vietnam war and me. Jesus, it's ridiculous."

I realized Hoffa had no concept of his role in the eyes of people outside the United States. What I did not realize was the extent of his defensiveness and feelings of inferiority. Jimmy Hoffa had ruthlessly carved his place in American labor, but he had no confidence in himself beyond the borders of his own direct power. In addition, the jail term and his tenuous grip on union affairs had shaken his normal dogged determination. Hoffa was operating much of the time on bravado.

"There's no damn reason why you can't just go to Nixon and tell him I want the conditions taken off. It's as simple as that," he said.

"If you think it's that simple, then you go to him yourself," I snapped. "I'll just forget about the whole business. I'll forget about Dorfman too if you like."

I walked out of his apartment and took the next plane to New York, terribly disappointed. I had not anticipated Hoffa's reaction. He was unable to see himself in any role but ruler of the Teamsters Union. I decided to wait and let time work on his ego. Knowing him, I was sure he would not be able to leave the idea alone now that it had been presented to him.

The days went by with no word from Jimmy Hoffa. Then a close friend of his called. "Jimmy wants to know if you're angry with him," he said.

"I'd say the answer is yes. If I take my time and get other important people to help me help Jimmy, I expect a better reception than I got. He may disagree with me, but I don't think I deserve to be told I belong in a nuthouse. If that's his evaluation of the guy who produced forty-five million dollars in bonds at the last minute to save his neck, of the guy who got him out of prison, then I don't want to waste his time and I don't want him wasting mine."

The message obviously got back to Hoffa because he telephoned me at home that night. He was downright obsequious, although he still maintained that my idea was preposterous. Finally he retreated enough to say, "If you think the idea's got any chance, hell—go ahead. Maybe I'm the one who's nuts."

It was as close to an apology as I ever received from Jimmy Hoffa, and I chose not to argue further. There would be more appropriate times to explain and convince. Not more than ten days after his apology call, a cable arrived from Claire Jourdan. It read: MR. HOFFA WILL PROBABLY BE REACHED THROUGH TEAMSTERS.

The North Vietnamese and their supporters had decided to explore the possibilities. It was imperative that I inform Hoffa of the full implications of the plan. Going to Miami had become as commonplace as crossing the street, and once again I found myself in Hoffa's apartment. This time I insisted on more than a brief meeting. I stayed in Miami for almost a week, meeting with Hoffa every day. We talked about the role of labor in China, North Vietnam, and most of the Eastern bloc countries. I delivered lectures on Marxist philosophy and politics. Hoffa, while quick-minded, had always been too busy struggling for power in his own world to take the time to understand the role of labor under Communist regimes or to comprehend his own image in other countries.

The meetings were productive and sobering. Slowly he began to realize the possible results of the plan. For the first time his thinking became more positive. "I still don't believe a damn thing will happen," he said, "but I'm sure you know what you're doing."

I felt a tremendous relief. Hoffa's deep feelings of inadequacy, a major and unexpected hurdle, had been overcome. Now he was at least facing in the right direction. Dorfman's appeal was proceeding well, and Hoffa had begun to feel more confident about everything. I had been making so many trips to and from Miami that I took his suggestion and rented a furnished apartment for a prolonged stay, making Miami my base for the Hoffa undertaking. I also hoped to get some rest and sunshine between those daily 8:30 meetings, which had felt like going to school even before my lecture series began. Instead of rest and sunshine, however, I ended up living in the air.

I received word from Claire Jourdan that a meeting with the North Vietnamese delegation in Paris had been scheduled. The Deputy Minister of Foreign Affairs of North Vietnam, Xoang An Lo, had confirmed it, and the delegation wanted me to give them a date for the meeting at the North Vietnamese Embassy in Paris. I sent Claire Jourdan several dates, and in a few days a time for our meeting was confirmed all around.

As I was due to go to Geneva to see Jean François, and to

Athens to attend to Dr. Patronikolas's financial headaches, I scheduled these trips around the meeting with the Vietnamese. Since the necessity for the utmost secrecy had been emphasized, I decided I wouldn't even let Hoffa know until the very last minute. Then, as I was making preparations for the meeting, I suddenly realized I had not given any thought to my own legal position. The United States was in a state of undeclared war. What laws applied, or did not apply, to the act of an individual citizen dealing with the government of a nation with which we were in combat?

Beset with an attack of second thoughts because I did not have an answer, I was unable to discuss my problem with any of the people I knew who might provide one. There was only one man I felt I could go to, and that was General Lucius Clay. I made an appointment with him at Lehman Brothers, New York, where he had replaced Robert Lehman as chairman of the board. I told him why I had come and the need for absolute secrecy.

"What you're doing has plenty of precedent," he assured me. "Offhand, I can think of several examples. William Samuel Johnson and Ben Franklin went to the English as special emissaries of Pennsylvania and Connecticut during the time the colonies were trying to unify.

"And of course there are countless examples of industries negotiating with other countries, like the fur trades, the railroads, mining interests—I'd say you're doing nothing unusual, provided no national secrets are being revealed. In fact, history proves the objectives of these private envoys nearly always paralleled the national interest."

He went on to offer me more than advice. "I'm very much opposed to our being in Vietnam. If there is even a remote chance that a meeting with the North Vietnamese will help shorten the war or help save American prisoners, I am prepared to give you all the help at my command."

I received more encouragement less than twenty-four hours later in the form of a phone call from the Vatican. The letter I had sent had been shown to His Holiness, and my caller said, "We wish you luck." Now I had the backing, as yet unofficial, of the Vatican.

When I went to Hoffa with the news, he was awed by the

increasing scope of the affair. Again I impressed upon him the need for secrecy. Then, with a letter of authorization from Hoffa in hand, I left for my meeting with the North Vietnamese. I first flew to Athens to meet Dr. Patronikolas regarding his business problems, but especially to be fortified by his thoughts on the impending meeting. After a day spent with him, I went to dinner with some old friends in Athens where I ran into Achilles Vlachopoulos. He approached our table and asked to speak to me privately. Although surprised, I was not really annoyed by his temerity. Achilles had often come into my thoughts since the kidnap-murder attempt, and after having read all the depositions, I had concluded he had not really plotted against my life. He had been drawn into the plot, true, but he tried to back out. It was fear that had kept him silent, I had deduced, as had the Greek authorities, who had given him a provisional release.

I also remembered his frightened attempt to warn me that day in Athens when I left to meet my would-be murderers in Switzerland. For a long time I had felt it was possible Achilles had been wronged, and I hadn't forgotten his valuable assistance when I was trying to get Theodorakis released. Therefore I was willing to talk to him privately that evening. He told me almost tearfully how badly things were going for him in Greece since he had gotten involved in the Theodorakis business. He had been out of work since his release from prison, and was desperate for money. He was no longer welcome at Olympic Airways and had given up on his show business career. He just wanted to find a job, any kind of job. "You know people all over the world," he said. "Maybe you can find someone who could use me."

When Vlachopoulos had stayed with me in Miami he had handled callers with charm and efficiency. I desperately needed an assistant, so I asked him to work for me. He was wildly grateful, and I told him to get in touch with me when I returned to America and I would see about bringing him to Florida.

When I told my dinner companions what I had done, they called me everything from softhearted to stupid. But I felt I had been a party to the harsh treatment Vlachopoulos had endured, and I felt sorry for him. I couldn't forget that he had warned me I was in danger at a time when he was obviously terrified for his own safety.

On June 11, 1972, I went to the Paris suburb of Choisy-le-Roi, where the North Vietnamese Embassy was located, surrounded by a hundred armed French police and twelve police cars. I was ushered into a living room with an Oriental motif where two members of the Vietnamese delegation greeted me. They were Xuan Thuy and Nguyen Mai, the chief negotiator in Paris. Both had been well briefed. They had seen *Mao's China* in Paris and asked me how I had managed to have the film shown at the White House before Nixon went to China.

"It would be good for Americans to see a film of North Vietnam," one of them said, and I understood his meaning, for North Vietnam was then under heavy American bombing.

More importantly, they knew who Hoffa was and knew he had recently been released from prison. The prospect of Hoffa meeting with Le Duc Tho, the head of the North Vietnamese delegation, was already a probability to them. However, when Nguyen Mai asked me about Hoffa's role at such a meeting, I understood his implication. He was concerned that Hoffa might be used as a propaganda tool by the United States. I chose my words carefully.

"I see Mr. Hoffa as a kind of bridge between two camps," I said. "He would come representing the hopes of people everywhere and not the policy of any government."

Nguyen Mai nodded slowly. My answer seemed to satisfy him. "Perhaps Mr. Hoffa should come to Hanoi for a personal visit. If someone such as Mr. Hoffa, a representative of labor and the common working man, were to see the devastation that has been caused in our country, it would help to make the world see how unjust Mr. Nixon and Mr. Kissinger are in continuing their prosecution of the war."

I backed away from being drawn down that path. "If an invitation were issued to Mr. Hoffa, there would be many beneficial results for the Vietnamese as well as the American people, I'm sure," I said.

"I don't know if such an invitation would be possible because of the practical problems. We can't guarantee the safety of visitors, for our country is at war," Nguyen Mai said. "We should, of course, like to arrange for a visit. However, as this is an exploratory meeting, our only authority is to transmit to Hanoi the results of our discussion. Le Duc Tho is arriving later this week. How long will you be in Paris?"

"I came especially for this meeting, to offer Mr. Hoffa's skills as a negotiator and his reputation as a labor leader in the service of peace and justice," I said. "I am prepared to stay as long as necessary."

"Very good," he remarked. "Please give us a little more time and we will contact you here in Paris."

As a preliminary discussion, the meeting exceeded my expectations. The North Vietnamese were eager to find a way to end the war while maintaining face, just as Dr. Patronikolas had maintained.

Things happened very fast. The next morning I received word to meet Le Duc Tho at three that afternoon. I had a quick briefing with Claire Jourdan and then went straight to the embassy. This time I decided to look like a statesman and hired a limousine. I was shown into the same room by Nguyen Mai and Xuan Thuy, but when Le Duc Tho entered, they vanished, and I was left alone with North Vietnam's top spokesman in Paris.

Speaking English with a faintly British accent, Le Duc Tho immediately launched into a tirade about the war. Perhaps it was his standard introduction, a form of staking out his position, although I did not doubt he passionately believed the things he said: Nixon was a ruthless barbarian, Kissinger was the new Hitler, and they were both utterly untrustworthy negotiators. He claimed there was no cause for the war, that the havoc inflicted upon his people was inhuman, that we talked about religion but didn't practice it. I attempted no reply. When he finished, he seemed to relax. In a conversational tone he asked questions about Hoffa and his willingness to take part in earnest discussions. He also asked about the official position of the United States on our mission.

I reminded him that the American authorities were not aware of my meetings with his delegation. He pressed me for an opinion, and I had to confess I didn't know. He thought about that for a moment, then continued.

"Because labor is the strength of the Vietnamese people, it would be fitting for Mr. Hoffa to take part in these discussions."

"I think Mr. Hoffa will come prepared with specific proposals," I ventured.

"That would be welcome. As you were told yesterday, the suggestions are being transmitted to Hanoi. You will probably hear directly from Hanoi, although I cannot hold out a great deal of hope. Conditions in my homeland are very bad. But let us hope for the best."

Le Duc Tho was most cordial and we shook hands warmly when I left. His conversation had been a curious mixture of political harangue, intense interest, quasi-invitation, and retreat, but when I told Claire Jourdan and Dr. Patronikolas what he had said, both felt the leaders in Hanoi would agree to meet with Hoffa. I was unabashedly excited.

Walking around New York the next day, my urge to buttonhole anyone, even strangers, and tell them what had happened was almost overwhelming. I did call Hoffa to tell him things had gone extremely well, and promised a full report in person.

Among my phone messages was a call from Clark MacGregor at the White House. I had learned that John Mitchell had resigned as Attorney General and now headed the Committee to Reelect the President and that Maurice Stans was chairman of the Finance Committee. When I called Clark MacGregor, he asked me to meet with Stans and Mitchell.

I could take an educated guess at what the meeting would be about. First I called Hoffa to get his views. "Go ahead and see what they want," he said. Therefore, I agreed to meet Stans and Mitchell at the headquarters of the National Finance Committee.

Before I left for Washington, however, I visited General Clay at his offices at Lehman Brothers. He was almost as excited as I was about my meeting with the North Vietnamese. "I'd say a substantial breakthrough has been made," he said, and again he cautioned me about secrecy, and that included his own involvement. Not even Hoffa was to know. "I think I can help you more behind the scenes," he said.

When I arrived at 1701 Pennsylvania Avenue, I was met not by Stans or Mitchell but by a man named Thomas Pappas. I'd once had some telephone conversations with him in Athens. His family was in partnership with Spyros Skouras at 20th Century–Fox, and he had sought me out in Athens to try to buy the hotels owned by Dr. Patronikolas. Later Pappas became heavily involved in CIA activities in Greece. He told me Stans and Mitchell had been called out of town and he would talk to me instead. I agreed. A man then came into our meeting who introduced himself as Ken Talmadge, part of the Nixon reelection committee.

Pappas was overly friendly, in fact irritating in his effusiveness. "How's Jimmy?" he said. "Jimmy and I are old friends, you know. How's he getting on these days?"

My reply was bland. Pappas continued to insist he knew Hoffa well and then he said, "I'd like to phone the fella right now. Do you want to dial or shall I? He's in Detroit, isn't he?"

"No, he's in Miami."

"I don't have the Miami number with me. Why don't you give it to me?"

"I'm sorry, I never give out Mr. Hoffa's number without his permission."

Pappas tried to convince me it was all right to give it to him, but finally he gave up on that approach. "Ken and I are handling campaign contributions in the absence of Mr. Stans and Mr. Mitchell," he said. "It's been decided it would be appropriate for you to ask Jimmy to contribute a hundred thousand dollars."

"You're talking to the wrong man," I said. "I don't represent Mr. Hoffa in that capacity." Before I could count to two, Pappas got aggressive.

"Who do you think you're fooling? Aren't you the one who got him released from prison?"

"I don't discuss Mr. Hoffa's affairs with anyone," I said.

He tried again to get Hoffa's phone number and became more hostile when I again refused. Then I closed up my briefcase and said, "Gentlemen, I have nothing further to say. I'd like to use your telephone to call Clark MacGregor at the White House."

"You'll have to use an outside phone," Pappas said.

I left forthwith. That night I found three messages from Hoffa at my Miami apartment. I was exhausted, but I called him.

"What did they want?" he said.

"Your phone number and a hundred thousand dollars." There was a long silence at the other end of the phone. "I met a man named Pappas who said you and he were bosom buddies, but I didn't give him your number."

"I know him," he said dryly. "All right, I'll talk to the guy myself. When I'm ready."

"That's just fine with me," I said and dropped the matter. I knew how difficult it would be to pry a hundred thousand dollars out of Jimmy Hoffa. After a sound night's sleep, I met him in the morning, and for the first time he was enthusiastic about our plan. However, his innate distrust and pessimism soon surfaced.

"Maybe the Vietnamese will come through," he said. "But how the hell can I do anything about it if they do? You're such a smart guy, you tell me how you're going to get the parole board and those bastards at the Department of Justice to let me go anywhere to do anything? You need a passport, you know. Jesus, I can't go anywhere except Miami to Detroit, Detroit to Miami. Senator Scott's been trying to get me permission to get as far as New York for three months and he can't get it, so you tell me how I'm going to get to Hanoi."

"That's my problem, Jimmy. Let me worry about it." The truth was, I hadn't decided how to tackle that problem.

Achilles Vlachopoulos arrived in Miami shortly after I saw Hoffa, and I acquainted him with what I expected of him. During that time a phone call came to my New York apartment from Geneva, the message garbled by the answering service. It took the better part of two days to unravel it, and when I did, I called Geneva at once.

My caller was a personal friend, a member of the royal family of one of the Middle East petroleum-producing countries. He was also, I discovered, a friend of Madame Mao Tse-tung. He told me I must meet him at once in an out-of-the-way place where his presence would not attract attention, for he had confidential messages to be delivered in person. We agreed on the Phoenicia Hotel in Beirut, which was then off the beaten path, and I left at once, telling no one anything.

If I had had any doubts about dropping everything and flying to Beirut, they were quickly dispelled. "I have been instructed to tell you that Madame Mao Tse-tung was made aware of your initial meeting with Le Duc Tho as soon as it had taken place," my friend said. "Since your meeting she has had fresh contacts with the North Vietnamese. An invitation will be forthcoming to you and Mr. Hoffa."

There was another message, from my "good friend Dorothy Ho-chan," as the royal gentleman put it. "Do you remember that mission she spoke to you about concerning applications and other such forms?"

"Yes, I certainly do."

"Well, as a result of your President's trip to China this year, she says you can withdraw the applications you made."

I gave a low whistle. I knew what the mission meant. It meant GOLD, but I was uncertain how much my informant actually knew, and asked no questions. Quite frankly, I was too excited about the message from Madame Mao to give a damn about Dorothy and the gold.

Back in New York I visited again with General Clay. I did not mention Madame Mao by name, but I did tell him it seemed most likely now that Hoffa would be invited to meet with the North Vietnamese. General Clay said, "If you ever need me to make a statement, I'll be glad to say I advised you during these initial stages." He was hopeful, very hopeful, and so was I.

In Miami, Hoffa was downright excited. He had a great belief in himself. It was one of his primary attributes, and I had been counting heavily on it all along. Now I had to worry that in his regained confidence he would talk too much. "Jimmy," I reminded him, "not a word about this to anyone."

At my apartment Vlachopoulos gave me a list of White House callers, among them Steve Bull, Dwight Chapin, and Maurice Stans. There was pressure on me, it seemed, to take a fund-raising role in Richard Nixon's reelection campaign. I kept my distance. I didn't want to be anywhere near the Washington circuit at this crucial time, for one wrong word, one error, could torpedo all that had been done so far for Hoffa.

Besides, I found myself involved in a new crisis with Hoffa. He had begun to sour on Allen Dorfman who, he had discovered, might be in even bigger trouble than Hoffa had thought. He even hinted broadly that I should stop my efforts in Dorfman's behalf. Knowing Hoffa's mercurial moods, I decided to take three days' rest in Miami to see if he would cool down.

Instead, he heated up. Hoffa called me from Detroit, his

voice shaking with fury. "Something's come up. I want you here at eleven tomorrow morning."

It was never "Could you?" or "Is it possible?" Just "Be here." I'd had enough. "Jimmy," I said, "I've been flying all over hell for you. Whatever is going on in Detroit can go on without me."

"Don't give me any of that shit. I need you here. I'm going to throw the book at Dorfman and I want you here to listen to it so you can know how to cut his head off. Eleven o'clock."

He hung up on me as usual, and I knew calling back and arguing would be useless. I had to go. With Hoffa in this kind of mood, there was no way of knowing what would come spilling out of him. I could see him telling everything about the Hanoi talks to show Dorfman he was the big shot and didn't need him. That was precisely what had to be avoided.

When I reached Hoffa's offices in Detroit a few minutes before eleven the following day, I found him still on the warpath. Bit by bit he had been finding out all about the huge sums that had been drawn from the pension fund while he was in prison. Dorfman and Nick Tweel arrived and Hoffa shut the door. Then the accusations and denials started to fly and I felt very uncomfortable.

Tweel interrupted. "Jimmy, what's this got to do with Bill? Why don't the three of us go into another office and have this out and Bill can wait here?"

Hoffa reluctantly agreed. Before he left, I took him aside. "Whatever you say in there, no matter how mad you get, keep your mouth shut about Vietnam. If you don't, you'll blow everything to hell and gone."

"All right, all right," he muttered after a moment. He went into the other room and I waited for two hours. Finally they came out, a silent and stony-faced trio. Hoffa assured me he had kept quiet about Vietnam. Dorfman returned to Chicago, Tweel to New York, and I went back to Miami, feeling I had wasted the day. When I reached my apartment, Dorfman had already phoned. He wanted to see me. It was urgent.

"You have your own plane, so why don't you fly down here?" I said. The idea didn't appeal to him. Obviously he feared Hoffa might see him there, and he plainly wanted to keep away from Hoffa for the moment.

"Let me think about a place. I'll be in touch," he said.

I went to bed, exhausted. I didn't hear from Dorfman during the following two days, but I did have numerous meetings with Hoffa. At one of them he complained Harold Gibbons was having a lot of trouble in St. Louis. Gibbons was a vice president and one of the members of the old guard.

"He's really having a hard time," Hoffa told me. "I think you ought to go to St. Louis and see him."

"I'm spending half my life in the air," I complained. "Let Harold come here to see me."

"His back went out on him yesterday. Be a good pal and go see Harold."

I agreed. Hoffa couldn't go to St. Louis under his parole restrictions and at least he was paying me for services rendered. Gibbons and I talked about the confidential matters Hoffa wanted discussed in person, and then I decided to call on Allen Dorfman because I was curious why he had never got back to me about a meeting place. Dorfman got excited the moment he heard my voice. "When can you get here?" he said.

I flew to Chicago that afternoon. Dorfman had a car waiting at the airport to drive me to his offices. There I found him and Nicholas Tweel. Dorfman insisted on taking us out to dinner. In the limousine it became clear Dorfman was on the verge of breaking down. As we approached the restaurant, he began to cry.

"After all I've done for Hoffa, getting convicted, fighting for my life—he's got no right to do these things to me," he sobbed. "He's trying to get you to stop helping me and I know it. He's trying to put me where he used to be. Well, don't pay any attention to him. If you stick with me, you'll never have to worry about a thing for the rest of your life."

"I don't know what's prompted all this," I said. "Whatever hell Jimmy is raising is something you ought to settle between yourselves. So far the appeal is doing well and it will go through as planned."

Dorfman calmed down, and over dinner he brightened up considerably. He didn't mention Hoffa again.

I had hardly been back in Miami an hour before Hoffa was on the telephone. "So you had dinner in Chicago with Dorfman, huh? You and Tweel?"

I didn't reply.

"We'll talk tomorrow morning. Be here at seven."

"What's going to happen at seven that can't happen at eight?" I said.

I compromised and arrived the next morning at 7:30. Hoffa was in a poisonous mood.

"All right, what did he want with you?"

"To convince me not to desert him. He's upset."

"Son of a bitch, he'll be a lot more upset when I'm finished with him. What else did he say?"

"Nothing I'd listen to. I told him I didn't want to get involved in these Teamster fights."

Hoffa picked up the phone and handed it to me. "Call Dorfman," he said.

"Jimmy, it's six thirty in the morning in Chicago."

"Call him. Tell him he's going to jail."

"I will not do that."

Hoffa gave me a vicious look and dialed the phone himself, getting Dorfman out of bed. Then he handed the receiver to me, pushing it into my chest. "Go on, tell him," he said.

"Allen, I don't know what to say to you. I don't know what's going on here except that Jimmy's mad as hell," I said.

Hoffa grabbed the phone from me and began to shout at Dorfman for seeing me behind his back. He ran down a list of things Dorfman had done in connection with the pension fund. "I put you where you are today, Dorfman, and I can tear you down just as fast." He slammed the receiver down, satisfied with himself. The gap between Hoffa and Dorfman was now a chasm.

I left Hoffa's apartment and a few hours later received a call from Harold Gibbons. He was acting rather odd. "I think you'd better come to St. Louis right away," he said. "There's something here I'd like you to see." I heaved a large sigh and headed for the airport.

"This just came,"said Gibbons, handing me a cablegram in the airport coffee shop in St. Louis. "What in God's name does it mean?" I stared at the piece of paper he handed me and felt the excitement rising in my throat. Slowly I read:

URGENT—HANOI—URGENT
HAROLD GIBBONS
300 S. GRAND AVE.
ST. LOUIS MISSOURI, USA
GLADLY INVITE JAMES HOFFA, HAROLD GIBBONS AND WILLIAM
TAUB FOR ONE WEEK VISIT—STOP—ARRIVAL HANOI JULY FIRST
OR FOURTH DESIRABLE—STOP—VISAS MAY BE OBTAINED IN VI-
ENTIANE OR PARIS—STOP
HOANG QUOC
PRESIDENT, VIETNAM TRADE UNIONS

It had come. I turned to Gibbons, aware of his confusion. Because Hoffa didn't want Frank Fitzsimmons to find out what was going on, the cablegram had gone to St. Louis rather than Washington. Moreover, Gibbons had once visited Vietnam with a labor delegation and was highly regarded there. I told Gibbons as much as Hoffa wanted him to know, and he listened in open-mouthed astonishment.

"Did anybody else in your office see this?" I said.

Gibbons shook his head. "It came directly to me and I opened it myself."

"Good. Keep it quiet." Total secrecy would be difficult to maintain from now on, I realized. Clutching the wire, I went to a phone booth and called Hoffa in Detroit and read the cablegram to him.

"I never believed it would happen," he whispered. "I just never really believed it. Let me talk to Harold."

Gibbons had a private plane at his disposal and Hoffa had him send me to Detroit. "I've got to see the cablegram for myself," he said. A few hours later I was in the Hoffa living room where he and Mrs. Hoffa read the cablegram, still in awe over what was going to happen.

From St. Louis Harold Gibbons sent an acceptance and gave dates when we would arrive to pick up the visas. In New York I shared the good news with General Clay. Something was starting to happen to me. While my original motivation remained, I was beginning to experience some unexpected emotions that had nothing to do with getting the conditions of Hoffa's pardon removed. A real possibility of finding a formula for prisoner exchanges and breaking the deadlock at the peace talks had emerged, and these goals now seemed predominant.

Two days later Claire Jourdan telephoned. Le Duc Tho wanted another private meeting with me before Hoffa went to Hanoi. I put everything else aside and prepared to go to Paris. Hoffa, however, had other priorities. He wanted me in Detroit.

"I have to go to Paris," I pleaded.

"You gotta come to Detroit first. You've got time."

"Not if I don't make my flight," I said.

"So they'll see you the next day if you're not there."

"That's not the way things work, Jimmy. Damnit, it's for you I'm going."

"Well, this is for me too," he snapped.

I went to Detroit. That night he spread a sheaf of papers in front of me. They dealt with Teamster pension fund loans.

"Just look at these, will you?" Hoffa said, and I quickly went over the documents, which were mostly loan approvals for real estate transactions in Las Vegas.

"You know who approved all these loans? Allen Dorfman did it. And he never cleared any of this with me. Not a goddamn word."

"What do you want me to do about it, Jimmy?"

"I just wanted you to see this," he said. "I want you to know that I'm not just imagining things. I told you there's so goddamn much of this stuff out there it's leaking out of the woodwork."

"The best thing I can do is go to Paris," I reminded him. "Your only hope is there."

Grim-faced, Hoffa put the papers into a briefcase and finally let me go. I was delayed at Kennedy Airport and when I rushed to Claire Jourdan's office in Paris, I was too late.

"Le Duc Tho had to go to Bulgaria," she said. "He wants you to telephone the delegation at once."

"Can you come to the embassy?" a spokesman there asked me. "We have private instructions from Le Duc Tho that can be given to you only in person, as they are highly confidential. Those are our orders."

Again I hired a car and chauffeur and drove to the embassy at Choisy-le-Roi. The member of the delegation who had spoken to me apologized for the absence of the top officials.

"They have accompanied Mr. Le Duc Tho," he said, "and he sends his regrets that he could not wait for you. However, he does very much want to meet you and has left word he will be in Sofia and hopes to meet you there. Please advise us if you can go to Sofia."

I hesitated. I had never been to Bulgaria and it was well behind the Iron Curtain. "I'll advise you within the hour," I said and drove at once to Claire Jourdan's office.

I was very apprehensive about going to Bulgaria. I was on a very private mission, representing no one in my government, and had no official status of any kind. Save for perhaps three people, no one knew my whereabouts, and I was suddenly aware how vulnerable I was. I asked Claire whether she would go with me to Bulgaria. "I can't possibly take the time," she said, "but I do feel you should go. I'll send word to my friend Maria Panova that you're coming. She will receive you as the Minister of Justice and my friend. I'm sure you will enjoy Sofia."

With those words of encouragement, but still not able to shake my apprehension entirely, I left for Sofia. When the plane landed there, Stephen Nedeltchev and Playmen Voynovsky, representatives from the Central Council of Trade Unions of Bulgaria, greeted me warmly. I was driven to the very modern Hotel Sofia where I was put up in a suite with fresh flowers in each large room, which I learned had been placed there by Maria Panova.

"Le Duc Tho is at a meeting that could last for some time," Voynovsky said, "but he will be in touch with you as soon as the meeting is over. This is our most important convention, you see."

The Convention of the International Labor Conference was in session in Sofia, dedicated to the ninetieth anniversary of the birth of Georgi Dimitrov, World War II hero and former Prime Minister of Bulgaria.

"If you would like to attend tomorrow's session," he continued, "we will gladly arrange for you to be there. Perhaps you would like to address the convention in the name of Mr. Hoffa."

I expressed my appreciation but quickly declined. I was certainly not prepared to enter the Communist arena. I quickly gathered as much information about the convention as I could, and spent the next few hours reading all that was available in

English. The convention was an international gathering attended by over one hundred delegates representing every country in existence. Most of the delegates were associated with Communist parties throughout the world, but others represented less parochial organizations such as the World Peace Council and the International Federation of Women.

Most of the delegates from the Communist labor groups were unknown in the West, yet they had come to Bulgaria to honor a man who had been imprisoned by the Nazis. Many of the delegates were also familiar with the inside of prisons. I began to see why Hoffa would be welcome. He shared these people's prison experience, and his conviction by an imperialist government could easily pass for martyrdom with them.

Since Hoffa was welcome, so was I, his representative. As I immersed myself in the unfamiliar doctrines in my hotel room behind the Iron Curtain, my nebulous plans for Jimmy Hoffa began to clarify. Jimmy would act in behalf of the American prisoners of war, a group no one had been able to help, not the President of the United States, not Henry Kissinger, not all the lesser emissaries with their cautious proposals. All these petitioners had been tainted by their politics. Jimmy, on the other hand, was a symbol of the working people of the world. He would not come to talk *quid pro quo* but to free American war prisoners in the name of humanity.

By the time Nedeltchev and Voynovsky returned that evening, my plan was firm. They told me Le Duc Tho was staying at the Hotel Rilla in Sofia and would see me at eleven o'clock the next morning. I bid them good night and went to bed, knowing precisely what I would say to Le Duc Tho.

A car arrived the next morning and I was driven to the Hotel Rilla. Le Duc Tho had been delayed and arrived at 11:30, inviting me to lunch with him and other Vietnamese delegates. It was a relaxed and pleasant gathering. He told me he had to return home that night, flying first to Moscow and then on to North Vietnam, and he invited me to go with him at least as far as Moscow.

I thanked him but declined, having no visa for Moscow. "That is no hindrance," he said. "I can arrange that." Still, I decided against the trip, and Le Duc Tho and I went into another room for a private meeting. I proposed that Mr. Hoffa's visit to Hanoi should result in a concrete humanitarian gesture: the release of American POW's. Le Duc Tho listened impassively, watching my eyes. There was a moment when I wondered whether he himself had entertained the same thought. If he had, we had come to very different conclusions.

"Such a gesture," I said, "would show the world the North Vietnamese leadership is interested in cooperation and in human lives. It would be an act neither the American people nor the world could ignore."

"How many?"

"Twenty-five," I said, holding my breath.

"One," he countered. "A symbolic gesture."

"More than a symbolic gesture. A real gesture, a meaningful one. One that will show a formula for future releases."

"Twenty-five would not be possible," he said. "Six might perhaps be arranged."

"I think Mr. Hoffa would find six to be almost as meaningless as one. For a man of his reputation to bring back only six prisoners would be demeaning."

Le Duc Tho was silent. "I will have to let you know," he said at last. "Where can you be reached?"

"I'll be in Rome, at the Excelsior Hotel."

"You will hear from me, or from a representative," he said, rising to signal the end of our meeting.

That day, after Le Duc Tho had gone, Nedeltchev extended an invitation to Hoffa, through me, to be an honored speaker at the labor convention the following year.

I telephoned the Vatican that evening. When my friend there heard where I was, he quickly realized I had something of unusual importance to tell him, and we agreed to meet at Rome's Leonardo da Vinci Airport.

The next morning he drove me from the airport to the Excelsior Hotel. He had already communicated with the Vatican secretary of state and everyone was waiting to hear what I had to tell them. I recounted all that had happened in Bulgaria. When the meeting ended, my good friend insisted I spend the weekend at his country place, and I agreed. The next morning he drove me to a lovely house in the Roman countryside, and we had a charming alfresco lunch. It was a little past noon when the telephone rang. To my astonishment, I was told that the Hoffa invitation to Hanoi had been brought to the attention of Pope Paul, who wanted all the details submitted in a letter by nine o'clock the following morning.

I had my friend rush me back to Rome where I managed to get hold of a secretary (no easy task there on a Sunday) and composed for His Holiness a letter covering every detail, including the agreement on the prisoners of war. The final item in the letter was a request that the Pope receive Mr. Hoffa.

A reply came back. The Pope would receive Hoffa and give his official approval to the mission. I was elated. Within a day, I received a telegram from Bulgaria instructing me to go to Paris for still another meeting with the North Vietnamese delegation.

I flew to Paris and met Nguyen Mai at the embassy. He presented me a letter to take to Hoffa. It read:

Today we have met with Mr. William Taub. Mr. Taub told us your suggestion on your trip to Hanoi. We will submit it to the Vietnam Trade Union in Hanoi for consideration. Due to the conditions of war, all trips to Hanoi suggested by our friends must be carefully considered for security reasons. We will inform you as soon as we receive the reply from Hanoi.

With best regards,
Nguyen Mai

The letter was a formality, most likely intended to satisfy the Vietnamese sense of propriety, for the cablegram inviting Hoffa to Hanoi had already been received and answered. Le Duc Tho's vital message was not in the letter. This was approval for Hoffa to bring back twelve prisoners of war. I felt this was as much of a compromise as I could expect in view of the original gap of twenty-four. It was, after all, twelve more than anyone else had brought home.

Much later I learned of the very large role Madame Mao Tse-tung had played in the decision of the North Vietnamese. With her characteristic long-distance view, she wanted the war ended, for it interfered with her own plans for United States–Chinese relations.

As the plane headed toward Kennedy Airport, I couldn't help feeling proud and deeply satisfied. My satisfaction transcended my own role and Hoffa's dilemma. I was about to embark on a mission that might result in breaking the stalemate.

At the very least, it would bring a dozen Americans home.

I slept later than I had intended the next day, and once again Achilles proved his value to me. He had every message ready for me in order of importance to scan and act upon. By afternoon I was beginning to appreciate the magnitude of the problems that remained. Chief among them was getting Jimmy Hoffa out of the country. Time was an enormous factor now that dates had been agreed upon.

Secrecy was no longer possible, I realized, nor was the need for it so vital now. I still didn't know how much Washington had learned. I consulted with General Clay, and he felt it was time to contact the President. Although I knew it would take extraordinary measures to get Hoffa out of the United States, I was apprehensive about going to the White House. Perhaps it was because I'd done so well on my own. Or perhaps it was because I had an undefined foreboding. Any reasonable person could only applaud what had been set in motion, I felt, yet I was worried.

A full "cabinet meeting" of the Hoffa camp was held in Detroit. Tweel, Dorfman, and Gibbons all flew in in their own jets. Hoffa's son James Jr. was there too, along with me. After too much discussion it was decided Henry Kissinger was the man to contact. Gibbons was the only one who knew him, and he called the White House. The call did not go through, we debated some more, and the consensus was that I should call General Clay to rouse Mr. Kissinger. The general was out to lunch, but Hoffa said no one could leave the meeting until General Clay had been reached.

He ordered lunch sent in from a nearby food shop—the usual sandwiches and coffee. It was the first time I had seen Hoffa dip into his pocket to buy anything for anyone. As we were finishing lunch, Clay returned my call. I told him what was happening and he said he'd do his best to reach Kissinger. He did. In a few moments the phone rang again and it was Henry Kissinger, asking to talk to Gibbons. I sat back with the others and listened as Gibbons answered a lot of questions.

"Mr. Hoffa is being represented in this by Bill Taub," Gibbons said, beckoning me to the telephone. "I'll introduce you to him now." As he handed me the phone, I heard Kissinger say, "I know all about Mr. Taub and what he's been doing."

Kissinger and I exchanged courtesies, and I asked him whether I could meet with him at once, that very day if possible.

"I'm leaving with the President within the hour for San Clemente. There is no way I could see you today, and the July fourth weekend is almost upon us. The first time I can see you would be Wednesday, the fifth, in San Clemente."

Having just returned from flying the Atlantic twice, as well as back and forth across half of Europe, the idea of another three thousand miles in the air was far from appealing. But I knew I had to go. We agreed that Harold Gibbons and I would go to San Clemente.

The meeting ended and I returned to Miami where Vlachopoulos had a list of callers who offered congratulations and asked questions. The startling news was traveling fast via Washington grapevine.

As the date for the San Clemente meeting had ended the possibility of Hoffa going to Hanoi over the Fourth of July, I sent a cable informing the North Vietnamese of the postponement and suggested a date some ten days later.

Harold Gibbons and I drove to San Clemente on July 5, and went through the elaborate security business that made visiting the President of the United States seem like an occasion of far greater moment than an audience with the Pope, the Queen of England, or even the powers that rule beyond the grave. Henry Kissinger greeted us, his arms open wide, and gave me a big kiss on both cheeks and then did the same to Gibbons.

"Come right in," he said. "I'll order coffee and toast." The only thing lacking was the brass band. He ushered us inside and then excused himself. A boy and girl came up and introduced themselves as Kissinger's children. Then Kissinger reappeared and said, "Someone has arrived unexpectedly to see the President. Why don't we go into my office and start the meeting without him. We'll join him soon."

We settled ourselves in his office and he said pleasantly, "It seems you're doing some of the things I'm supposed to be doing."

"Not that I know of," I said. "I represent Mr. Hoffa. Do you?"

He gave me a sly half-smile. My remark had knocked him off base a little. "On the contrary, Mr. Taub," he said. "I represent the President of the United States. I have had a good many meetings with the North Vietnamese, and in all those times the name of James Hoffa has never come up. Who did actually ask Mr. Hoffa to Hanoi?"

I had anticipated such a question, and brought out a slim white booklet that contained all the pertinent documents. I showed him the telegram from the Vietnam Trade Union inviting Hoffa. I presented the letters from Nguyen Mai, the cable from Nedeltchev, and a synopsis of the brief I had prepared for His Holiness. Kissinger looked carefully at each document. Then his intercom buzzed. It would continue to buzz every three minutes or so until we were called into Nixon's office. Kissinger said a few words into the phone and then continued, "What I fail to understand, and perhaps you can illuminate me, is why did the Vietnamese pick Mr. Hoffa? Why didn't they pick the President or myself or any number of other people who would have been more appropriate?"

"Because there's only one James Hoffa," I said.

"You seem to back up Mr. Hoffa very much."

"That's correct. That's why Mr. Nixon released him from prison." That floored him. Fortunately for him, Nixon was on the intercom again.

"I think your idea is the best one I've heard," Kissinger said, after dispensing with Nixon's call with a few inaudible words. "There's one major problem, however, and that is the timetable. A visit by a man of Mr. Hoffa's prominence right now would cause very much comment in the press and might possibly jeopardize the peace talks that are imminent."

"Mr. Kissinger, I must object. I don't think even Congress would deny him the right to go as soon as possible. In fact, I think they would consider his visit an asset to the peace talks."

At that point Nixon called and asked us to come into his office. As Kissinger briefed him on what had transpired, I could tell Nixon didn't like it one bit. In fact, he sat in his chair like a stone and didn't say a word while Kissinger and I argued about the timetable.

"I would like you to postpone your trip until July eighteenth or after. It is my opinion, based on everything that has occurred at the peace talks to this point, that a postponement is advantageous to all."

"I would prefer submitting this to Congress. The North Vietnamese expect us immediately. We have already postponed the trip once," I said. I caught Gibbons's wink, and could tell he felt I should agree to the July 18 date. I also saw the expression on Nixon's face and got the feeling he wished he'd left Hoffa in jail. I think he was jealous. Hoffa, Gibbons, and I were trespassing on his imperial prerogative to run the world and he didn't like it one bit. Still he said nothing, and I finally relented. I said I would present the postponement request to Hoffa.

"When are you planning to see Jimmy?" Kissinger asked. "You know there are some rather sizable problems involved concerning Mr. Hoffa's leaving the country."

Then Nixon spoke. "Why don't we have John Dean handle all this?" he said to Kissinger.

"Yes," Kissinger agreed at once. "Splendid idea."

Then we were invited to stay for lunch, during which our discussion continued. We finished with the following agreement: If we would to to Hanoi after July 18, the government would facilitate the trip in every way possible. Kissinger cautioned, "Naturally, when you go, you will not in any way be representing the government. You must realize that."

"We have never made that implication," I assured him. "Mr. Hoffa is going on a humanitarian mission to the prisoners of war." I said nothing about the number of prisoners it had been agreed would return with him. That was still a private understanding between Le Duc Tho and me.

The meeting was over. Kissinger conducted us to our car and began kissing us all over again. Everything was fine and wonderful. Except that I couldn't quite believe it.

As I flew to Detroit to see Hoffa, I couldn't understand why I felt so uneasy abut the San Clemente meeting. There was something in the attitudes of Nixon and Kissinger that disturbed me. Kissinger had overreacted, I decided, and Nixon had been too quiet. And who the hell was John Dean?

I decided not to share my misgivings with Hoffa. They were nebulous, based on nothing, I told myself. I should be elated rather than depressed. Maybe Hoffa's paranoia was rubbing off on me.

Hoffa was eager to know the practical details. "What about a visa? How is this going to go through the parole board?" he demanded.

"We haven't worked that out yet. That's all been turned over to a man named John Dean."

"Who's he?"

"He's on the President's staff," I said, for that was all I knew. For the rest of the month Hoffa was like putty. I hadn't seen him so optimistic since his release from prison, and although he continued to be as ornery as ever about other matters, on the Vietnam mission he was almost pleasantly cooperative.

When I arrived in Miami there were three messages from Kissinger. I called him and he said he'd been to the State Department. Attorney General Kleindienst was working on the passport. Other people were working on other things. Everybody was doing everything under the sun to get Hoffa to Hanoi.

During the next three days I received at least twelve more calls from Henry Kissinger. Each time he questioned me about my reactions to Le Duc Tho, the atmosphere of our meetings, my estimates of the negotiator's response to several potential proposals. I realized he was trying to extract as much helpful information from me as he could before his next confrontation with Le Duc Tho. It was a perfectly reasonable thing to do, although I wished he would be less circuitous. Still, I could not reveal Madame Mao's behind-the-scenes help, which was unfortunate for Kissinger, for he could have used that knowledge in his negotiations.

Meanwhile, word had been sent to Hanoi that Hoffa's visit would have to be postponed. I was afraid it might be misinterpreted as reluctance or lack of resolve. However, they readily confirmed July 25 as the new date. A week went by before I finally heard from John Dean. I found him very affable and willing to help. He wanted to see me to go over all the necessary clearances for the trip, such as the parole board release, passport, and visa, and we named a meeting date.

That day a call came from Dean's secretary. The meeting had to be postponed, as Mr. Dean had been unexpectedly called away. "How is July 13?" she asked. I was unhappy about the delay, but had no choice but to agree to the new date.

On July 13, Dean's secretary called again, this time to cancel. No future date was offered, and I felt a twinge of apprehension.

Other people I didn't know started calling to ask questions. They all said the same thing. They even all sounded the same, and later I discovered they all looked the same. Nixon had apparently hired a matching set of nice-looking, clean-cut, well-spoken young men to carry out his orders.

Henry Kissinger's aide, Richard Campbell, also called to ask me whether all the documents were being processed. There seemed to be a great deal of motion but no progress, and I began to dislike the sound of it more and more. On July 14 I reached John Dean and had an abrasive conversation with him. His affability had been replaced by evasiveness.

"The President told me you yourself would be handling this matter," I said. "Now I'm getting calls from all sorts of people, all supposedly pursuing one thing or another. This is not the way we planned it at all."

"A number of people are needed. The technicalities cover a lot of different areas," Dean said.

"Nonsense. It's not that complex. It needs only one person to tie up the loose ends, not a small army. I want as few people involved in this as possible."

Dean would give me no assurances, and I hung up. Not only was Hoffa on edge, but I was becoming nervous too. I knew intuitively that nothing was really moving.

Later that evening, sitting in my living room with Nick Tweel and two others, all friends of Hoffa, I got a call from Rancho La Costa, the big resort complex built in California with Teamster pension fund money. It was Harold Gibbons.

"A funny thing's going on," he said. "Allen Dorfman is sitting in the restaurant having dinner alone."

"What makes that so strange?" I asked.

"Frank Fitzsimmons is sitting at another table, also having dinner alone, only a few dozen feet from Dorfman. It's like they don't know each other."

"That's impossible," I said. "You know Allen Dorfman's supposed to be in Chicago tonight."

"Well, he's not. He's having dinner here by himself. I thought you'd like to know." Gibbons rang off and I told Tweel and the others what he'd told me.

"I think maybe you ought to call Jimmy," Tweel remarked.

When I called Hoffa, he said, "Impossible. Call La Costa,

get the captain in the dining room, and have him tell Dorfman to come to the phone. Then I'll believe you."

I made the call. In a few moments Dorfman was on the wire, astonished to hear my voice. "What are you doing at La Costa?" I said. "I just talked to Jimmy and he told me you were in Chicago. How the hell can you be in both places?"

Dorfman stumbled around for a while, then said he was in California for a golf tournament coming up soon. I thought his reply was pretty transparent, called Hoffa back, and told him about the golf tournament story.

"And you say Fitz is there too?"

"That's what I was told."

"Call again. Talk to Fitz," he said and hung up.

Once again I called the restaurant, this time asking for Fitzsimmons. I had never met him but he knew very well who I was. "This is Bill Taub," I said. "Jimmy wanted me to call you to talk about setting up a meeting between us, but he didn't believe you were at La Costa."

"So why the hell didn't he call me himself?"

"I can't answer that question. Perhaps he thought it very strange that Allen Dorfman, who is supposed to be in Chicago, is having dinner alone at the same restaurant you are."

"So what the fuck business is that of yours?" he exploded. I hung up on the barrage of abuse that followed and called Hoffa once more.

"Son of a bitch," he said. Apparently after he slammed down the phone on me, he called Fitzsimmons himself, because it wasn't long before Fitzsimmons called me, enraged that I had told Hoffa about our telephone conversation.

"I saw nothing wrong in that, Mr. Fitzsimmons. Was there any reason Jimmy shouldn't have known you're where you are?"

Then Fitzsimmons hung up on me, and for the next hour my phone continued to ring. It would have reminded me of school boys bringing home tales had I not known the danger that was imminent if the battle escalated. Finally my guests and I went out to dinner just to get away from the telephone. We returned at 11 P.M. and the battle resumed. I picked up the phone and it was Hoffa.

"You're not going to believe this," he roared. "Dorfman

and Fitzsimmons left separately, met outside, and together they went to San Clemente to meet Nixon."

"Why?"

"Don't worry. I'm sure as hell going to find out."

We all found out the very next morning when the newspapers carried the pictures of President Richard Nixon and Frank Fitzsimmons standing side by side, grinning from ear to ear, and the announcement that the Teamsters Union had endorsed Nixon for reelection. A few days later the White House dropped plans for antistrike legislation in the transport industry, but I was to find out soon that there was more to the mutual back scratching than that.

Hoffa, in a monumental fury, tried to call Dorfman at Rancho La Costa, but found he had checked out.

"I told you that son of a bitch Dorfman should have gone to jail," he said. "And it's your goddamn fault for helping him."

"Wait a minute. You were the one who insisted I help him in the first place."

"But later on I told you to stop. He never told me he was going to pull this. Not one goddamn word. That shithead thinks he can do whatever he likes. Well, he's going to find out he can't. Where are those trip papers anyway?"

His last question was one I had been asking myself every hour of every day. I couldn't tell Hoffa there would be no papers forthcoming. He was suspicious enough already. But it was clear to me the understandings of the July 5 meeting at San Clemente had been thwarted. It was even possible the whole thing had been a sham from the beginning.

As time had not completely run out, I called General Clay in the hope that he might have a fresh approach. Clay's advice was to go to Paris at once.

"Tell them as much about the situation as you can, before the trust you've built up is endangered. Let them know you've acted in good faith. Maybe there's some pressure that can be applied from their end."

It was a route I hadn't considered, but it appealed to me. I called Claire Jourdan immediately and had her arrange an urgent meeting with Le Duc Tho. I took the first flight out and was in Paris within twenty-four hours, facing Nguyen Mai.

"Mr. Hoffa very much wants to accept your invitation to

visit Hanoi. I want to come. Mr. Gibbons wants to come. The understandings reached with Mr. Le Duc Tho are in no way changed, but we're having difficulty getting permission for Mr. Hoffa to leave the United States." I drew a deep breath. "Not everyone is in favor of Mr. Hoffa's visit. Certain forces are making it very difficult for him to leave."

I knew I was not being impressive. All I could offer were suspicions, nothing specific.

Nguyen Mai gave me a small, wise smile. "There are always forces," he said softly.

"I simply do not think we will be able to visit Hanoi on the twenty-fifth. I hope you understand we are both very disappointed and frustrated."

Nguyen Mai's smile disappeared and his voice became stern. "I understand your position, but the government of the Democratic Republic of Vietnam is highly disturbed at this development. We feel this turn of affairs requires a statement from us. If you can give me one hour, I will have a more definitive answer for you."

I agreed to wait and was shown into another room and offered tea. Nguyen Mai returned and read me the first draft of his letter. As I listened, I felt myself growing hopeful again. His letter might turn the thing around. I was told to return the following day and pick up the official letter. When I did, the North Vietnamese strongly urged me to call a press conference and read the letter to the world.

I backed away from that commitment and returned to Paris. The letter, never made public until now, read:

July 18, 1972

Mr. William L. Taub
116 East 60th Street
New York

Dear Mr. Taub:

We have received your letter informing us that Mr. Hoffa is not permitted by the U.S. Government to legally visit North Vietnam.

As you are aware, many Americans from different organizations have visited the Democratic Republic of Vietnam. These trips have contributed to enhance the mutual understanding between the peoples of our two countries.

As we told you during the meetings we had with you yesterday and today, we would like to confirm once again that the Vietnam Trade Union is prepared to welcome Mr. Hoffa, Mr. Gibbons and you in Hanoi on July 25 for this visit, and we hope you will not meet with difficulties from the U.S. government on the question of passport for Mr. Hoffa.

With best wishes,   Sincerely,

Nguyen Mai, Secretary
Vietnam Committee for
Solidarity with the
American People

It was clear to me from the tone of the letter the North Vietnamese wanted to end the war and were making no bones about it. Still, I disliked the idea of a press conference. I had no desire to publicly embarrass my government, and besides, I felt the letter itself might be enough to effect a change.

I went to the American ambassador in Paris with the letter. "I'm about to call a press conference and it's going to be devastating for the United States when I do," I said.

The ambassador made it clear he knew I had just been to the North Vietnamese delegation, and I assumed I was being followed in Paris. "Be good enough to hold off for an hour to give me a chance to transmit this letter to Mr. Kissinger," he said.

In less than an hour he called me back into his office. His attitude was greatly changed. This time I was treated with much cordiality. "I talked to Henry," he said. "Henry sends his regards along to you and says if you will refrain from releasing the letter and return directly to Washington, he will see you at once and work everything out with you."

Then I made my only real mistake in the entire affair. I agreed to Kissinger's request. Confident the letter had ended White House delaying tactics, I indulged myself and stayed in Paris an extra day. That night I picked up the midnight edition of the Paris *Herald Tribune* and did a double take. There on the front page was a photo of Henry Kissinger disembarking that morning from a plane at the Paris airport. The accompanying story told how Mr. Kissinger had called for an emergency meeting with Le Duc Tho.

I did some calculating. In order to arrive in Paris that morning, Kissinger had to have left Washington within a few hours after talking to the ambassador. He must have gone straight to Nixon, who must have told him to gas up and go. I called the North Vietnamese delegation and I was told more or less, "We told you so. We told you to release the letter." The only conclusion I could come to was that neither Richard Nixon nor Kissinger wanted to end the war.

I was sick at heart all the way to New York, where in a few days my worst fears were confirmed. No call came from Kissinger. No concrete steps were taken by anyone on Hoffa's papers. John Dean continued to play hide-and-seek, July 25 came and went, and the doors to the White House were closed to me.

I showed Senator Ted Kennedy the letter. "Release it," he said. "Unfortunately, my name won't get you even as far as yours will at the White House." He did try to get through the White House switchboard but to no avail. I almost took his advice, but at the last moment decided against it, for once the letter was released, the trip would go down the drain. Unreleased, it remained a threat. Had I known the facts I was soon to learn, I might have torn up the letter for all the good it would do to stop the forces that were working against Hoffa's trip.

After I saw Senator Kennedy I stopped trying to contact anyone at the White House. I wanted time to assess my options, if I had any.

A day later Hoffa phoned. "Who the hell is General Haig?" he said.

"He's deputy to Kissinger. Why?"

"Who gave him my number?"

"I haven't the slightest idea."

"Last night I was watching TV and a man calls me and says he's General Haig. Then he starts asking me a lot of questions. Why do you want to go to Hanoi? What do you think you're going to do there? Then he asks me who the hell you are."

"What did you say?"

"I said, 'Who the hell are you?' and he said he was at the White House. Big deal, I said, and I told him not to bother me again and I gave him your number."

"Well, he is at the White House, Jimmy."

"I don't like people calling me I don't even know, bothering me at night. I don't care what kind of big shot he is. You talk to him. You're running this show."

Knowing how rude and peremptory Hoffa could be, I felt somewhat embarrassed about calling General Haig. I needn't have. His tone was easily as crude as Hoffa's. Furious, I called Rose Mary Woods. I told her I wanted to find out what had happened to our July 5 agreement. "I'll ask the President about that," she said coolly, and I was no less angry when I hung up.

Hoffa was now convinced his initial misgivings and pessimism had been correct. Once again his first concern was looking after Teamster affairs, and his first move was to try to smooth the waters with Dorfman and Fitzsimmons. He wanted me to be his emissary. "That's not going to be so easy," I said. "I don't think I should be the one."

"Dorfman will listen to you."

"He knows I'm involved with you," I said, "and I've told him I don't want to get into the middle of Teamster battles. You know, you've been saying a lot of rough things, Jimmy."

"And I meant them. But now I want to move in a different way. Look, I'll set up the meetings with Dorfman and Fitz in Washington. You just start the ball rolling, that's all I'm asking. Christ, this Vietnam thing has fizzled and I've got to come up with something else."

"It hasn't fizzled. I'm not writing anything off yet," I insisted, reluctant to give up entirely on the extraordinary plan I had been so near to bringing off. However, I didn't want Hoffa to lose confidence entirely, so I agreed to help him try to patch things up with Dorfman and Fitzsimmons. I flew to Chicago to see Dorfman first. When his number-one aide, Mike Breen, picked me up at the airport instead of the usual driver, and when instead of taking me to the Teamsters' executive dining room he steered me into one of the airport restaurants, I was immediately on my guard.

Breen asked me a lot of questions about Hoffa's mood, ambitions, opinions. I gave noncommittal answers as we drove through winding back-country roads to Dorfman's home. I was thinking about that night in the French Alps, and I was quite relieved when we drove up to Dorfman's magnificent home. As I was being ushered through the front door, I saw a heavyset man leaving through the back door and stepping into a limousine, which immediately drove off. The man at the door said, "Did you see Fitz?"

"Fitz?"

"Frank Fitzsimmons. That was him getting into the car."

I was totally unprepared for this information, and tried to figure out what was happening. After seeing Dorfman, I was supposed to go to Washington to see Fitzsimmons, as Dorfman knew because Hoffa had told him. I walked into the large foyer and Dorfman soon appeared. We went into his studio for a private talk.

"You know how angry Jimmy is," I told him. "And you know better than I what he's angry about. My advice is you and Fitzsimmons ought to meet with him and try to resolve whatever it is."

Dorfman balked. "I don't see that doing much good. You shouldn't pay so much attention to what Jimmy says. He's been out of touch a long time, you know." That was not at all accurate, and Dorfman knew it. Hoffa had remained very much in touch all through his prison term. However, I did not want to get into that.

"You know," I said, "I'm seeing Fitzsimmons tomorrow in Washington about this." I paused and watched his face. He said nothing, and the silence spoke volumes. Had he been in favor of the peacemaking overture, Dorfman would have had Fitzsimmons stay. Instead, he rushed him out before I arrived. I decided two could play this game and I didn't let on I had seen Fitzsimmons hurtling himself into the limousine. After some inconclusive discussion, our meeting ended.

"Are you going right back to the airport?" he asked, and I said I was. "Good. There's someone else here who's going back too, so my driver will take you both."

A man whom I instantly recognized appeared in the foyer. He was owner of a Las Vegas nightclub and had been meeting with Dorfman when I arrived.

The man wedged his huge bulk into the front seat of the limousine and I sat in the back. "You know, Jimmy and I have been friends for a hundred years," he said. "I wish he'd take a more active interest in the Las Vegas scene." I told him I thought that was unlikely. "When you see him again would you do me a favor?" he said. "Tell him I gave Allen three hundred thousand dollars in cash that he gave to Fitzsimmons, who turned it over to Nixon."

"Fitzsimmons gave three hundred thousand dollars cash to Nixon?" I said, as impassively as I could. "Are you sure about that?"

"I'm sure. Fitzsimmons took it to the White House himself. He went there with Mitchell and Dean. Just tell Jimmy, will you?"

"I will. I certainly will," I said.

We parted at the airport and I boarded a flight to Washington. I was dazed. A casual remark had changed everything. I now saw what we were up against.

When I picked up my room reservation at the Hay Adams in Washington, I was handed a message. *Mr. Fitzsimmons will not be in D.C. for the rest of the week.* I was furious. I called Dorfman and said, "Damnit, here I am in Washington and I just got word Fitzsimmons isn't going to be here for the rest of the week. What's going on?"

"I could have told you that. He's going to Boston for a checkup at the hospital."

"Why didn't you tell me that when I saw you?"

"Why didn't you ask me?"

"Look, Allen, I'm a little weary of all this. Why didn't you tell me when I arrived that Fitzsimmons was just going out your back door?"

"Where'd you hear that?"

"What difference does it make?"

"If it doesn't make any difference, then it's none of your business," he snapped.

I hung up and called Hoffa.

"That's nuts. Fitzsimmons wasn't in Chicago today," Hoffa said, and I had the feeling I'd come into the middle of a movie I had seen before.

"He was there. And maybe this won't make you feel any better, but I rode to the airport with a man who said he gave three hundred thousand dollars in cash to Dorfman, who gave it to Fitzsimmons, who gave it to the President. Jimmy, they beat us to the punch."

Hoffa was too stunned to say anything. "Stay where you are," he finally demanded. "I'll call you back."

By the time I had unpacked, Hoffa called. "Fitzsimmons isn't in Boston, he's in Washington. And you were right. He was at Dorfman's house and he did walk out the back when you walked in the front." In the silence I could almost hear him thinking. "Stay in Washington overnight," he finally said, "and I'll call you first thing in the morning."

When I heard the following morning that Fitzsimmons refused to see me, I took Hoffa's advice and got out of Washington. Hoffa's olive branch had been refused for some reason—or 300,000 reasons. Before I left, however, I decided to do a little investigative work. I knew I would have to play cagey, making it appear I knew more than I did. John Dean was the man to call.

"Have the Hoffa papers been put on the shelf entirely?" I asked him.

"No, not at all," Dean said earnestly. "I'm still working on them."

"Well, I've about had it with the whole business. It's my understanding there was a special meeting last week with Frank Fitzsimmons, John Mitchell, the President, and you. Mr. Fitzsimmons was in Chicago yesterday and so was I. He confirmed that meeting took place."

"Right. We did go see the President. He told you why we went, didn't he?"

"He did. I was given to understand the funds were handed over at that meeting."

"Right, that's right." Then, after a hesitation, "I didn't know you were in on that." He was a bit alarmed at the indiscretion.

"I'm in on a lot of things. Keep in touch, will you?" I hung up quickly, pleased with myself for outwitting Dean but depressed at confirming my suspicion. The same friends who had been unable, or unwilling, to free Hoffa from prison were now hard at work keeping him from going to Vietnam. And they had persuasive bargaining powers and the most powerful allies in the land. I remembered Morris Shenker turning down every idea I suggested to Jacques Schiffer to get Hoffa out of prison. I remembered Fitzsimmons's strange ineffectualness, too. Everyone talked of wanting to get Jimmy out, but Jimmy stayed in. Now that Dean had confirmed that Allen Dorfman had just given $300,000 in cash to Nixon via Fitzsimmons, I knew the obstacle that lay between Jimmy Hoffa and Hanoi.

Not long after that bombshell I learned Kissinger's meeting with Le Duc Tho had been arranged expressly to destroy everything I had done. Kissinger (whom Le Duc Tho had warned me was a "Nazi") had told the North Vietnamese that Hoffa didn't represent the United States, that they had no right to deal with him or with me, and that he was not to be trusted, having recently been released from prison. With monumental arrogance, he deprecated the very things about Hoffa they admired. It was little wonder that his dealings with the Vietnamese were so unsatisfactory.

That afternoon on the way to Miami I was sick with despair. Everything I had done had been subverted. A good chance to free a dozen prisoners of war and set up a formula for the release of more had been brutally cast aside for selfish reasons. Even as Richard Nixon was making indignant speeches to the POW families about the plight of captured Americans, he was intriguing to torpedo the first concrete proposal to bring some of those prisoners home. Nixon had found to his delight that $300,000 was not too high an asking price for keeping Hoffa's hands tied. As he had once bargained with Hoffa, now he bargained with Hoffa's enemies. But then, Richard Nixon was never shy about playing both ends against the middle.

11

TURNABOUT

In the first hot days of August another member was added to the team of White House spoilers. His name was Charles Colson. "Don't you dare do anything that will cause embarrassment to Mr. Kissinger," he threatened me. "No one has given you any authority to butt in. You're interfering with his delicate peace negotiations."

"You mean the ones that aren't getting anywhere?" I asked.

"If you try to deal directly with the Vietnamese, you could be violating the Constitution, you know."

"Is three hundred thousand in cash delivered to the President's desk also considered a violation of the Constitution?" I retorted.

That was one of the milder exchanges that invariably ended with Colson hanging up on me. Despite their success, the White House team was nervous, and I could think of nothing to do but wage a battle of nerves, basically a futile exercise.

My thoughts turned to General Lemly in California. Since his first letter after the kidnap-murder attempt, we had had many conversations. His neighbor and friend, retired Admiral R. W. Woods, had a son who was a prisoner of war. I called

General Lemly and told him I needed his help. "If I flew out to see you privately, could a meeting be arranged?"

"As soon as it takes you to get here," he said.

That was enough for me. Saying nothing to Hoffa or Gibbons, I flew to Los Angeles and drove to Rancho La Costa, which was five minutes from Lemly's home. My visit would appear to be just another business trip if I stayed at the Teamster resort. When I arrived at La Costa, I telephoned General Lemly at once and asked him to come to a luncheon meeting in my suite. He promised to be there at noon the following day. Then I called Admiral Woods. He told me it wasn't possible for him to travel, but he wanted to know what he could do.

"I've been blocked at every turn," I told him. "Everything I've begun is just crumbling away. As you know, I did get an agreement for Mr. Hoffa to visit the prisoners of war."

"I know. I had hoped great things might come of it. I thought of writing a letter for you to take to the Vietnamese. None of my other letters have been answered. I don't know if my son is dead or alive. I thought maybe a letter delivered by you personally might get through to my son. Then we would at least know if he's alive."

"I'd be happy to try," I said, thinking of the thousands of other Americans who were engulfed in the same anguish.

"What can I do to help?" he said.

"You can think how pressure might be brought upon Mr. Nixon to allow Mr. Hoffa to make that trip. That's the key to the entire problem."

Later that afternoon I took a walk around the La Costa property and the golf course with one of the resort's top managers. He paused frequently to point out the numerous parcels of land owned by Dorfman.

"Allen owns most of the land surrounding the club," he said proudly. "He bought it all up a few years ago and now it's worth three times as much."

I stared at the acres and acres of valuable land. "It must be worth millions of dollars," I said.

"At least."

Two hours before General Lemly was to arrive for lunch Dorfman called from Chicago, alarmed and abusive. Who did I think I was, going to Rancho La Costa as if I were Hoffa himself, he demanded.

"I didn't come here thinking I was anybody but myself," I said.

"Who told you to go in the first place?"

"Nobody told me to go."

"Then what are you there for?"

"Because it's convenient, that's all."

"And nobody sent you?"

I decided to toss another log on the fire of his suspicions. "I'm not obliged to tell you where I'm going or what I'm doing," I said. "It's none of your damn business, frankly."

I hung up on him, and five minutes later Hoffa called from Detroit. His radar screen had picked me up and he was even more belligerent than Dorfman.

"What the hell are you doing at La Costa?"

"I'm here on business," I said, angry that he sounded as suspicious as Dorfman. However, suspicion was bred into Jimmy just as social graces are bred into other people.

"Just what kind of business are you on?" he said.

"Important business. You'll have to take my word for it." Of course, he was in no mood to take anyone's word for anything, although I did feel I had earned the right to be trusted. "I'm not going to talk about it now," I said. He ranted a few minutes longer, then hung up.

My visit to La Costa was less discreet than I had hoped. I was beginning to suspect my room phone was bugged and I was nervous about General Lemly's arrival. Something told me to go down to the lobby and check on things. Sure enough, Lemly had arrived and had been told by the desk clerk I had checked out. He'd had the good sense to wait around for me, and I found him and his aide in the lobby. Even in civilian clothes he looked very much the Marine Corps officer. He was tall, commanding, erect, and exuded authority. We began our luncheon meeting at once.

"What can I do?" was his first question.

"I would like you and Admiral Woods to approach the President directly. Our progress has been sabotaged by the forces I described to you. I don't think Mr. Nixon would be able to ignore a personal appeal from two friends of high military rank, and it might change his mind about permitting Mr. Hoffa to go to Hanoi."

"I'll do it," Lemly said gravely. "I've never believed we

should be involved in Vietnam, and I can assure you Admiral Woods will back me up, even though Mr. Nixon is still our commander-in-chief. However, I want one thing understood. You know what I thought about the Geneva episode. Well, I do not regard Mr. Hoffa's pardon as making up for the neglect at Geneva."

I nodded and said nothing about what I thought were the real reasons for Hoffa's pardon. Then he continued. "When I speak to the President, it will be in behalf of you and what you have begun, and not for Mr. Hoffa. It will be for the soldiers in prison over there. Not for Mr. Hoffa."

"That's how it should be," I said.

He kept his word. A few days after our meeting I telephoned him. "I saw the President," he told me. "You know, I've known him well for many years and I laid it on the line. Maybe it was no way for me to talk, but I did it. I told him if Mr. Hoffa or anybody could obtain the release of prisoners of war, it was his duty to help him. I told him freeing the prisoners is all that matters and not who does it."

"What did he have to say?"

"You'll be hearing from the White House directly, Bill."

That was exciting news. I flew back to the East Coast, stopping in New York, where I saw Nick Tweel at the Hampshire House. He had a different kind of news for me. "There's more going on around Jimmy now than when he was in prison," he said. "I don't know if you stirred it up, but there's a real battle taking place."

"What kind of battle?"

"Between those for Jimmy and those against him. Simple as that," Tweel said.

"And how do you tell the players without a scorecard?" Tweel didn't answer. Maybe even he didn't know.

I went on to Florida the following day, where the Republican convention was just ending. I watched the festivities on television and got sick. There was Nixon getting hugged by Sammy Davis, Jr., and everybody applauding wildly as if they were at a grand party, while the war went on, and on, and on.

Early the next morning I put in a call to Kissinger at the Nixon Key Biscayne headquarters. I was told he was breakfasting with the President and would return my call. He never did. An hour passed and I called again. This time I was told Nixon and Kissinger had left for San Clemente but Kleindienst wanted to speak to me. I called him at the Doral Hotel, and he set up a meeting in Washington for the following Monday. I decided I would tell no one except Vlachopoulos where I would be that Monday or whom I was going to see.

The following morning I spoke with General Lemly. "I heard from the President," he said. "He assured me he had acted on the things I spoke to him about, and he said Mr. Hoffa is indeed going to Hanoi." It was more than I had expected, and I told him how grateful I was for his help. He said he was sending me Admiral Woods's letter to his son and hoped I would be able to get it to him.

"You have my word," I said. For the first time in a long while I felt hope and excitement rising in me. When I arrived at the Justice Department for my appointment with Kleindienst, I was met by Deputy Attorney General Elaine Crane, who proved to be as charming and gracious in person as she had been on the telephone. She took me in to meet the Attorney General. Once we were alone, he quickly came to the point.

"The entire Hoffa matter is now in my hands," he said. "I've assigned Deputy Attorney General Ralph Erickson to expedite everything and work closely with you. One thing, however, and this is of utmost importance. There must be no word of this to Mr. Rogers at the State Department or to Mr. Kissinger. The arrangements must be kept secret from them at all costs. Those are the President's direct orders."

"As you wish," I said. I had the feeling I had been plunged into the middle of a court intrigue, and could not help being reminded of the conspiracies among the Teamsters. The machinations of the mighty implied by the Attorney General made me speculate. Would Kissinger and Secretary of State Rogers really object so strenuously? Had Nixon given Kissinger an exclusive mandate to negotiate the Vietnam stalemate?

Nixon personally ordered Kleindienst to keep it that way and he directed me to so inform Hoffa.

Kleindienst must have seen something of what I was thinking on my face, for he said, "I'm sure you know what the complications of government are. Everything in this instance must come from this office."

"But under the law we're obliged to tell the Secretary of State when going out of the country under these conditions."

"Never mind that. I'm the Attorney General and I'm telling you it's all right to go. Don't write a letter to Rogers."

"In that case, I'm prepared to honor your instructions," I said.

"Miss Crane will take you to Mr. Erickson," Kleindienst said. "I must leave for the White House at once."

I felt as comfortable with Ralph Erickson as I had with Elaine Crane. Both were obviously in favor of any attempt to free the POWs and shorten the war, and they told me I could reach them twenty-four hours a day. Feeling I was working with allies for a change, I decided to probe a little and see how deep their understanding went. "You know, if Mr. Hoffa succeeds in bringing back a number of prisoners, that would be a real achievement," I said. "We would hope such an event would cause the President to remove the conditions of Mr. Hoffa's pardon."

Erickson took a moment to answer. "I couldn't speak for the President on anything like that."

"Naturally not, but as an official of the Justice Department, do you see any reason why such conditions could not be removed following such an event?"

"Well, the proper papers would have to be submitted," he said carefully.

"I'm very confident Mr. Hoffa's trip will be a great success, especially when it comes to releasing some prisoners of war. I'd like to see those papers prepared," I said.

"All right, we can assist you in your recommendation for removal of the conditions of the pardon. By the time you return, they can be on the President's desk."

"Fair enough," I said. "Now, what is the first thing I should do?"

"We need a letter from Mr. Hoffa to the parole board," Erickson said, "requesting permission to travel to Hanoi. It should be hand-delivered to the parole board, and then I'll expedite it."

For two hours I took notes on the complex procedures that had to be meticulously followed to avoid any more delay. Elaine Crane said, "I'm going all out on this. I'm going to write the petition on releasing the conditions myself. Meanwhile, I'll give you a duplicate set of all the forms you'll need to fill out. It's a long flight to Vietnam, and maybe you can work on them coming and going."

On the flight back to New York I decided it was time for a no-nonsense meeting with James R. Hoffa. I hadn't spoken to him since his infuriating call to Rancho La Costa when he accused me of treachery. When I telephoned him in Detroit he was suspicious as always, then astonished, then confused. "I don't get it. I don't trust anything with the name Justice Department on it."

"You don't trust anything period," I said. "Either you start trusting me completely or we can forget the whole thing."

"Why does this have to be handled by the Attorney General?" he said, ignoring my reprimand.

"I don't know why Nixon is doing it this way, but damn it all, this is the way it is."

"I still don't get it."

"You don't have to get it. What you have to do is write a letter tomorrow morning to the parole board in Detroit."

"And that's going to do it?"

"So I'm told."

"Somebody's feeding you a crock of shit," he exploded. "Senator Scott still hasn't been able to get them to let me get as far as New York."

"Look, Jimmy, either you want to go or you don't. This is your last chance. Nixon is going along with it, maybe because of what General Lemly and Admiral Woods said to him, maybe for his own reasons. Who knows? All I know is this is it. Do you want to go or don't you?"

Inwardly I felt far less confident than I sounded. Hoffa reluctantly agreed to submit the letter. A few days later, after going through numerous drafts and fighting with Hoffa over semantics, a letter that met everyone's approval was delivered to the parole board, and Hoffa was granted permission to leave the country and travel to Hanoi. Elaine Crane told me Hoffa must come to Washington at once for his passport. I thanked her for the speedy action and relayed the news to Hoffa. He picked up the approval from the parole board and was on the phone instantly. "It's no good," he said.

"Now what's wrong?"

"It says I'm supposed to be back in the States by the fifteenth of September. That only gives me ten days. Suppose I get there and can't be back in ten days? They can toss me back in the slammer. I'm not taking the chance."

"Jimmy, for God's sake, you're dealing with the Department of Justice."

"Yeah, I know. I've dealt with them before. They sent me to prison."

"All right, all right. What do you want?"

"Thirty days."

"I'll see what I can do."

I called Ralph Erickson at his home and told him what Hoffa was demanding. "Tell him to go back tomorrow afternoon. There'll be a new letter of permission waiting for him," he said. Hoffa got his thirty days.

Because of the shortness of time, Hoffa's audience with Pope Paul had to be cut out, but the Apostolic Delegate in Washington called and offered his assistance. Labor Day was approaching, and Erickson had called many times urging haste because the President kept asking whether he had gone. Nixon was concerned about a leak to the State Department or to Henry Kissinger. Or perhaps he had another reason. In any case, he was now terribly eager for Hoffa to be on his way.

A passport was the next important item. I called Hoffa and told him to get to Washington right away. I arranged to meet him there and go to the passport office with him.

"I can't go till next week," he said.

"What are you talking about?"

"It's Labor Day this weekend. I'm entertaining my grandchildren."

It took me a moment to find my voice. "I don't believe this. What's more important, entertaining your grandchildren or getting the conditions of your pardon lifted? You can entertain your grandchildren any time."

"No, I can't. You don't have grandchildren. You don't understand."

"And you apparently don't have any damn brains." We argued bitterly and I finally ended the conversation in disgust and anger. After I had calmed down I realized something very important. For some reason Jimmy was afraid to go. I called Elaine Crane and she made special arrangements for Jimmy to get his passport the Tuesday after Labor Day. "We're terribly afraid Mr. Kissinger or Mr. Rogers is going to find out about this. If it's necessary, we'll have the office open at night."

Hoffa and I were to fly from Washington to New York, where Hoffa would stay overnight, in secret, at the Warwick Hotel. Hoffa, Gibbons, and I would then fly to Paris the next evening. Again I impressed upon Hoffa the need for secrecy. "The Justice Department emphasized that with every sentence," I said.

"I still don't get all this secrecy," he grumbled.

"Let's not get into that again. You're leaving the country and going to Hanoi and that's all that matters."

"How much money should I take?"

"You're limited to five thousand dollars by law," I said.

Harold Gibbons had reserved our tickets to Paris on a commercial Pan Am flight that would allow us to depart without undue attention. He had also chartered a private Pan Am jet to wait in Vientiane for us when we returned from Hanoi with the twelve prisoners. The only passengers on the flight home were to be Hoffa, Gibbons, the twelve prisoners, and me, plus whatever members of the press we decided to include. Only one item remained undecided, and that was whether the jet would land in New York or Washington. Hoffa favored Washington so Nixon could meet the plane, but the final decision was up to the President.

The American consulates along our route had received coded messages from the Justice Department, acting under Nixon's orders, alerting them to our passage. They were to assist us along the way. The consulates in Paris, Bangkok, and Vientiane must have been wondering why the message came from Justice instead of State.

On September 6 I arrived at the passport office. Hoffa arrived a half-hour later with his birth certificate, parole documents, photo, money, and suitcase, looking, as always, like a yokel. Hoffa never gave a damn about his clothes or making an impression. He left all that to Dorfman. Many times I had given him neckties as gifts. He never said thank you and he never wore them. So there he stood in his off-the-rack suit and cheap necktie, ready to go to Hanoi on the most important mission of his career. I had to remind myself that appearances are deceiving, for no one on this earth could negotiate like Jimmy Hoffa.

Everything was processed by the time it took to drink the coffee they served, and going down the elevator, Hoffa shook his head in amazement. "In all my years of going in and out of Washington, this is the first time I've ever received a decent reception from anybody in government. I don't know what you did, but it's a good feeling. Nixon must really believe in you."

I kept my mouth shut. Although Richard Nixon's interest in seeing Hoffa off to Hanoi had escalated tremendously, I wondered whether that might be directly related to the Watergate scandal, which was also escalating despite the administration's efforts to disparage the entire affair. It wasn't too hard to see how much benefit Nixon could derive from backing a successful visit to Hanoi by Hoffa or anyone else. Such a breakthrough would overshadow Watergate and take care of George McGovern once and for all. Nixon had had too many close calls at the polls, often winning or losing by a hair, to ride easy two months before election day.

We reached the main floor. "There's Davidson," Hoffa said, pointing to a man nearby. "I told him to meet me here."

"You what?" I gasped. Irving Davidson was a Washington publicist/lobbyist. I watched aghast as Hoffa pulled out his passport and showed it to the man. Davidson was a close associate of Hoffa.

"I'm on my way to Hanoi," he boasted loudly.

I pulled him to the side and hissed, "You weren't supposed to tell anybody anything. What's this all about?"

He shrugged. "I figured it'd be all right now to tell a few people."

"Good God no. Not now, not later, not any time until you're in Hanoi. What are you trying to do, wreck the thing at the last minute?"

Hoffa said nothing, but his face was set. "I told Davidson I'd go to his office for a little while."

"Meet me at the Attorney General's office at two o'clock sharp," I said. "And keep your trap shut!" I stalked away from Hoffa and his friend exasperated, for at that time I didn't understand Jimmy's fear.

At two o'clock Hoffa met me at Richard Kleindienst's office. Elaine Crane and Ralph Erickson were also there to wish Hoffa *bon voyage* on behalf of the President. Nervous at first, Hoffa grew calm as the climate proved to be as friendly as it had been at the passport office. Everyone wished him success and he began to expand in his new role of hero.

"You'll get the Congressional Medal of Honor if you pull this off, Mr. Hoffa," Elaine Crane said. "Just bring back some prisoners and you'll be everybody's hero."

Hoffa shot me a look. I said nothing. I still hadn't told anyone about the agreement I had reached with Le Duc Tho. "Mr. Hoffa will not come back empty-handed," I promised.

Then we flew to New York. My next surprise was waiting for me at La Guardia Airport where three labor goons met us with a car to take us to the Warwick. "Jesus, who else did you tell?" I said.

Hoffa refused to meet my eyes and folded himself into the seat alongside one of the goons. I got out of the car at my apartment and told Hoffa I'd come to his suite after dinner to go over last-minute things. I forced myself to think positively. In less than twenty-four hours I'd have him on board the flight to Paris. Things had proceeded too far for anything to go wrong now, I told myself.

But when I arrived at Hoffa's rooms he was not alone, as I had expected. Instead he was entertaining a roomful of Teamster bosses. One of them turned to me and said, "I don't think a man like Jimmy should leave the country unless he's got it in writing about bringing back the POW's." Several of his fellow Teamsters concurred. They all felt Jimmy should have the deal on paper.

"Maybe you fellows would like to take over my job," I said, and got up to find Hoffa, who had spent much of the evening ignoring my furious glances. I told him I'd be back at 8:30 for breakfast.

Back in my apartment, I couldn't sleep. At 2 A.M. I called Claire Jourdan in Paris and told her we were ready to go. She confirmed the final arrangements for our flight from Vientiane. The Russian government had arranged an Aeroflot plane to fly Hoffa, Gibbons, and me from Vientiane to Hanoi. Shortly before it was time to get up, I floated into an uneasy sleep, having no idea the new day was about to explode in my face.

The first sign came right after breakfast. Hoffa and I had just talked to the doctor who had been in to see Gibbons. He said Gibbons was too sick to go. Then the telephone rang. It was the *Detroit Free Press.* Would I confirm that trip to Hanoi? I would not and turned to Hoffa. "How did they know? How in hell did they hear about it?"

Hoffa's face was impassive. "That paper has always been good to me."

"You were the one who told them, goddamnit!" I raged. "You leaked it to them yourself."

"Yeah, I told them," he snapped. "Why not?"

"Oh my God, how can you say that? How could you even think that?" I was ready to go out the thirtieth-floor window when the telephone rang once more. It was the *Detroit Free Press* again, and again I refused to talk to the reporter. But he had been making other calls and the Warwick's switchboard was about to be deluged. The first caller to get through was Charles Colson. I listened to eight or nine choice words and then hung up on him. I wasn't in the mood for his comments. The next time Colson got through, Hoffa hung up on him. But I knew the cat was out of the bag. I made a desperate call to Nguyen Mai, my North Vietnamese contact in Paris, and told him to tell Le Duc Tho we were leaving at seven that night.

Then I tried to cheer the both of us. I managed until Nixon's communications director, Ken Clawson, called. He was obviously in the dark about everything. He sailed into Hoffa.

"Who did you get your visa from? How did you get the parole board to give you clearance?" he demanded.

"Go screw yourself, whoever you are," Hoffa said, and slammed down the receiver. "That bastard told me Rogers was revoking my passport," he exclaimed, and he looked scared.

"He can't do that, Jimmy. I'll call Kleindienst right now." Kleindienst was at a meeting with Nixon in the Oval Office at the White House. Erickson was also unavailable, but he called back soon enough. "Elaine Crane and I just spoke to the President," he said. "He said to tell you to get Mr. Hoffa out of the country and on his way to Hanoi if you have to chloroform him."

That was enough for me. The arrangements still held.

"Jimmy, you're to get on that plane tonight and that's that."

Hoffa glowered. "Then why the hell is everything still so secret?"

I decided to call Tweel in Fort Lauderdale, thinking perhaps he might be able to reassure Hoffa. But as Hoffa listened to Tweel, his expression hardened, his eyes narrowed with suspicion. I then spoke to Tweel myself.

"Get him out of the Warwick," he said. "Take him to my apartment at the Hampshire House or take him to your place."

By that time the lobby of the Warwick was a welter of reporters and television cameras, all waiting for Jimmy to appear. Word had spread through the town and everything was wildly out of control.

There were three bedrooms in Hoffa's suite, plus a living room and kitchen, and every telephone in every room was ringing.

"Jimmy," I said, "we've got to get out of here. We can sneak out the back and be on our way to the airport, free and clear." Then he said what I'd been afraid to think about.

"I'm not going."

"What did you say?"

"I'm not going to Hanoi," he said softly. "You go. Here, take the money." He reached in his pocket and took out the $5,000. "Take this and go to Hanoi. I'm going down and talk to the newsmen and then I'm going back to Detroit."

"Why?" We were both talking in hushed tones now. My question seemed to be coming from another person, a stranger in a strange dream.

"I don't like it, that's all. I don't like the smell of it. If I go, I'll never get back into the country. I'll never have my family around me again."

I stared at him a long time and saw he meant what he said. "That's crazy, Jimmy. Just crazy. Everything's been taken care of just the way you wanted it. Nixon is the President, not Rogers. And Nixon wants you to go."

"I'm not going," he repeated. "You go." I looked at his face and saw it was hopeless. As he continued to fidget in his chair, I realized he was deathly afraid of leaving on that plane. Something had scared him, and he wouldn't tell me what it was —if he knew himself. I saw the look in his eyes and the set of his jaw and I knew I had lost. Then he got up and walked out of the room without a word, and I knew he was going downstairs to the lobby to talk to the reporters.

I stayed where I was because I didn't want to hear him tell the press he wasn't going to Hanoi. I sat in my chair feeling hollowed out until I figured the lobby would be clear, and then I walked slowly back to my apartment.

The next day I unhooked my telephone. I was amazed at how many people knew my unlisted number until I learned Hoffa had been handing it out right and left. In the blizzard of accusations and disclaimers, evasions and indignant protests, no one, especially Hoffa, was telling the truth. The official version, unveiled at a White House press conference held by Ronald Ziegler, would have been laughable had I been in a laughing mood. Ziegler's remarks revealed he was totally in the dark about what had happened, but he blundered his way through the lies and the slander he had been provided.

A story appeared on page two of the New York *Daily News* on September 8: "White House Press Secretary Ronald Ziegler said that President Nixon's National Security Affairs Adviser Henry Kissinger had met with Teamsters Vice President Harold Gibbons and Teamsters lawyer William L. Taub of New York in San Clemente, California, on July 5." Then Ziegler had to convince the press that Kissinger met us secretly at San Clemente under the very nose of the President.

"You mean to say the President knew nothing about the meeting until Kissinger told him about it later?" one of the reporters asked incredulously.

"That is correct," Ziegler had to say. Like a man standing in front of an elephant and solemnly denying its existence, he was once again made to look like a fool by those on high. I felt sorry for him. He also told the press that at the July 19 meeting between Kissinger and Le Duc Tho in Paris, Kissinger had made it clear Hoffa was not representing the United States in any way. The explanation that Kissinger had gone all the way to Paris just to tell Le Duc Tho Jimmy was "simply a private citizen" was pretty ludicrous. But then, Ziegler had so little credibility by the fall of 1972 that no one expected him to tell the truth about anything.

When I came to Ziegler's statement that the government

had provided no assistance to Hoffa, I was so furious I called the *News* and told them that not only had the government provided all sorts of assistance, but that Kissinger himself had approved the plan, with the proviso that it be postponed until after July 20. They printed my statement. It was one of the few I made during that terrible time.

But the biggest mystery about the whole affair was, in the words of the *News,* that "Neither the State Department nor Ziegler was able to explain why Secretary of State Rogers did not know of the case until yesterday." I could have explained that. Rogers didn't know because Nixon took elaborate pains to keep him ignorant. But I did not clear up that mystery, or protest the other lies being fed to the press. For one thing, I wasn't absolutely sure what had happened. For another, I had to protect confidential ties. I couldn't very well involve Generals Lemly and Clay and Admiral Woods. But primarily, I was afraid that if I told all I knew, the doors I had labored so hard to open would be irrevocably closed. Crazy as it may seem, I hadn't stopped hoping.

Throughout this period of explanation and denial by Ziegler, Kissinger, et al., Richard Nixon's name remained unsullied. The President "did not know" or was "not informed." He was sublimely above the clamor. It was a trial run for the Watergate battle, when Nixon would again remain aloof while lives and reputations were ruined all around him.

And there remained the matter of Jimmy Hoffa's change of heart. His last-minute refusal to get on the plane had exasperated me at the time, but now I was beginning to think he had been instinctively right. Hoffa was no stranger to deviousness and intrigue. I found myself trying to think as he thought. Three hundred thousand dollars in cash had halted our first attempt. Then Nixon had suddenly reversed himself with great urgency and secrecy. "Get him to Hanoi if you have to chloroform him," he had said. Why? Because of General Lemly's plea? Because he had seen the need for something spectacular to offset the Watergate business? No matter how I cut it, the reasons didn't seem valid.

Hoffa had been highly suspicious of the sudden reversal and the secrecy surrounding it. Then, when he finally refused to go, he said it was because he was afraid he would never be allowed to return. Had the same powers who had stopped the first attempt supported the second because it was advantageous to their own interests?

I still don't have the answer, but knowing what happened to Hoffa three summers later, I have to believe that when Jimmy started listening to his instinct, it was telling him the truth.

12

TREACHERY

Jimmy Hoffa did what he usually did in tight circumstances. He pleaded ignorance and referred everyone to me. I had three sequential phone numbers in my apartment. All three started ringing the next morning early and continued until finally I disconnected them. I had made an agreement with the Justice Department, acting on behalf of Nixon, not to talk. And I had made a private agreement with myself not to jeopardize my confidential relationships with Madame Mao and others. There was also the long list of people who had believed so fervently in the attempt, not for Hoffa's sake but for the sake of shortening, maybe even ending, the war: Dr. Patronikolas, Generals Lemly and Clay, Claire Jourdan, Admiral Woods, Ralph Erickson and Elaine Crane, my friends at the Vatican. Every one of them was now bitterly disappointed.

The war would go on. The Christmas bombings would become Kissinger's new mode of diplomacy. But in early September I still couldn't relinquish my desire that something might come of our plan yet, if only I didn't give up hope.

After Hoffa backed out, he suffered an attack of ambivalence. He talked about going to Hanoi in the same breath he said he'd never go. At one point he seemed so sure he had made a mistake I flew secretly to Paris to try to resurrect the trip plans. While waiting in my Paris hotel room for Jimmy to make up his mind, I had an attack of severe pain caused by a strangulated hernia I had been neglecting while consumed by the Hanoi mission. While the hotel doctor shot me full of painkillers, Jimmy Hoffa continued to vacillate, now calling in Morris Shenker.

"Shenker says he's got to see all the details of the new plan before I can go," Hoffa told me on the phone.

This was the same Morris Shenker who couldn't get Hoffa out of prison. I was sickened to hear Hoffa was turning to Shenker for advice, and I refused to tell him anything. "I'm your only representative in this," I said. "It's between you and me and nobody else. If you want to know where I think you stand, you'll be in violation of the parole board order and in violation of the special visa arrangements the passport office made for you. You're in violation of everything, and I don't want to hear any more about Shenker."

The hotel doctor wanted me to check into the American Hospital in Paris at once for surgery, but I couldn't do that so I asked him for more painkillers. That week I had run across an old friend, Phillip van Dyke, and we had spent a wonderful evening at the Ritz Bar, a place with much nostalgic connotation for us both. We had reminisced about Hermione Gingold's first New York stage appearance thirty years before, when I had sent Phillip to London to prepare her for that debut. Now I was overwhelmed with a longing for sane people and tranquil times.

At 2:30 in the morning, as soon as the doctor left, I called Phillip and said, "Can you come and get me at this ungodly hour?" He came straight over in his Peugeot. I climbed in, baggage and all, and he drove me down the deserted streets to his secluded villa near Paris. I badly needed to get away from Hoffa's turbulent phone calls and think.

Hoffa's latest plan was for me to go to Bangkok or Vientiane, alone. I would proceed to Hanoi. In Phillip's tranquil villa, away from the telephone and all the insanity, it didn't take long to decide this was a futile idea. I was too ill, for one thing. For another, it could be dangerous. As far as the Thais or the Laotians were concerned, I had no business in Bangkok and Vientiane. In Hanoi I might be a man without a friend. The North Vietnamese might decide they had been deceived, and conclude I was one more treacherous American.

In the morning I sent a cable to Le Duc Tho, ending the affair once and for all. I telephoned Phan Mai in Paris and told him about the cable, then presented Claire Jourdan with the shameful news. My last call was to Achilles Vlachopoulos in Florida, telling him to contact my doctor and reserve a room at the hospital for me. "Hold the room in another name, not mine," I said. "If the press calls, you don't know where I am or when I'm coming back. That goes for everybody, Hoffa included."

On September 15 I returned to Miami and closeted myself in my apartment. Three days later I had crawled out of my depression enough to call Elaine Crane at her home to thank her for all her efforts. Then someone named Jack Smith from CBS called, but I refused to speak to him.

While I was having dinner, the telephone rang again. It was Hoffa. I groaned, then took the receiver. He was mild, even affable, and wanted to talk about an interview, something to do with Walter Cronkite. I told him I was in the middle of dinner and would call him back.

I didn't. The whole fiasco had become too painful to discuss. At 11 P.M. Hoffa called me, angry because I had refused to talk to Jack Smith from CBS.

"It's all been arranged with Walter Cronkite. They're going to interview you for a full-hour TV special with Cronkite. You can knock the shit out of Nixon and throw in Fitzsimmons and Dorfman for good measure."

A terrible weariness settled over me as I listened to him. "Jimmy," I cut him off, "this has gone far enough. You were the one who backed out. Not Nixon or Dorfman or Fitzsimmons. You cooked your own goose."

"Wait a minute. You've got to do it. You know, *Life* magazine is going to nail you to the wall. If you don't put a stop to it, they could put you out of business forever."

"Not going into the hospital will put me out of business a lot sooner, so that doesn't frighten me one bit."

Once more he launched into his reasons for not going and I hung up. When the phone rang again, I had Vlachopoulos disconnect it. The silence was a balm. Two days later I was in the hospital under an assumed name with a security guard outside my door. Only Vlachopoulos and an old family friend knew I was there. After the surgery I stayed in the hospital for nearly two weeks, mending my equally ravaged body and mind.

When I returned to my Miami apartment, I learned *Life* had published a truly irresponsible piece on me and the trip. I wanted to strike back, but an old and valued friend, a retired justice of the New York Supreme Court, visited me and ordered me not to say a word in retaliation, reminding me I would have to prove malicious intent. But *Life* was obligated under the law to give me an opportunity to reply. A formal press conference was held, after which *Life* printed my denials.

The press conference turned out to be important for reasons that had nothing to do with the *Life* article. On the morning it was scheduled, Achilles Vlachopoulos refused to drive me to the conference. His reasons were so unconvincing I was baffled, and wondered what had suddenly come over him. This was only the first of many disturbing incidents. Within a day Claire Jourdan telephoned from Paris to tell me Ernest Keiser had been arrested in Monte Carlo. Under French law, I had to appear at once to press charges. I was still swathed in bandages and unable to travel.

"Then you must send me a cablegram notifying me of your inability to travel," she said.

I had hardly sent it off when Vlachopoulos came to tell me he had to leave for Athens to attend a wedding. "Just for twenty-four hours. Just one day," he said. "I'm to be best man for an old friend of mine."

"All of a sudden like this? You've never mentioned anything about a wedding or an old friend."

He shrugged. "Guess it just slipped my mind." Something was off-key.

"I can't let you go. I can't even get around yet. It just isn't the time for you to leave, even for twenty-four hours."

Vlachopoulos was displeased, but he said no more. The next night the manager of the building where I had my New York apartment telephoned and told me a strange story. Two men had buzzed him from the lobby at one o'clock in the morning and said they had orders to enter my apartment to obtain some documents. He had insisted on identification and they had disappeared. I was unable to figure out who they were or what they were looking for.

Vlachopoulos continued to sulk. He insisted he had to go to that one-day wedding. Then he started disappearing at odd hours, once leaving me stranded in the middle of nowhere with a friend after having driven us to a movie. Finally, thinking my refusal to let him go to Athens was the reason for his sullenness, I relented. I decided he could carry two important letters for me and deliver them personally in Athens. Although I was still quite ill, I arranged to fly with him to New York to check up on things in my apartment. I would return to Miami when he came back from Greece. After he left for the airport, I found the two letters, forgotten or purposely left behind.

The following day he called from overseas, claiming he had lost his return ticket and needed money or a prepaid ticket. "I'm going back to Miami," I told him. "You stay in Athens and I'll be in touch with you when I get there."

"I don't want to stay here," he wailed. "I want to be on my way back to Florida."

"You'll have to stay until I get back to you," I said. I hadn't been back in my Miami apartment a full day when in walked Vlachopoulos.

"Give me ten dollars," he said. "I've got to pay the cab driver downstairs." I gave him the money, he hurried out, and returned in a few minutes with his bags.

"A very difficult trip," he said.

"How did you get back from Athens without a ticket?"

"Oh, that. I found the ticket, fortunately."

"Really? Did you enjoy the wedding?"

"Yes, I had a wonderful time."

His answers were far too glib. Achilles was an excellent dissembler, but I knew him well. However, I was too exhausted to play games and went to bed.

The next day I got a surprise call from an old friend, Larry Brill. He was in Miami and suggested we have dinner at the Jockey Club. "You won't have to do any running around," he promised. "I'll pick you up in my car." It was an appealing idea and I agreed, but before I went out I decided to move some important papers I had locked in a closet. I was apprehensive about Vlachopoulos, who was still hostile and erratic. When Larry Brill picked me up, I took some of the papers with me to leave in a storage box at the Jockey Club until morning, when they could be transferred to a bank vault.

As we drove, I told Larry about Achilles' strange behavior. He reminded me of the many friends who had told me it was a mistake to hire him back, and as he continued to admonish me, I became more apprehensive about the papers I had left behind in the closet. Finally I asked Larry to drive me back to the apartment to get the rest of the documents.

When we returned, we found the door to Vlachopoulos's room open. In his closet I found one of my suitcases, locked. I hunted around for a key, and when I finally unlocked it, I found it was full of those important papers I had been so nervous about. Most of them concerned the Hanoi trip and were correspondence relating to Hoffa. To my astonishment, I also found a letter from Allen Dorfman regarding his legal troubles. The envelope was addressed to Vlachopoulos at a post office box in Miami.

"What in hell is he involved in now?" Larry said. I could only shrug, but I intended to find out why he had stolen papers from my files. I unpacked the suitcase, took out of it all the papers that were mine, and brought them to the Jockey Club.

Vlachopoulos had returned by the time Larry Brill brought me home that evening, but I said nothing to him. He was plainly unaware I had been in his room. Two days later, however, he locked his closet. So now I knew he knew that I knew. Still he said nothing, and the tension became almost palpable.

When the time was right to confront him with the theft of the papers, he was evasive and stony-faced. "What about the post office box?" I said, enjoying the astonishment on his face. "Why, when you're living in Miami in my apartment and under my sponsorship, are you getting mail at a post office box?"

"I'm leaving tomorrow," he said petulantly, avoiding an answer.

"You can leave tonight if you wish," I said. I was trembling with anger on my way to my bedroom when I felt myself go dizzy. Then I collapsed. When I woke, I was in bed and Vlachopoulos was over me.

"You must have had another heart attack," he said. "I'll call a doctor."

"No, I don't think so," I said. I was quite sure my collapse had been precipitated by pent-up anger and exhaustion. Vlachopoulos watched me, frowning.

"I think I'll make you some tea," he said. "That would be good for you."

I nodded, and he returned in a few minutes with a cup of tea. I had a few sips and fell into a deep sleep. I woke at 3 A.M., rose to a sitting position, and found I was still slightly dizzy. I called for Vlachopoulos and got no answer. He was not in the apartment. Sitting on the edge of the bed, I telephoned the garage and asked whether my car was there.

"No, Mr. Vlachopoulos took it." I lay on the bed half awake until I heard him return at 5 A.M. Then I slept. At eight the doorbell rang, and I was surprised to see Larry Brill.

"What are you doing here at this hour?" I said.

He looked at me, puzzled. "Don't you remember talking to me last night?"

"I didn't talk to you last night."

"Bill, what's wrong? At midnight you telephoned me and told me to come for breakfast at eight this morning."

Vlachopoulos stepped into view at that moment. He had obviously been listening behind the door. "That couldn't be," he said stiffly. "I took the receivers off the hooks so Bill wouldn't be disturbed by phone calls."

Larry's face tightened. "That's a damn lie," he said. "I spoke to Bill at midnight." He looked at me intently, well aware of my apprehensions about my assistant. "Why Bill doesn't remember calling me is what I'd like to know."

I didn't know either, but suddenly I remembered the cup of tea. While Vlachopoulos disappeared into his room I told Larry, "I think I was drugged last night. When I woke up at three and called the garage the phones weren't off the hook like he said."

Then Vlachopoulos reappeared, fully dressed, luggage in hand. "I'm leaving," he announced.

"You know, you're a liar, Achilles," Larry said. "Whatever you've been up to, you ought to be ashamed of yourself."

"I think maybe I ought to find out just what it is you've been up to," I said.

Vlachopoulos's face turned red, he dropped the bags, and came at me. Before I could move, he grabbed me and lifted me up and would have thrown me out the window had Larry not been there. Brill was six foot two and an ex-football player. Recovering from his surprise, he leaped forward and flung Vlachopoulos halfway across the room, where he lay dazed while Larry called the police and I gingerly picked myself up.

Then Larry called the FBI. As he was waiting to be connected with someone, Vlachopoulos said, "Please let me talk to them. They know who I am." Larry ignored him and handed me the telephone.

"We know who you are, Mr. Taub," a voice said. "We're not interested in the matter."

As Larry and I were absorbing the FBI response, Achilles tried to sneak out the door unnoticed. He was nearly felled by four policemen who arrived just as he got to the door.

He was arrested and taken to the county prison. Given the choice of deportation, prosecution, or leaving the country voluntarily, he took the easy way out. But he left a legacy of frightening proportions. Soon after I got a call from an assistant United States attorney in Tampa.

"How well did you know Achilles Vlachopoulos?" he asked.

I told him I had known him for several years and had hired him to work for me upon the recommendation of Aristotle Onassis.

"Are you aware of certain connections he had?"

"What connections?" I asked, thinking immediately of the secret post office box.

"Are you aware Mr. Vlachopoulos was working for Donald Segretti while he was living in your apartment?"

"Oh, my God. No, I didn't know that," I managed to say. Segretti, chief of the Nixon Dirty Tricksters, had recently been apprehended in Florida.

"Mr. Vlachopoulos had papers having to do with your client Mr. Hoffa," the assistant U.S. attorney continued, and I realized the papers I had rescued from Vlachopoulos's room were not the only ones removed from my files. But my surprises continued.

"Did you know money was transferred from the Bank of Miami to an account held by Mr. Vlachopoulos outside the United States?"

"No. How did you learn of this?"

"We found the records among Donald Segretti's things.

The money was sent from America over a period of time. It came to twenty-five thousand dollars in all. One thousand went to the Bank of Greece in Athens, and twenty-four thousand went to the Credit-Suisse Bank in Geneva. The checks were signed by Segretti, and among the evidence we've gathered, we have records written in Vlachopoulos's hand of the twenty-five thousand paid out to Vlachopoulos."

I was speechless. The twenty-four-hour wedding trip, the lost ticket, the forgotten letters—everything was cleared up by the United States attorney. Vlachopoulos had not gone to Athens but to Geneva to pick up the money, a fact later confirmed by my Swiss banking contacts. I thanked my caller for his information and assured him of my cooperation.

Then I sat down and tried to digest what I had been told. Donald Segretti had paid Achilles Vlachopoulos $25,000 for services rendered. What services? I could only assume spying and stealing. It now seemed possible that Achilles' hard-luck story, which had caused me to rehire him, had been scripted by Segretti.

The frightening question behind who paid Vlachopoulos was who paid Segretti. The Dirty Tricks operation was not limited to frolicsome political sabotage. Segretti must have operated on many fronts, and the question I most wanted answered was: Who was so interested in my activities that it was worth $25,000 to have me watched? Had the money been allocated because of my relationship to Hoffa, or did it reach all the way back to *Z?* Or somewhere in between, like the China gold business or my secret meeting with Madame Mao? There were many possibilities, each conjuring up a whole different set of questions, many of them relating to the CIA and the private concerns of some very powerful people in and out of government.

I remembered how afraid Jimmy Hoffa had been to go to Hanoi, and more than ever I felt his fears were justified.

Donald Segretti was convicted on charges involving his activities as head of Nixon's Dirty Tricks Department, but I kept wondering what else Segretti had been delegated to accomplish. To this day I don't know why he chose Vlachopoulos to spy on me, or what Vlachopoulos had been able to supply him besides the documents he stole. I don't imagine I'll ever know if he was worth the $25,000 he was paid.

Several years later Senator George McGovern asked the Senate Intelligence Committee to investigate unresolved questions about CIA support of the Greek dictatorship at the time of the film Z. Among those to be questioned was Thomas Pappas, the man who had received me at the Nixon reelection headquarters in place of Mitchell and Stans and who had told me Hoffa was expected to give $100,000 to the campaign.

This meeting with Thomas Pappas, political fund raiser and Greek junta sympathizer, supplied a motive for the spying, if it had been instigated by the CIA. Another hypothesis related to Hoffa and was, I felt, just as credible. Several months after the Hanoi trip failed, another White House participant in that debacle was revealed to be a Teamsters Union bedfellow. In December 1972 the Teamsters Union disclosed plans to transfer its legal business to Charles Colson who was leaving his post as Nixon's special counsel and labor liaison. Unfortunately for Colson, before he could resume law practice, Watergate had caught up with him.

Harold Gibbons, the only top Teamster official to support George McGovern, was ousted by Fitzsimmons, either for his politics or for his close relationship with Hoffa. It was obvious the Fitzsimmons camp was doing everything possible to solidify its allegiance with Nixon.

There was more. Richard Kleindienst had been the man assigned by Nixon to speed Jimmy Hoffa out of the country. In testimony before the Securities and Exchange Commission, Kleindienst described his warm relationship with Frank Fitzsimmons during the time that he was Attorney General.

Perhaps. A lot of relationships were described in those terms during the Watergate era, including the one between Richard Nixon and Fitzsimmons. However, during Kleindienst's tenure as Attorney General, a number of decisions made by the Justice Department were of unusual benefit to Mr. Frank Fitzsimmons, both personally and in his position as union head.

For over a year while Kleindienst was Attorney General, the Department of Labor had worked hard to amass evidence concerning the illegal use of pension funds by an officer of a Teamster local in Detroit. That officer was Fitzsimmons's son, Richard. The mountain of evidence was turned over to the Justice Department for prosecution. The Justice Department did not move on the evidence. The Labor Department demanded action. Finally Justice flatly refused to prosecute the case, and this refusal so outraged people in the Labor Department that some of them went directly to Kleindienst's boss, Richard Nixon. It was a hopeless appeal, for the President had the same interests and the same friends as Kleindienst when it came to the Teamsters.

Only a few months before Richard Kleindienst resigned from Justice in 1973, when the dark night of Watergate was beginning to descend on those around the President, another very interesting decision was handed down from the Attorney General's office. The FBI had been maintaining electronic surveillance on Teamster activities for forty days under the rules of the Crime Control and Safe Streets Act. The evidence the agents had gathered had so alarmed them that they requested permission to continue further surveillance, submitting a lengthy and detailed affidavit of all that had been learned. It was sent to Kleindienst's office. The most urgent request related to continued surveillance of Frank Fitzsimmons and known crime figures at La Costa Country Club. The affidavit also presented evidence of a plan by organized crime figures in Chicago and Los Angeles to defraud the Teamsters pension fund of tremendous sums in return for kickbacks to cooperating union officials.

Kleindienst's Justice Department refused to allow continuance of the electronic surveillance on the grounds that the investigation had not been "sufficiently productive."

Jimmy Hoffa, on the other hand, remained under constant surveillance of every kind by agents of the federal government. Conversations between agents assigned to Hoffa were monitored, and the procedures were so secret that mention of Hoffa's name was forbidden. He was watched and listened to twenty-four hours a day, everywhere he went—except on one afternoon. For a reason I am still unable to fathom, all the watchers and listeners seemed to melt away that day. No one followed him, and no electronic devices were playing. On that day Jimmy Hoffa was just an average citizen on his way to a business meeting.

By 1975 the Teamsters Union's connection with people in

high government office was as widely acknowledged as its connection with organized crime. Even after the high officials fell, the post-Hoffa leadership retained its strength, and its control over the union became more entrenched than ever. Hoffa's chance of regaining power diminished as the months went by and he continued to remain under the strictures of his pardon. But Hoffa was a desperate and tenacious man, and he would do anything to get his power back. Anything.

13

THE
END OF
JIMMY HOFFA

It had been a while. The call came on a night I least expected to hear from him. Disdaining the amenities as usual, he launched his conversation in midair.

"There's something I want to tell you. Something big," he said. "Go to a public phone booth and call me back."

He gave me an unfamiliar number and hung up. I muttered something appropriate and looked off into space. I didn't want to deal with Jimmy Hoffa again. The mere mention of his name could give me a two-day headache. Besides, I was busy with other matters and Jimmy still owed me the bonding money.

On the other hand, I was intrigued, for in all the years I had done business with him, he had never acted so secretive. I was tired. I had worked very late the night before on Onassis interests in the Middle East, and the last thing I wanted to do was leave my air-conditioned apartment on a hot night to go look for a public phone booth. But I did, for two reasons. One, I was curious, and two, I knew if I didn't return his call, my phone would ring all through the night.

I took the slip of paper with the Detroit number on it and my credit cards and went down the elevator to the street. New York had been a steambath all that day and night had brought very little relief. I walked to a phone booth on the corner of Sixty-ninth Street and Lexington Avenue alongside a Chinese restaurant. Using my credit card, I called the number Hoffa had given me. The line was busy. I hung up, waited, tried again, but still the line was busy. It was getting very hot in the phone booth, so I took a walk, found another booth, and tried again with the same results. I started for home, deciding to try phone booths on the way.

Then I began to think about Hoffa's furtiveness. He plainly did not want a record of his call to me. It occurred to me I might not want the call recorded on my end either, so I went into a drugstore and prevailed upon a clerk to exchange a five-dollar bill for a pocketful of change.

When I returned to the phone booth I found it was being used by someone with a huge supply of coins. The next one I found didn't work and my frustration was beginning to heat me up more than the weather. At last I found an empty booth with a phone that worked and placed the call to Detroit. The line was still busy. Slowly I counted to ten and redialed. This time Hoffa answered.

"Goddamnit, what took you so long?" he said. In place of the furtiveness, there was a note of expansiveness in his voice. Whatever calls he had made since his one to me had pleased him greatly. "I want you to listen carefully, Bill," he began. "Something big is going to happen. You know that appellate court decision?"

"Yes. What about it?"

"I'm going to win this time."

"I see," I said, unconvinced. He was referring to his latest attempt to have his pardon conditions removed. Time and again I had argued it was an error to try to get the conditions lifted by a federal court. Hoffa always became furious, spewing out accusations, disloyalty the least of them, and I often had to walk out of those meetings to avoid a fistfight. The long history of those battles flared in my mind as I said, "I've heard all that before, Jimmy. What else is new?"

"Yeah? Well, you may not believe it, but I'm gonna win. Anyway, that's not important now."

"How do you figure that?"

"I'm taking over again."

"Taking over what?"

"The union. What else? By the first of August I'll be back on top."

"How are you going to manage that?"

"It's all set. One of my people in a local here will be up front for me. He'll replace Fitzsimmons."

"Wait, what do you mean, he'll replace Fitzsimmons?"

"Do you remember the man you met in my apartment in Miami? He was from New Jersey."

I thought about that for a moment. I hadn't met many people in Hoffa's Miami apartment. Except for Hoffa's wife, Josephine, we were nearly always alone at our regular 8:30 meetings. But I did recall one morning meeting a white-haired man whom Hoffa talked to privately in his dining room. After he left, Hoffa had told me the man had been in prison with him.

"I remember somebody vaguely," I said.

"You know, Fitz is a sick man. By August first there'll be no more Fitzsimmons."

I was silent, trying to absorb the meaning of his cryptic words. "It's going to cost a million big ones, cash," he continued, "but the sick man will be gone and I'll be back running the show."

Gone. One million dollars paid out, and then Fitzsimmons would be gone. The man from Jersey would carry out the job. In my small hot cubicle I suddenly went cold. Then I recalled another conversation I had had with Hoffa. It was in Detroit. We were going down in an elevator together, he to get his car and return to his home at Lake Orion, and I to catch a cab to the airport on my way to Washington.

"Did you ever hear of the Purple Gang?" he asked.

I had heard the name, always in connection with organized crime, but that was all I knew.

"Well, this is my town. In this town you can disappear and nobody will ever hear from you again. Your body will be put in the trunk of a car, the car soaked in gasoline. Light a match, and your ass goes up in smoke. Nobody will ever know what happened to you."

I had wondered at the time whether the story was a veiled warning to me not to cross him, or an attempt to impress me with his power. Now I knew it was a simple statement of policy.

August first was ten days away.

"Are you there?" he said.

"Yes, I'm here. What's all this got to do with me?"

"I want you to go to Washington and tell all those people you worked with back in seventy-two about lifting the pardon restrictions—you know who I mean—tell them I'm going to withdraw the litigation because by the first of August I'll be back in charge of everything. The union, the pension fund, everything. Let them know Jimmy Hoffa's going to be back in the driver's seat."

"I can't do that, Jimmy. In ten days I'm going to the Middle East and I'm swamped with work I have to finish here." While my answer was entirely true, it was equally true I wanted nothing to do with Hoffa's plan.

"Do me a favor. Think about it and someone will be in New York this week to fill you in on all the details."

Then he hung up and I walked back to my apartment, unwilling to believe what he had said. I needed something concrete to go on so I started looking through my files. I took out everything that had to do with Hoffa while I thought about the man in Miami, the one who had been in prison with Hoffa and was now going to help him get rid of "the sick man." Hoffa had been convicted in 1964 for jury tampering, but he hadn't been imprisoned until 1967.

Although a considerable body of evidence had been gathered to prove the jury tampering charge, Hoffa fought the conviction all the way to the Supreme Court. I glanced through the file of that final argument. Then I went through the other file folders until I found the one for the presidential pardon in 1971. I reread the specific act on pardons, on the removal of legal obstacles, what the Justice Department and the U.S. attorney required, and all the other pertinent documents. Elaine Crane and Ralph Erickson had given me all the forms I would need to file after our anticipated success in Hanoi. The conditions of the pardon had been very stringent and Hoffa had agreed to them, although he later tried to claim otherwise. I could not see the remotest possibility that the appellate court would remove them.

Suddenly everything became clear. Jimmy Hoffa wasn't going to wait for a court ruling because he had another solution:

one million dollars, one murder, and a return to power. I wished very much I had never gone out of my apartment to call him back.

Before the week was out I did speak with Hoffa's emissary, but he didn't change my mind. The best thing for me to do, I concluded, was to put the entire matter out of my mind and concentrate on the preparations for my August 1 departure to the Middle East.

On July 31, 1975, I turned on the "Six o'Clock News" and heard about the disappearance in Detroit. I sat down very suddenly and stared at the television screen. I could have sworn the newscaster had said it was Jimmy Hoffa and not Frank Fitzsimmons who had disappeared. Then he repeated Hoffa's name and I saw members of the Hoffa family being interviewed.

There was little information. Hoffa had last spoken to his wife when he telephoned her around 2:30 on the afternoon of July 30 from the Machus Red Fox Restaurant in suburban Detroit. He was supposed to meet Anthony Giacalone there, and had complained that Giacalone was late. Mrs. Hoffa had not heard from him since. His car had been found in the restaurant parking lot. No one seemed to have a clue to what had happened to him.

I tried to absorb the meager details and fit them into what I already knew. It was the very day that was to have been Frank Fitzsimmon's last, according to the scenario Hoffa had described during our last conversation. The script had been followed down to the last detail, but at the final moment someone had switched the leading man.

Of one thing I was certain: Jimmy Hoffa was dead. I didn't need to wait for further details on the "Eleven o'Clock News" to figure that out. I had only to recall the personal habits of the man I had come to know so well to conclude he was no longer alive.

Hoffa was a suspicious man who listened to his instincts. I recalled his sudden, infuriating change of mind as we were about to board the plane for Hanoi. The man had never favored his intellect over his gut feelings. On the day he vanished, he was on his way to meet a man he had no reason on earth to trust.

Jimmy never rode in anyone else's car. In all the times we traveled together in many parts of the country, we always went in his car. Under no circumstances could I believe a man so rigid in his habits had suddenly changed them on his way to meet a dangerous man he knew had murdered his way into the Teamsters hierarchy.

Jimmy always knew who his enemies were. He also knew when he could deal with them to his advantage. Hoffa may have dared to negotiate alone and unarmed with people he didn't trust, but there was only one way he could have left that parking lot in someone else's car and that was by force.

More ominous than the discovery of Hoffa's car in the Red Fox parking lot, however, was the fact that no one had heard from him in twenty-four hours. Josephine Hoffa lived with a man who lived by the clock. He called her several times a day to give her the latest bulletin on his activities and to provide her with the exact time of his arrival home so she could rush dinner to the table as soon as he walked in the door. This went on every day of their married life. I couldn't believe Jimmy Hoffa would let twenty-four hours go by without checking in.

Hoffa had gone to the Red Fox Restaurant to meet Anthony Giacalone, an old family friend who had been named a top Mafia figure during the 1963 Senate hearings on organized crime. Giacalone had well-established ties to the Teamsters, as well as to Anthony Provenzano.

Provenzano was the other man Hoffa was supposed to meet that day, ostensibly to discuss his support of Hoffa in his bid for the union presidency. Giacalone had been late. Or never showed up. I had very little to go on, but I was able to deduce the following: The Red Fox was not the meeting place, for Hoffa had mentioned only Giacalone's name in his call to his wife. I guessed the plan was for Hoffa and Giacalone to meet in the parking lot and then proceed in separate cars to a prearranged location, where they would meet Tony Provenzano.

This would not be an unusual precaution for three men who were under constant surveillance by the local police, the FBI, and, probably, the Justice Department. Assuming Hoffa had been forced into someone's car in the parking lot, I tried to piece together what might have gone wrong. I knew the way he conducted business, and could readily construct some possibilities.

Jimmy Hoffa was to have brought $1 million in cash to a

meeting where he would arrange to have the "sick man" disappear. Ordinarily Jimmy never paid for favors in cash. Compensation was always in the form of a deal—a hotel deal, a franchise, a union job—something that would enable the payee to make money. I never saw Hoffa with cash in his hand but twice. Once was when he reached into his pocket and brought out the money he had been given permission to take to Hanoi after deciding he wasn't going. He told me to take the $5,000 and go to Hanoi myself. I took it, but when I got back to my apartment and counted it, I found there was only $2,000. The other time was the day he bought lunch for us in Detroit while we were waiting for Kissinger's call. Those two times were the only times I had ever seen Jimmy's hands touch money in all the years I knew him. Nevertheless, he had promised the "man from Jersey" a million in cash.

One possibility was that Jimmy had arrived empty-handed. Maybe he had had unexpected trouble raising the cash, and in a desperate attempt to stall for time had agreed to get into someone else's car. But why wouldn't he have been able to raise the cash? Jimmy had at his disposal at all times a million-dollar letter of credit that could be converted into cash within twenty-four hours. He also claimed to have $350,000 in a suitcase in his Miami apartment.

Then there was his friend Allen Dorfman, who controlled the pension fund. Dorfman was in Europe and it was remotely possible that Hoffa, unable to raise the cash on his own, had somehow failed to keep Dorfman informed of the timetable, resulting in a last-minute slip-up. Or equally possible, a deliberate stall.

In all my scenarios something was wanting. Either too many people were acting out of character, or there was a lot I didn't know. I was positive it was the latter.

The following morning I got a call from a reporter in the Washington Bureau of *The New York Times*. I had worked with the man on other matters and considered him one of the fairest and most trustworthy newsmen in the business. He didn't waste any time getting to the point. "Bill, what do you think happened to Jimmy Hoffa?" he said.

"I think he's dead."

"Are you serious?"

"Would I joke about a thing like this?" I said, a little annoyed. Equating Hoffa's disappearance with his death shouldn't have been so improbable to someone with his experience.

"What makes you so sure? The guy's only been gone two days."

I told him the two things I knew about Jimmy that made me so sure. I told him he never rode in other people's cars, and he called his wife a hundred times a day so he wouldn't ever have to wait for his dinner.

"I don't know," he said. "I'm not ready to believe he's dead." Neither was the *Times,* apparently, for the Hoffa disappearance story appeared that day buried on page fourteen.

The next day another *Times* reporter called, this time a Detroit correspondent. He asked me the same question and I gave him the same answer.

"How would you feel if I were to tell you Jimmy Hoffa's son has just announced he's going to hold a press conference at two o'clock and his father is going to be there?"

"I'd be very much surprised," I said.

"Well," he said rather defiantly, "that's what's going to happen and you should know about it before you tell anyone else Jimmy Hoffa's dead."

"I regret that I'll miss the press conference because I'll be out of the country by then. But believe me, when I arrive in Paris tomorrow, I'll be the first one out of that plane to get a copy of the *Tribune* to read about Jimmy Hoffa's appearance at that press conference of yours."

"I gather you don't believe he'll show."

"Not only don't I believe it, but someone has a very macabre sense of humor. Hoffa's not going to be at the press conference or anyplace else because he's dead."

I left for Paris and the Middle East but kept abreast of the news as the investigation continued, increasingly amazed at the meager information and the errors that went uncorrected. It was weeks before the press stopped referring to Charles O'Brien, who had been Hoffa's bodyguard for years before allying himself with Frank Fitzsimmons, as Hoffa's foster son. Hoffa had no foster son, and the error was only one among many made about a man whose every move, telephone call, and piece of mail had been monitored by law enforcement agencies for years. It seemed the ground had opened and Hoffa had been swallowed up without a clue to who was responsible or why.

Unknown to the public, the carefully laid plans of the man from Jersey had begun to unravel almost immediately after Hoffa's murder, but it would take three years before the facts would emerge. I can now reconstruct what happened on July 30, 1975, on the basis of my knowledge of Hoffa and what has been told me by others. There had been no miscalculations, no errors in the timetable for the delivery of the $1 million. Jimmy Hoffa had kept his part of the bargain and had made only one mistake. He paid the million to the man from Jersey for his own funeral.

During that last week in July while I was in New York trying not to think about Hoffa and the "sick man," a number of men were converging on Detroit. All of them were connected with Hoffa, the Teamsters, or organized crime, and, in my opinion, their presence in Detroit that week would either directly or indirectly relate to Hoffa's death.

Anthony (Tony Pro) Provenzano, head of Teamster Local 560 in Union City, New Jersey, was seen in Detroit around the end of July, although he was later to deny to a grand jury that he had been there. Tony Provenzano joined the Teamster hierarchy in 1961 by having his rival for the presidency of Local 560, Anthony Castellito, executed. Provenzano promised a man named Salvatore (Sally Bugs) Briguglio a $30,000-a-year union job to do the killing. Castellito's body was never found, and Provenzano became head of Local 560.

He rose with astonishing speed. In 1962 he was making a mere $25,000. In 1963 he prodded his fellow union members into raising his salary to $55,000. When that same year an additional $40,000 a year was approved at a very select membership meeting, Tony Pro was about to become the world's highest paid union official.

I first became aware of Provenzano in 1963 when I saw his name on the list of Teamster officials to be bonded. Although he was only twelfth vice president and held no other office, I noticed he was making an awful lot of money.

Provenzano had extorted that high salary only to use it as a concession. He preferred, he said, to live on his current salary, provided it would be allowed to accumulate if ever he were sent to prison on—appropriately enough—an extortion indictment. He was convicted, and while he was in Lewisburg Penitentiary with Hoffa, they had a row. Provenzano wanted Hoffa to change the pension fund bylaws to allow him to collect his pension as well as his salary for the years he spent in prison. Hoffa refused to make an exception, and Provenzano carried a grudge against Hoffa for years, even though he never lost a day's pay from 1963 to 1969, when he was released from Lewisburg.

In 1975 Provenzano was already stalking Frank Fitzsimmons. He had plans to unseat him as president at the June 1976 union convention. As a suspected member of the Vito Genovese crime family and long-time head of Local 560, whose jurisdiction covers highly strategic truck lanes, Provenzano was a real threat to both Hoffa and Fitzsimmons.

By the summer of 1975 Hoffa and Tony Pro had apparently patched up their Lewisburg differences. They had the basis for an alliance in their mutual desire to unseat Fitzsimmons. Or so Jimmy Hoffa thought.

During that July another man very important to the story appeared in Detroit. Anthony Giacalone came up from Miami, where he had allegedly been forced to relocate by his rivals in the Detroit Mafia, to visit his son Joseph. An unusually large number of toll calls were made by Tony Provenzano to Giacalone the week before Hoffa disappeared.

Giacalone—or Tony Jack, as the Hoffa family called him —visited Hoffa at his Lake Orion summer home around July 27. It may have been that during this visit arrangements were made for the July 30 meeting with Provenzano.

Also making his way to Detroit at this time, from his home in Arkansas, was Charles O'Brien. He had sometimes acted as Hoffa's bodyguard, although I had never met him and I didn't think he was particularly close to the Hoffa family. He was close to Giacalone, however, whom he referred to as Uncle Tony. O'Brien, according to Hoffa, was a traitor, and he was outraged a man he had been good to had turned on him. Chuck O'Brien had been involved in some trouble while organizing agricultural workers against Cesar Chavez's United Farm Workers Union, but he appeared to be back in the good graces of the Fitzsimmons camp, and stayed with the Giacalones during part of his Detroit visit.

It was Joseph Giacalone's car Charles O'Brien was seen driving near the Red Fox Restaurant on the afternoon of July 30. He was also seen at seven o'clock the following morning being driven away from the Red Fox parking lot in a car belonging to a Teamster official.

On July 26 Frank Fitzsimmons appeared on the scene. Around midnight he checked into the Fairlane Inn in Dearborn, Michigan. He later told a grand jury he was visiting relatives. The man Jimmy once used to strike matches on, the man he had trusted to run the union on an interim basis while he was in prison, had become his greatest enemy.

Jimmy was still plugged into his union on all levels, and his radar screen was as effective as ever. I imagine he was pleased to find out Fitzsimmons was nearby and making things easy for him.

Three other men from Local 560 out of Union City also came to Detroit that week. One of them, Sally Bugs Briguglio, had been a member of the assassination squad Tony Provenzano had hired to kill Anthony Castellito in 1961.

Still other men were spending that week in Detroit. Their presence may or may not have been coincidental. From upstate New York came godfather Russell Bufalino, known to be connected to Teamster operations for many years. He was particularly close to Provenzano. Bufalino said he was in town for his cousin's daughter's wedding. Driving him to Detroit was Frank Sheeran, a Teamster official from Wilmington, Delaware.

The word had gotten out: Jimmy Hoffa was taking over. Fitzsimmons would be eliminated, and Hoffa said he had the goods on Allen Dorfman. "It's all come out of the woodwork," he had said to me many times when talking about Dorfman and the pension fund. In the book he was writing, *Hoffa—The Real Story,* he charged Dorfman with looting the pension fund, while at the same time cheating union members out of their pensions on small technicalities. Everything was going to be exposed. Jimmy planned to leave nothing out.

The book also charged that Fitzsimmons had conspired with John Dean and Charles Colson to prevent Hoffa from regaining office. Hoffa was also going to tell all he knew about Fitzsimmons "selling out to the mob," as he put it. In 1975 the looting of the New York and New Jersey pension funds had not yet received widespread attention, overshadowed as it was by the Chicago pension fund scandals. This revelation was all part of Hoffa's plan to return to power. He vowed he would put an end to the abuses and tighten control everywhere, making it tougher for organized crime to infiltrate union activities.

Throughout the Northeast Jimmy Hoffa had become an anathema to the mob. His threats translated into millions of dollars in lost income. Hoffa had to go.

The following reconstruction of the last day of Jimmy Hoffa is based on my intimate knowledge of Hoffa as well as previously undisclosed information that has come my way in the three years since his death:

On July 30, 1975, Jimmy Hoffa left his home in Lake Orion, forty miles north of Detroit, and drove to the Red Fox Restaurant in suburban Bloomfield Township to meet Anthony Giacalone. The restaurant, a suit-and-tie place, was one of Hoffa's favorites, but he wasn't planning to lunch there because he was dressed in a blue shirt, blue pants, and no tie.

Instead, he drove into the parking lot and waited for Giacalone. Around 2:30, frustrated because he had been kept waiting, he called his wife. "Where the hell is Giacalone? He's late," he said, knowing of course that Josephine wouldn't know, but it always made him feel better to complain to someone. Then he made a second call to an old friend he had tried to contact earlier in the day. "I've been stood up," he said. He wanted someone he trusted to know where he was that day, and especially whom he was going to see. The man who last spoke to Hoffa remembered the names of the men Hoffa was meeting. They were Tony Pro and Tony Jack.

Tony Giacalone never showed up. Instead, someone else drove up in his son's car. My guess is it was Charles O'Brien, for he had been seen driving in Joseph Giacolone's car near the Red Fox Restaurant that afternoon. Hoffa was alarmed at once upon being told Giacalone had been delayed and was waiting for him at the arranged meeting place. Hoffa didn't like the change one bit. But he had $1 million in cash beside him in the car, Frank Fitzsimmons was in Dearborn, and the assassination squad from New Jersey had arrived. If he backed out, he might never have a chance to reassemble the cast. On several occasions he had admitted having big regrets over backing out at the last minute on the Hanoi trip.

If he did something rash, it wouldn't have been the first time. The man had blind spots and one of them was an overly developed sense of his own omnipotence. But most of all, he was desperate.

Most likely he drove in his own car to the secluded site everyone had agreed upon for the exchange. The house lay back from the road and was hidden by foliage, and the grounds were of estate proportions. Nobody was home. Hoffa got out of his car as a car with New Jersey license plates came up the driveway. Three men climbed out of it and not one of them was Tony Provenzano. They looked like low-echelon hoods. Hoffa was outraged. He didn't negotiate with goons. Then he recognized Salvatore Briguglio and his rage turned to fear. Jimmy Hoffa knew he was in big trouble.

He never carried a gun and he was one man against three. Nevertheless, he fought like a bull. He was the strongest man I ever knew, and the assassination squad had a hard time killing him. He wasn't shot, because no human blood was found in the borrowed car. Salvatore Briguglio had a preference for piano wire, and Jimmy was probably garroted. They stuffed his body in the trunk of the Giacalone car, and sometime during the night disposed of it Purple Gang fashion, igniting it in an abandoned car, just as Jimmy had described to me in the elevator.

As far as how Hoffa's car got back to the Red Fox parking lot, I guess that Charles O'Brien drove it there the following morning, and it was then picked up by a fellow Teamster. O'Brien dropped from sight. Provenzano and the assassination squad returned to New Jersey. Fitzsimmons checked out of his motel. And Mrs. Hoffa called the police.

On August 4 O'Brien surfaced in Washington, D.C., where he met with Frank Fitzsimmons. When Fitzsimmons was asked to confirm the visit, he said he had urged O'Brien to turn himself in to the Detroit police.

The police had a lot of questions for Chuck O'Brien, such as where the bloodstains came from in Joseph Giacalone's car. O'Brien said they were fish blood. His entire explanation revolved around a forty-pound salmon. On the day Hoffa disappeared he had been delivering a fish to a friend, and it was only coincidence the trip took him past the Red Fox. The salmon bled all over the car seat and he had to drive to a car wash to have the stains cleaned before they smelled up the car. At seven o'clock the following morning, he said, he was dropped off near the Red Fox to wait for a ride to work. He saw the Hoffa car but didn't think anything of it. He said he didn't know Hoffa was missing.

The only part of O'Brien's fish story that could be confirmed was that the wiped-off stains in the Giacalone car did appear to be fish blood. The police, who had gone over every inch of the car, decided to have trained dogs go over it too. The dogs detected Hoffa's scent in the back seat and, most incriminating of all, in the trunk of the car.

By then the case was so thick with conflicting testimony and bizarre coincidence that investigators called for a grand jury. The coincidences multiplied. The manager of the car wash, who had denied to the press that O'Brien had come to his establishment to have his car cleaned, was found dead. Police said he died of natural causes. And it was revealed an old trusted friend of Hoffa, whose house some thought might have been used as the murder site without the owner's knowledge, had been dining with his wife at the Red Fox while Hoffa waited in the parking lot.

The denials continued. Before a grand jury that convened September 5 in Detroit, Tony Provenzano swore his July appearance in that city was the first time he'd been in town since he had come in for Hoffa's daughter's wedding in 1963. He said he hadn't seen Hoffa since Lewisburg Prison. I knew that was a lie.

O'Brien denied he'd been anywhere near Hoffa during his visit to Detroit. He also denied being allied with Fitzsimmons. Frank Fitzsimmons said he had only come to Michigan to visit relatives. Giacalone didn't have to deny anything. He was under indictment for mail fraud and tax evasion and took the Fifth Amendment.

Russell Bufalino denied coming to Detroit for anything other than a wedding, and Frank Sheeran also took the Fifth. Two items that appeared in the news around that time interested me greatly. One was the statement by a Hoffa friend that Jimmy had told him a week before he disappeared, "Something big is going to happen." They were the very words he had used when he talked to me that hot night in the phone booth. The second was the rumor Hoffa had withdrawn $1 million either from a union fund or from his personal account two days before he vanished.

Then, unknown to the newspaper-reading public, a convict named Ralph Picardo decided to talk. Serving twenty years for murder in a New Jersey prison, Picardo had once been a member of the Union City assassination squad. He knew all about Tony Provenzano and the murder of Anthony Castellito in 1961.

A few days after Hoffa vanished, Ralph Picardo had a visitor who had some big news for him. "Do you know who it was who went to Detroit to kill Jimmy Hoffa? It was our guys— Sally Bugs and two others," his friend bragged.

Soon after this visit Ralph Picardo decided to become a government informant. It was Picardo's testimony that helped convict Tony Provenzano on June 14, 1978, of the murder of Anthony Castellito. Salvatore Briguglio had originally been a co-defendant in that case, but he had been gunned down in front of the Andrea Doria Social Club in New York's Little Italy two months before the trial. Dining nearby was Tony Provenzano.

The weeks went by and the investigation into the mysterious disappearance of Jimmy Hoffa went nowhere. Some officials still felt he had arranged it himself. Many others were starting to admit he must be dead, but they seemed no closer to discovering who might have killed him than they had been in August. All over the country people were busy digging for Jimmy Hoffa's body as if it were buried treasure.

I kept wondering about all the coincidences. If I have learned anything in my life, it is that there are no coincidences. And still they continued to unfold.

A few weeks after Hoffa vanished, Tony Provenzano was going around telling people Frank Fitzsimmons had given him a choice position in the union that allowed him virtual control of the North Central States pension fund. He dropped his campaign to unseat Fitzsimmons at the 1976 convention. However, he was not able to take up his new assignment because after Ralph Picardo started to talk, Provenzano was indicted.

Hardly a month after Hoffa's disappearance, Fitzsimmons

was reunited with another erstwhile enemy who I knew was part and parcel of Hoffa's assassination plans. This individual obtained a multimillion-dollar pension fund loan through Dorfman, whose relationship to Fitzsimmons also seemed to be as close as ever.

How surprising to find these three men returning to the bosom of Fitzsimmons so soon after allegedly being part of a plot to do him in. I can only conclude they all subscribed to the favorite saying of John Mitchell: "Watch what we do, not what we say."

As of this writing no one has been arrested for the murder of James Hoffa. Of the men who traveled to Detroit the week he disappeared, Salvatore Briguglio has been murdered, Tony Provenzano has been convicted of murder, and nearly all the others have been convicted of crimes ranging from car theft to extortion to tax evasion. All have been harassed by law enforcement agencies. The looting of the New York and New Jersey pension funds has come under closer scrutiny, but by no means has mob influence within the Teamsters Union abated.

As for bringing the killers of Jimmy Hoffa to trial, eventually, inevitably, someone will talk. Meanwhile, Hoffa is dead —some might say a victim of his own treachery—and in the world most people know, that would be a fair statement. But in the byzantine world Jimmy Hoffa lived in, things are viewed differently.

I would call his end a fatal case of bad judgment. He was a victim of his own bravado, driven to extremes to get what he wanted and dying at the hands of his fellow conspirators after having paid them $1 million in cash for his own funeral.

14

THE WOMEN

CHIANG CH'ING

In February 1976 an announcement was made at San Clemente that made me feel the world had fallen into a science fiction writer's time warp. Overnight, February 1976 had become February 1972, for once again Richard Nixon was going to China. Although he had been forced to resign the presidency in disgrace, the People's Republic of China had invited him to revisit the scene of his greatest triumph. The Chinese government would even send one of its jets to Los Angeles to pick him up, an unprecedented courtesy.

Although Nixon stressed over and over that his visit would be strictly private, his itinerary sounded like a state occasion. The press was stunned. The Republican party was outraged, for the timing couldn't have been worse. The crucial New Hampshire primary was coming up, and Nixon's successor, Gerald Ford, had enough election-year problems without the man he had pardoned going to China and impersonating the President of the United States. "Mischievous," "peculiar," "Nixon's ego trip" were typical editorial responses. Barry Goldwater put it more vividly: "Do the United States a favor. Stay in China," he said.

If the timing was ill-chosen for the United States, it seemed even more so for the People's Republic. Premier Chou En-lai had died the month before, and China watchers everywhere were trying to figure out what the current poster wars signified, particularly relating to the surprise succession of a low-ranking Deputy Prime Minister named Hua Kuo-feng over Chou En-lai's own apparent choice, Teng Hsiao-p'ing. As Charles Bohlen put it, "It's not a mystery, just a secret."

The editorial writers speculated endlessly, but most of them simply couldn't figure out why Nixon was going back to China. I, of course, had some ideas.

On February 20, 1976, a Chinese Boeing 707 landed at Los Angeles International Airport, three hours before its scheduled departure. The jet had a capacity of 118. A total of forty, including Mr. and Mrs. Nixon and their party, boarded and flew to Peking for the mysterious return visit of Richard Nixon, private citizen.

In Peking the Nixons met with Mao Tse-tung and went to a cultural program at the Great Hall of the People with Madame Mao, who made one of her rare public appearances. A nine-course banquet for three hundred was also held in the Great Hall in honor of the Nixons, the first time a private citizen had been so honored.

The Nixons returned to San Clemente on February 29, and the columnists and editorial writers speculated some more. No one came up with anything more illuminating than the fractured logic of Daniel Moynihan, who wrote, "China invited Nixon because it is trying to speak to a position of greater U.S. strength in the world." I read that over about three times and then became more convinced than ever that I had the only explanation that made any sense. The matter soon disappeared from everyone's minds. It didn't make any sense. It was more Nixon skulduggery. Forget about it, was everyone's attitude. On to something that could be understood.

I also intended to visit China in 1976, and correspondence with Madame Mao had begun through the Chinese Embassy in Paris, only to be interrupted by the huge earthquake in China. I got word that "conditions were not safe" in China, and could only speculate whether the conditions referred to were geological or political.

Then came the news of the death of Chairman Mao on

September 9. I knew my trip would have to be postponed indefinitely, and wondered whether Madame Mao would become the new leader of the People's Republic. I was sure the woman who had played such a dominant role during her husband's decline intended to take over after his death, and had made careful plans for the transition.

I was stunned, therefore, to hear that within a month after his funeral she was under arrest. It was obvious she had been outmaneuvered. She was accused of everything imaginable, from murder of her husband to sexual perversity to the old familiar charge of falling victim to libertine Western influence. She was even accused of being responsible for the tedious and long-winded characteristics of the newspaper prose.

The most serious charge was that she had been part of a cabal that plotted the overthrow of the new Prime Minister. I thought that could very well be true. She was undeniably shrewd and clever, but she was, after all, a woman who commanded loyalty primarily because she was the wife of the most revered man in China. Now she was merely the great man's widow.

Chiang Ch'ing, who did so much to shape Chinese culture, is still in prison. It is a tragedy to my mind that the internal politics of the People's Republic of China are so remote and difficult to comprehend that her imprisonment has gone virtually without comment or clamor. There are no Free Madame Mao movements, and no impassioned protests by heads of government, although it has been proved many times that governments, no matter how totalitarian, are subject to outside pressures. The release of Theodorakis came during the most repressive period of the Greek dictatorship. There are many other examples.

Madame Mao, a once beautiful woman with many artistic talents, endless personal ambition, and great skill in maneuvering through the treacherous waters of Chinese politics, was a ruling force in her country for nearly forty years. It is hard to understand why the world has ignored her plight. Any other woman of equal stature would not have been allowed to languish in prison without voices raised in protest. I have the strong hope she will be heard from again.

FLOR TRUJILLO

The same summer I was planning the trip to China that never happened, I was also pursuing a suit in behalf of Flor Trujillo against the United States government regarding the CIA-sponsored slaying of Generalissimo Trujillo. I had been able to learn the identity of the two CIA operatives who had been working out of Miami with the Dominicans who actually killed Trujillo. One of them was someone I will call Nick Anzalone, a run-of-the-mill hood, and the other was Johnny Roselli.

Roselli was an exceptional hood. He had been a well-known underworld figure for forty years and was the number-one man in the Mafia-Hollywood connection. His influence went all the way back to the birth of the Las Vegas entertainment scene. Starting out as Jean Harlow's bodyguard, he was quickly elevated to a position more suited to his talents. At one time he was actually employed by the Hays Office, and was responsible for the mob ownership of big-name entertainers.

But that wasn't all. Roselli the mobster was also Roselli the CIA man. It was Johnny Roselli who spirited Howard Hughes to Boston in 1966 after the satellite proposal failed, and it was Roselli who was given the assignment to arrange the killing of Rafael Trujillo.

Late in the spring of 1976 I learned through someone in Florida that Nick Anzalone wanted to meet me and talk about the murder of Trujillo. I passed the word along that I would see him in my New York apartment. Flor said she wanted to be at the meeting, and I finally did agree to that, although I did not like it.

Anzalone arrived. He was at least six feet tall, weighed two hundred pounds, and had a beefy face. His speech pattern was city street. He could have been an extra from a crime film they were shooting downtown for all I knew, and I asked him for his CIA identification.

"I didn't bring it, but I've got it. I've worked for the CIA for years. Both of us did, Johnny Roselli and me. We were partners and Johnny says I'm supposed to tell you I'm here because he sent me."

"What does that mean?"

"Anything I say, I'm saying it for Johnny too. Any deal I make comes from him."

"Fine with me," I said, and I invited him to sit down. Flor sat across from him.

"This is Flor Trujillo," I said to him. He nodded briefly in her direction.

"Let's hear your story," I said.

"Johnny says we can nail your case down for you. We were there. We planned the thing with the Dominicans who were into it. They'd come to our house in Florida and we'd go over the plans. You know, maps, approaches, where we could most likely kill him while he was out riding in his car. Schedules—that sort of thing. When the time was right, we flew to the Dominican Republic in a camouflaged CIA plane with the guns and ammunition and the plan."

"Tell me something," I said. "Why did Roselli send you? Why didn't he come himself?"

"Johnny had to stay in California. Business."

"Is that the only reason?"

"Johnny doesn't like to travel these days. Don't worry. If we can work something out, he'll fly in for a meeting."

Then I excused myself, motioned to Flor, and we left the room. "I don't want you in there, Flor," I said. "I've got to find out if this guy is telling the truth, and I don't want you to have to listen to it."

"Bill, you know what you're doing, but my advice is, don't do it."

I nodded and returned to the room where Anzalone waited, thumbing through a magazine. Then I asked him a lot of questions only someone thoroughly familiar with certain unpublished aspects of the assassination would know. He answered all of them satisfactorily. He told me about Wimpy's supermarket, where the automatic carbines were smuggled in, concealed inside cases of food, and other aspects of the operations known only to a handful of people, some of them pretty gruesome.

At the end of his recitation he said, "Johnny wants cash. In a thing like this nothing comes cheap."

I made no comment.

"We want ten thousand in cash up front and another fifteen thousand before we go to court to testify." Still I didn't respond.

"That's the deal. Take it or leave it."

I had already decided to leave it, but I wasn't ready to tell him. I said I'd need more time to discuss the matter further. He gave me his Miami telephone number and left.

Flor came back into the room. "I will not deal with that man," she said.

"You're not going to," I said. "I wouldn't let you pay him one red cent. We don't need his testimony anyway."

The matter was settled as far as I was concerned, but Anzalone didn't even wait for me to call him. He phoned me collect a few days later from Florida.

"I've talked to Johnny Roselli and a lot of other people," he said. "You can count on a lot of cooperation."

I told him it didn't matter because Miss Trujillo and I had decided to turn down his proposal. He was furious.

"It's called criminal conspiracy when someone pays someone else to testify in court," I said. "Tell Mr. Roselli that." He ignored my comment and started telling me things about my private affairs—names, dates, places, and details—that left me speechless. If he was trying to frighten me, he was doing a good job.

Then I got two more telephone calls. In the middle of the night Johnny Roselli called me from California. The first time he called I heard the operator ask me if I would accept a collect call. I was dead tired and told her to have the party place the call in the morning. Then Roselli called me back on his own dime and started right in on me.

"What's the matter? Are you too cheap to accept a collect telephone call?"

"Do you know it's the middle of the night in New York?"

"I know what time it is all right, and I also know you're in big trouble if you turn down my offer." He then proceeded to tell me all about the kidnap-murder attempt, and hinted broadly I was risking my life again. He told me details about that event no one but the authorities knew, and if I had ever seriously wondered whether there was a CIA connection somewhere, I didn't any longer. After a few more out-and-out threats on my life, he hung up.

Deciding to ignore Roselli's threats, I proceeded through the Justice Department, meeting with lawyers there concerning the suit.

In August 1976, a few months after my visit from Anzalone, some fishermen came upon a fifty-five-gallon oil drum bobbing in the waters of Dumbfoundling Bay near Miami. They called the harbor police. The drum was towed to shore, and when they opened it up, they found the badly decomposed body of John Roselli curled up inside it. Speculation was the underworld had decided he'd been talking too much. I found that a ridiculous assumption. Roselli was seventy years old, he had been involved in the Syndicate all his adult life, and he had never talked. Why should he suddenly become careless?

However, Roselli undoubtedly had enemies of many kinds, in the underworld, the CIA, and elsewhere. He should have limited his dealings to the underworld, whose codes he knew. It was my hunch he had stepped outside to play in another league and found they had their own rules of *omertà*.

My relationship with Flor lasted through forty years, ten husbands, and a lot of bad times for both of us. As the spouses came and went, she always had me to turn to in friendship. She died of cancer in February 1978. I miss her very much, and when I dream of her, it's always about the good times.

DOROTHY HO-CHAN

For six years the woman connected with the Chinese gold was out of my life. I thought it was for good, and then one day in the spring of 1977 she was back. I ran into her in New York, where she still kept her apartment on Fifth Avenue. She was as effusive as ever, and said we had to get together to catch up on all that had happened since 1971.

Over tea in my apartment she told me she had become heavily involved in philanthropy. "People change," she said seriously. "I'm not so frivolous as you remember. Right now I am deeply involved in an education project for my people."

"For the Chinese? Where?"

"I am helping raise funds for a Chinese university that we hope to build downtown. There will be nothing like it, and it will bridge the gap between the two cultures. We will welcome exchange programs. It is time the Chinese stopped clinging to their isolationism and reached out to others in order to be better understood. I am terribly proud to be a part of this. In fact, I must leave soon. I have a meeting to attend across town. We are planning a big fund-raising soirée."

I could scarcely believe my ears. Was this the fun-loving, irresponsible Dorothy who gambled the night away and never stayed in one place long enough to learn her room number? Then she asked to use my phone. She spoke to a woman named Clare and told her she was on her way.

"Yes, I'll bring the check. What? Oh, my goodness, wait a minute. I'm having tea right now with a good friend of mine. Maybe he can help us out."

She put her hand over the mouthpiece and said, "Bill, I have a big problem. I'm going to a meeting of the benefit committee and have promised them a check for five thousand dollars, but it's drawn on my San Francisco bank account and it will take five days to clear. They need the cash right away. Could you help me out?"

I told her we could exchange checks. She relayed the good news to the woman on the phone and departed in a great hurry with my check. Later that afternoon she called me from her meeting.

"Bill, I'm sorry to be such a bore, but the committee has just drawn up a budget and we realize we'll need more money in order to get things rolling."

"Is it all that urgent? Can't it wait the five days?"

"Oh, Bill, you know how these benefits go. Everyone is so busy and things always get done at the last minute. Most of the reservations have to be paid in cash, and very rashly I've made all these promises I can't keep because of my crazy banking system. If you could help me out with another check, I'd be eternally grateful. I can send a messenger over right away with another check of mine."

"How much?"

"I'm not sure. Certainly not more than the first one."

"All right," I said, unable to say no because she seemed so earnest about her new charity. I was certainly more willing to underwrite the benefit than her gambling. The messenger came at once with another $5,000 check. I was a little surprised at the amount, but I sent him back with another check of mine.

Both of Dorothy's checks bounced. I couldn't get hold of her and kept leaving messages with her service. She didn't return my calls. Finally one night she called me. I brought up the two bounced checks.

"Oh, them. Submit them again. I'm sending a big check out to San Francisco on Monday."

"Oh no you don't," I said. "I'm not playing waiting games with a bank clear across the country. Don't you have a bank account in New York?"

"Of course I do. Look, this is all silly talk. It's not why I called. You'll get your money, and if you're so all-fired anxious about it, I'll take care of it first thing Monday. What I called about is something else entirely. I must see you as soon as I can about something terribly important. How about tomorrow morning?"

Tomorrow was Sunday, but I agreed as she seemed so excited. She arrived promptly, looking as elegant as ever. She was in her fifties and still very attractive, but now she had a harried look I didn't remember seeing before. She took out of her bag a certified check for $35,000 drawn on a Zurich bank.

"See this?" she said. "There's your money. I'm depositing it on Monday. I receive a check like this every three months from a trust fund. Can you imagine how messed up my bookkeeping gets with all these banks? One in Zurich, one in New York, and one in San Francisco? I tell you, it just drives me wild. It's not my fault about the bounced checks, I'm sure you can see that, and I'm dreadfully sorry if they've caused you any embarrassment. The fact is my trust fund is being mishandled and there isn't a thing I can do about it."

I told her I wanted her to go to her New York bank on Monday, present the certified check for $35,000, and repay me my $10,000 with another certified check. "I'm not going to wait around anymore," I said.

"You're being ridiculous and petty," she said. "Can't you see how harried I am over all this money nonsense?"

"I want the money—and I want it from the New York bank tomorrow," I said. "I've been very helpful to you. Now it's time for you to be considerate of me."

I thought she was going to cry, but she controlled herself. "Oh, Bill," she said, "I'm in such a mess with all these money matters and I'm so embarrassed. I have no choice but to tell you everything." With that she took another envelope out of her purse and gave it to me. It contained documents relating to a lawsuit brought against her by Caesar's Palace in Las Vegas. My eyes nearly popped out when I saw she owed them in excess of $10 million in gambling debts.

"That's nothing. You should see the letters I get from the I.R.S."

"You don't seem very worried about it."

"I'm not. And you won't be when I'm through telling you about my unbelievable luck. Now, you must know this is very private and very confidential. Not a soul knows about this yet."

I settled back and waited for her story.

"Last year I was in the Middle East. I met a most incredible man there and we fell in love. For many months now he has been pursuing me like you wouldn't believe. He wants very much to marry me. All the time I'm not so sure. Our cultures are so different, I've been free to come and go as I please for so long, and I just wasn't so sure I wanted to be possessed. For this man is one who loves to possess, I can tell you that. He is terribly passionate and a little overwhelming. He would insist on my belonging to him utterly. Sometimes I feel suffocated by his personality. But, Bill, I have changed. I want to settle down now and make him happy. Now here's the big surprise and nobody knows but me, you, and him. We are going to marry in September 1977."

Her eyes were glittering. She was waiting breathlessly for me to say something.

"Who is this man?"

When she told me his name, I was speechless.

Dorothy Ho-chan had gone and gotten herself engaged to Crown Prince Fahd of Saudi Arabia, richest and most powerful man in the world.

"So you can see why I'm not so terribly concerned over these gambling debts," she said.

She then told me she wanted me to become her financial adviser. I would receive 40 percent of all the moneys she received. The first item of business would be a trip to London to take care of a welter of business matters relating to the impending marriage as well as to a diamond ring she had pawned there for $250,000. On the basis of our new agreement, I gave her another check for $10,000, which she said she needed desperately because a credit card was about to be revoked.

We went to London in July. She couldn't find the pawn ticket. The matter was dismissed as temporarily unimportant. Other matters were supposed to materialize but didn't. We returned to New York, and she began to make preparations to leave for Riyadh on the royal passport she said the prince had given her.

"We have to firm up all the wedding plans," she told me. "I have just talked to Henry Kissinger, and he will be coming. I also have a list as long as my arm of other people I want to come, but of course my fiancé must approve them first."

On the day she was to leave she called me. "I've just talked to the crown prince. He was planning to send his private plane to bring you and me and our honored guests to Riyadh for the wedding, but now he has changed his mind. He wants only me to come." She sounded worried. I told her not to let it concern her. I'd see her after her marriage.

I flew to Paris and then to London, where I had occasion to call her on a business matter. I called the private residence of His Royal Highness in Riyadh and asked to speak to Dorothy. No one there had ever heard of her. Then I sent a cablegram to His Royal Highness, requesting that his fiancée call me at once in London.

"I have instructions for you from His Royal Highness Crown Prince Fahd in Riyadh," the Saudi Arabian ambassador from Washington said, sitting gingerly on the edge of the damask sofa in his Waldorf Towers suite. "This is a most unusual and strange business. His Royal Highness Crown Prince Fahd has never heard of a lady named Dorothy Ho-chan, and he is very disturbed to hear he is engaged to be married to her. Any representation she made regarding her relationship with him is utterly false, and she must refrain from making these statements. Please convey this to her."

Not long after that meeting I was given a similar message from the U.N. ambassador from Saudi Arabia. "I have never met or heard of this mystery woman," he said.

When I again met Dorothy, she brought up the matter of her gold assets, which were "a little tied up" but which she was seeking to untie.

"You know, since we first talked about the gold, it has gone from thirty-five dollars an ounce to nearly two hundred dollars an ounce. Isn't that fabulous? I am in a very good position, don't you think?"

"Only if you can get your hands on the gold," I said.

I had been taken in by the most successful liar I ever met, and she believed her own lies.

Dorothy lived by her wiles. She had to. A tax-free income of $140,000 a year would have been ample for most people, but not for someone who was a compulsive gambler as well as a liar. Thus ended my association with Dorothy Ho-chan, who was not to become Her Royal Highness.

15

ONASSIS

I was in London with Hermione Gingold. She was playing in a West End production, and we were having a roaring good time as always, but my conscience bothered me every time I read a newspaper. Finally I flew to Paris to pay my respects to Aristotle Onassis, who was dying.

I walked down the halls of the American Hospital, not sure of where he was, looking into rooms until I found him. His door was wide open and the room was dark. A door leading into an adjoining room was also open, but both rooms were empty except for the comatose man lying on the bed. No wife, no daughter, no family whatsoever was in sight. No private nurse, not even a security guard was with him, and Onassis looked as if he were already dead. His face was yellow and sunken and his body was shriveled up. He looked so small and helpless that anyone so inclined could have put him in a bag and carried him off.

The scene was a replica of the last days of Onassis's brother-in-law, Dr. Patronikolas, who lay gravely ill for some time in a New York hospital. When no wife or family members came from Athens, I paid some of his mounting medical bills myself, and then arranged through the Banque Romande in Geneva for power of attorney to enable me to pay the rest. Then

241

Patronikolas was flown to Athens, where he died in late 1972. The bad blood between him and Onassis had never been resolved.

At the time of Patronikolas's abandonment I had said to myself, How could this possibly be, that a man could die all alone? That day in the American Hospital it all came back to me, the shock and wonderment and lack of understanding. If ever there was a family that played out its tragedies in the ancient Greek style, it was this family, and all too often I had been caught in the thick of the strife.

And if there was one figure around whom the many recurring elements of my life revolved, it was Aristotle Onassis. Oil, Nixon, the CIA, Saudi Arabia, the Kennedys, Eisenhower, Howard Hughes, Josephine Baker, William Rogers, Achilles Vlachopoulos, *Z*—all were bound together in my association with this intensely difficult, larger-than-life man who now lay alone in his bed like a pile of neglected bones. It was only his wealth that remained vital; his physical self had already become insignificant.

My association with Aristotle Onassis went back to the 1950s, when he was having big legal problems with the U.S. Department of Justice. The source of these problems remained a secret until 1978. Had I known before, the mysteries that bedeviled me all those years would have been clarified. Everything makes sense now that I know the deep involvement of that now-familiar combination: the giant oil multinationals, the CIA, whose agents performed for the multinationals as if they were on their payroll, and Richard M. Nixon. The plans to ruin Onassis were carried out in the name of national security. Call it a dry run for Watergate.

In 1954 Aristotle Onassis was already a millionaire many times over. He had just signed an agreement with King Abdul Aziz ibn Saud of Saudi Arabia that would enable him to ship 10 percent of the oil flowing out of the kingdom. The king, however, died shortly after the contract was signed, and the giant oil companies in America were outraged that their hegemony had been threatened by a man whom they feared they could not control.

Then a mysterious and alarming chain of events began that nearly did Onassis in. He was indicted by the U.S. Department of Justice under Attorney General Herbert Brownell. The indictment was prepared by Warren Burger, head of the Justice Department's Civil Division. Onassis was accused of violating the Merchant Ship Sales Act, which forbade the sale of American surplus ships to foreigners. His legal problems were soon compounded by what seemed to be a plot to destroy his character. He was called anti-American, that pervasive fifties charge, as well as a Nazi sympathizer *and* a Communist sympathizer who intended to ship all that Arabian oil to the Russians. The character assassination went on all over the world, and Onassis was unable to find out who was behind it.

Then private information concerning his business affairs began leaking everywhere. Onassis had the utmost confidence in his top executives. Many were family members or close lifelong associates. Suddenly their confidential transactions were being made public. It didn't take him long to conclude the telephones in his offices in America, Europe, and Saudi Arabia were tapped. Several of his executives also told him they thought they were being followed.

Matters got even worse. The Saudis, under the new king, reneged on their agreement. Onassis's whaling fleet was attacked by Peruvian planes, and all over the world his tankers lay empty, the result of a concerted boycott by the oil companies. Once his agreement with Saudi Arabia had been revoked, the pressure subsided, but the Onassis empire was still reeling from the full-scale war directed by parties unknown and therefore impervious to counterattack.

Shortly before Eisenhower's second inauguration, and at Onassis's request, I discussed the savage attacks on him privately with Eisenhower, telling the President they seemed to emanate from within the U.S. government. In his usual perfunctory way Eisenhower reached for the telephone and called Attorney General Herbert Brownell. He asked Brownell what the situation was with the Onassis indictment. I don't know what Brownell told him, but it was short and sweet. Eisenhower hung up the telephone and said, "I don't know what's going on, but Brownell is going to talk to William Rogers and get back to me."

I thanked him and left. Several days later, on a Sunday, I had lunch with Onassis, Johnny Meyer, and Darryl Zanuck in

New York at the King Cole Room in the St. Regis Hotel.

"It's all set," Onassis said to me cryptically. I knew what he was referring to. "Call me at the Pierre tonight at eight."

When I called him that evening he told me his troubles with the Justice Department would soon be over, though he had no more insight into why the persecution had ended than why it had begun. He believed one very hefty contribution to the Republican party had been part of the solution at that time.

My association with Onassis in the following years was always difficult because I resisted his pressure to work for him as an employee. I preferred to remain his representative on certain business affairs, particularly those involving Saudi Arabia, where I could be useful to him. He offered many incentives, even throwing in Maria Callas at a time when I was trying to get a commitment from her for a musical production. Callas had been as unreachable as the moon. Suddenly she was practically in my lap, a paragon of sweetness and cooperation. However, when I still refused to go to work for Onassis, her cooperation dissolved. Aristotle Onassis was a firm believer in mixing business and pleasure. Marriage was also a matter of commerce.

My association with him was further complicated by my deep friendship with Professor Gerasimas Patronikolas, who was also the great favorite of Onassis's son, Alexander. Patronikolas was warm and giving. Onassis could be unbelievably remote, even cruel, toward his family. He was estranged from his son. When Alexander died in the airplane crash, Onassis belatedly realized how much he had lost. However, the enlightenment that came with grief did not result in a renewal of ties with his brother-in-law. In fact, the enmity increased. As in a Greek family tragedy, the daughter was just like the father, and consequently there was something of a bond between them.

In 1973 a new business relationship, again with Saudi Arabia, this time under King Faisal, rekindled our friendship. Shortly before his final illness I told Onassis that I had paid for many of Patronikolas's medical expenses myself and had received no reimbursement. After his death I expected Christina to honor his pledge, as she was well aware of her father's promise. I gave her all the necessary documents, which she looked over without a word, cold as an icicle. I have yet to see any repayment—and don't expect it.

This year, 1978, the complete story of the plot to destroy Aristotle Onassis surfaced. It sounds sadly familiar. All the usual names are there: Howard Hughes, William Rogers, every big American oil company, John Roselli, the CIA, the FBI, the Justice Department, the State Department, and Richard Nixon. The game plan: to maintain the American corporate stranglehold on Arabian oil under the cover of national security. Richard Nixon was Vice President, and the orders came directly from his office. Onassis was to be smeared, bugged, indicted, physically threatened, and destroyed in the name of free enterprise and the safety of the free world.

Nixon succeeded in having Onassis's contract with Saudi Arabia broken. The plan was carried out by agencies of the United States government without the knowledge or approval of anyone but Nixon and his underlings, and paid for by the United States taxpayers, all for the benefit of the giant oil companies and Richard Nixon.

William Rogers succeeded Herbert Brownell as Eisenhower's Attorney General, surfaced again as Nixon's Secretary of State, and is now the representative of the Shah of Iran. John Roselli went on to plan the aborted assassination of Castro and the effective assassination of Trujillo. He was brought into CIA employ by Robert Maheu, who soon rose to prominence in Howard Hughes's Sanctum Sanctorum. The American oil companies continued to pour money into Nixon's campaign coffers as freely as they siphoned oil out of Arabia.

The CIA went on to involve the multinationals in other assassinations, other coups. Warren Burger was appointed Chief Justice of the U.S. Supreme Court by Nixon. Aristotle Onassis went on to even greater wealth and a marriage of commerce to Jacqueline Kennedy, catapulting himself into the very lap of the gods. Still, he died a very bitter, lonely, disillusioned man. Richard Nixon went on to the Oval Office, where he assembled a similar but much larger cast with a much more ambitious intent, and he came very close indeed to success. How close he came is the part that sometimes keeps me awake at night.

A book about a person still caught up in the thick of living is difficult to end. Recent events, flowing as they do out of the names and places described in my story, are hard to put in perspective: my life remains open-ended, unresolved, subject to surprises and change of heart.

The greatest change for me has already taken place. My decision to tell about the things that have happened to me up to the present has meant that for the rest of my life I can no longer be what I have always preferred to be: an anonymous man.

ACKNOWLEDGMENTS

There are many important people in my life whose names appear only in passing or not at all in this book. I cannot write about myself and not acknowledge the relationships that have so greatly enriched my life.

My enduring friendship with Hermione Gingold is one such relationship. Our friendship goes back to World War II and has been a deep joy to me for more than thirty years. It was Prince Philip who introduced us. There are others, some living and some dead, whom I must name: Rossano and Lydia Brazzi, Ilona Massey, Miriam Hopkins, Gina Lollobrigida, Juliette Greco, Sheik Abdullah al Khalifa and members of the Saudi Arabian royal family, the Honorable Judge Thomas Weaver, Percy Sutton, Rose Morgan, Dr. Patronikolas, Cardinal Ottaviani, Jerry Bradshaw, Judge Herbert Evans, Nicholas Tweel, Anne Sabella, Oscar Ornstein of Rio de Janeiro, Catherine Revland, who assisted me in writing this book, and a special tribute to my trusted lawyer and friend, Claire Jourdan, Paris.

Also, my appreciation to Harold Roth, president of Grosset & Dunlap, for his patience and assistance during preparation of my story.

247

INDEX

249